THE BATTLES THAT SHAPED AUSTRALIA

The Australian's Anniversary Essays

edited by
David Horner

ALLEN & UNWIN

© *The Australian*, 1994

This book is copyright under the Berne Convention.
All rights reserved. No reproduction without permission.

First published 1994
Allen & Unwin Pty Ltd
9 Atchison Street, St Leonards, NSW 2065 Australia

National Library of Australia
Cataloguing-in-Publication entry:

The Battles that shaped Australia

Includes index.
ISBN 1 86373 704 9.

1. World War, 1939–1945—Campaigns. 2. Australia—History,
Military—1939–1945. I. Horner, D.M. (David Murray), 1948– .
II. Australian (Sydney, N.S.W.: 1964).

940.5412

Set in 11/12½ pt Bembo by DOCUPRO, Sydney
Printed by MacPherson's Printing Pty Ltd

10 9 8 7 6 5 4 3 2 1

THE BATTLES THAT SHAPED AUSTRALIA

Foreword

One of Australia's most enduring and powerful traditions stems from its achievements on the battlefield. Australia's military tradition is important both in its own right and as a dynamic force which has moulded the national character.

This military tradition should not be exaggerated beyond its proper place but nor should it be downgraded in any assessment of our national achievement and character. As a nation however, we have not always honoured this tradition or tried to explain its relevance to the latest generation of young Australians. Too often it has been caricatured by contemporary writers or it has fallen into disrepair because it did not coincide with the latest fashion.

As the country's only national newspaper for the general reader, *The Australian* has sought to reinvigorate this tradition. Our purpose has been twofold. First, to commemorate those men and women who established and enhanced Australia's reputation in various theatres of war around the globe. Second, to inform and remind our readers of these momentous events and to identify their significance for today's Australians, who face very different challenges but who will require the same qualities of courage and perseverance.

The Australian has embarked on this commitment not because we are preoccupied by war, but because we are interested in explaining our history, our progress and our identity as a people. The paper has sought to highlight important anniversaries of national events. We found that this was nowhere more appropriate than in our military history. Australia's achievements in World War I, World

War II and other conflicts have been revisited by *The Australian* in a series of special supplements over the last few years.

In particular, we have commemorated the outstanding 50 year anniversaries from World War II including the attack on Pearl Harbor, the fall of Singapore, the Battle of the Coral Sea, the Siege of Tobruk, the Battle of El Alamein and the fighting on the Kokoda Track and at Milne Bay. The paper's approach to these issues has been guided by a commitment to the best historical analysis available, supplemented by first-hand accounts and an effort to understand the pressures at home. We have published these specials relying on the resources of our own staff and distinguished outside contributors.

These specials have been a privilege for us to publish and we have been delighted by the overwhelming response to them by Australians of all generations. I cannot think of another undertaking which has been more appropriate for a national newspaper or which has brought us into such intimate contact with our readers or the nation.

I was delighted that one of Australia's foremost military historians, Dr David Horner, participated so fully in our projects. I am equally delighted that David Horner has edited with care and precision the following series of articles and chapters which capture these turning points in our military history and watersheds in our national development.

Paul Kelly
Editor-in-Chief
The Australian

Contents

Contributors

Peter Badman is a former Army Officer and the author of several works on Australian military history.

Bryan Boswell is former foreign correspondent for *The Australian*.

Carl Bridge is an Associate Professor in history at the University of New England, Armidale.

Paul Burns is a freelance writer from Armidale working on a history of the Brisbane Line.

Peter Charlton is a former associate editor of the *Brisbane Courier Mail* and the author of several books on Australian military history.

Chris Coulthard-Clark is a professional historian who has written numerous books on Australian military history.

David Day is an Australian historian and author of several books on Australia in the Second World War. He is currently working at a university in Ireland.

Christopher Dawson is a former journalist for *The Australian*.

Sylvia Dropulic is a former journalist for *The Australian*.

Bill Evans is an author, naval officer and historian.

Tom Frame is a former naval officer and presently an Anglican priest. He is the author of several books on Australian naval history.

Sir David Griffin was a sergeant in the 2/3rd Motor Ambulance Convoy in the Malayan campaign. He is a company director and author of several books.

Alec Hill is a former senior lecturer in history at the Royal Military College, Duntroon. He served on Morshead's staff at El Alamein.

Les Hoffman, the son of Leslie Hoffman senior, a newspaper correspondent in Singapore during the Second World War, is Syndications Manager for News Limited.

David Horner is a Fellow in the Strategic and Defence Studies Centre, Australia National University.

Gary Hughes is a former journalist for *The Australian*.

David Jenkins is an author and associate editor for the *Sydney Morning Herald*.

Gavin Long was the General Editor of the Australian Official History series of the Second World War and author of several key volumes of that series.

James Morrison is a journalist working for *The Australian*.

Michael O'Connor is the Executive Director of the Australian Defence Association and a defence columnist for *The Australian*.

Gregory Pemberton is a lecturer at Macquarie University and the author of several books on Australian foreign and defence policy.

Sado Seno has written for several Japanese and US publications.

Cameron Stewart is the defence and foreign affairs writer for *The Australian*..

Denis Warner is a former war correspondent and editor of the *Asia–Pacific Defence Reporter*. His wife Peggy is also an author.

Introduction

THE period of twelve months that began with the Japanese attack on Pearl Harbor on 7 December 1941 and ended with the fighting on the north coast of Papua in December 1942 marked a turning point in Australian history. Suddenly Australia's focus moved from the war in Europe to a new, more pressing danger at home. Within a few months, and for the first time, modern Australia faced the direct threat of invasion.

The new war had many dimensions. From the military point of view it was marked by Japan's remarkable advances into South-East Asia. It brought about the defeat of the British and Australian forces in Malaya and Singapore. It saw the advance of the Japanese to the shores of Australia with air attacks on Darwin and even a submarine attack on Sydney Harbour. It resulted in the crucial naval battles in the Coral Sea and at Midway. There was the bitter fighting at Guadalcanal, on the Kokoda Track, and at Milne Bay. Eventually, the Japanese were driven back and suffered defeats at Guadalcanal and at Buna, Gona and Sanananda on the north coast of Papua. No longer was it likely that they might invade Australia. The war was far from over, but the possibility of defeat had receded.

In the midst of these battles close to home people in Australia knew that across the world other mighty battles were being fought which would have a bearing on the outcome of the war. One of these was at El Alamein, in Egypt, which became the turning point of the war in the Middle East. Australians played a key role in this battle, just as they played key roles in Malaya and on the Kokoda Track.

The war had other dimensions. The Labor Government, under John Curtin, had to reconcile Australia's requirements with the wider strategic aims of Britain and the United States. This struggle for Australian sovereignty was complicated by the presence in Australia of not just thousands of American troops, but also General Douglas MacArthur, who had operational control over all the Australian armed forces in the South-West Pacific Area. The Government had to make difficult political decisions, such as conscripting Australian men for service outside Australia, while at the same time it had to mobilise Australian industry. Politically and socially it was a turning point for Australia.

In recognition of the effect that these events had on the development of the nation, *The Australian* newspaper commissioned a series of articles which were published on the fiftieth anniversaries of the major events. Some of the articles, written by the newspaper's staff, attempted to provide an outline of the events, and drew on first-hand, personal accounts. Most of the articles, however, were written by leading Australian military historians, who sought to put the events of 1942 in historical perspective, making use of recent scholarship. Some of the views presented by the historians might be seen as controversial, certainly they are thought provoking. Together they provide a valuable and contemporary assessment of these crucial episodes in Australian history.

In view of the importance of these articles, and the events they discuss, *The Australian*, in collaboration with the publisher, Allen and Unwin Australia, has reprinted a selection of the articles, in almost the same form as when first published. They do not represent a comprehensive, all-encompassing history—that was never the intention—but together they do provide some illuminating snapshots and a valuable commentary that should be of interest to most Australians.

Nothing can change what happened fifty years ago. But history is not static. Historical events are viewed through the prisms of past experience and present-day attitudes. This book shows that what happened fifty years ago was a turning point in the development of the nation, and that Australians today are still living with those experiences.

1
Pearl Harbor

Bryan Boswell

The day of infamy that changed history*

THE sun had risen with its usual splendour over Oahu on Sunday 7 December 1941. The eight battleships of the Pacific Fleet rode at their moorings around Ford Island, rising in the gentle swell of the finest harbour in the eastern Pacific. They sat in line like limousines parked in orderly rows, the USS *Nevada*, *Arizona*, *West Virginia*, *Tennessee*, *Oklahoma* and *Maryland*, alongside each other in pairs, the outboard ones closer to Kahua Island. Further down the waterway the USS *California* was at solitary station and on the opposite side of the island the USS *Utah*, once a proud battleship, now a target vessel, was tied to other ships. All around them, scattered over the shallow waters, more than 90 other warships rolled with the morning breeze, many of them only half manned, some still with unpacked guns or ammunition stored in cases.

On board, crews were recovering from hangovers after celebrating the Battle of the Bands on shore the previous day or attending the ball game that was a highlight of traditional pre-Christmas celebrations in Hawaii. Some had gone to Mass, others were still wiping the sleep from their eyes. Harvey Milhorn, on board the USS *Arizona* was on the port side of the boat deck talking to his buddy Russ Tanner about whether to go and see Tyrone Power in

---

* First published under the same title in *The Australian Special Edition*, 7 December 1991.

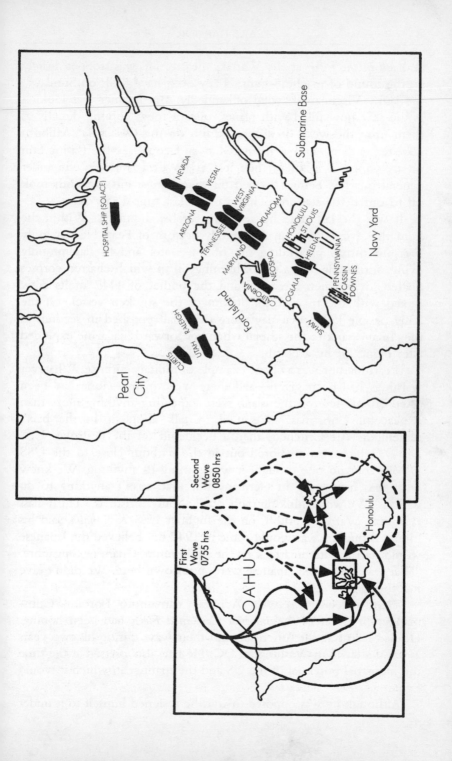

A Yank in the RAF at the Waikiki theatre. He was stopped briefly by the sound of machine-guns. 'They even have drills on Sundays', the lanky Virginian drawled offhandedly. But Tanner was looking at the sky, now filled with planes, one of them coming directly at them from the west. 'It dropped a fish on the *Oklahoma*', Milhorn now remembers, 'and as it banked away I could see the Rising Sun on its wings. We knew then it was no drill. I don't remember general quarters being sounded on the *Arizona* but we both took off to our battle stations. That was the last time I saw Russ.'

It was the last time he saw most of his shipmates. Within the hour the *Arizona* was on the muddy bottom of Pearl Harbor, only the gun turrets protruding out of the water and its flag proudly flying, surrounded by a sea of burning oil in which charred corpses floated, dying men screamed and the bodies of 1117 of its crew mixed with the mechanical flotsam of the stricken vessel. Of the 2409 people killed that day more than half perished in seconds as the *Arizona* sank to the seabed when her forward magazine exploded after being hit by a bomb.

Pearl Harbor was a classic example of military surprise. Whatever warnings had been given—and there were many—none had been acted on and few on the island were expecting anything more than a peaceful Christmas. 'We used to talk about it in the bars', remembers Art Critchett, then a deckhand on the destroyer USS *Dewey*, which was anchored out in the harbour close to the USS *Dobbin*, 'but no one thought it was coming to anything. We knew what was happening in Germany but that wasn't anything to do with us. We were thinking most of all about Christmas.' Third-class radioman Warren Verhoff, on the tugboat USS *Keosanqua*, said his friends thought a war would come in 1942 but believed the Japanese would start it with an attack on the Philippines, Guam or Singapore. 'That was where the Japanese were, not down here. We didn't give it a thought.'

That, indeed, was what Admiral Yamamoto Isoroku, Commander-in-Chief of the *Imperial Combined Fleet*, had been hoping. He had learnt about Americans and their ways during his two years as naval attaché in Washington DC. He had also assessed at the time the industrial potential of the US and the manner in which it would fight.

Although he was opposed to war, he resigned himself to it under pressure from the military-ruled Japanese Government and then applied his tactical brilliance to its execution. Yamamoto believed Japan could not fight a long, defensive war. It needed to take the offensive with a shattering blow that would eliminate the US as a player in the Pacific early, giving the army the chance to seize the Philippines, the Dutch East Indies and other points within what it considered its 'cooperation' zone.

In April 1941 Japan had created the First Air Fleet, which brought together a number of aircraft carrier divisions into one operational unit capable of launching several hundred planes at one time. It was put under the command of Vice-Admiral Chuichi Nagumo and, to make up for his lack of naval aviation experience, Rear Admiral Ryunosuke Kusaka was made his chief of staff and Commander Minoru Genda, a pilot, became air officer. Under them, the Japanese fleet spent the summer of 1941 practising dive-bombing and short torpedo runs at remote sites to overcome the problems presented by the relatively shallow waters of Pearl Harbor.

Yamamoto finally picked the date—Sunday 7 December—a time when he believed most of the US fleet, including its aircraft carriers, would be in port for the weekend as was its peacetime custom. The imperial force assembled in Hitokappu Bay in the Kurile Islands on 22 November and sailed four days later, heading north to avoid detection by other ships or aircraft. Carriers steamed out in two parallel columns, with battleships protecting the rear, submarines, cruisers and destroyers protecting the flanks and other destroyers far ahead to warn of any other ships.

It was an inauspicious start. Gales and high seas washed men overboard and ripped away signal flags. Sudden fogs almost stopped progress and there were collisions during refuelling. But by 3 December the fleet was moving south, with an expeditionary force of 27 submarines ahead to send back reconnaissance, torpedo any ships that might escape the attack and to send five midget submarines into the harbour on suicide missions to torpedo anything they could. Spies in Honolulu had already detailed the position of the US warships more or less correctly. They had also reported that the US carriers were not there—the one great disappointment for Yamamoto and the Imperial High Command.

The USS *Independence* was scheduled to be in Pearl Harbor with its task force on the 7th after taking supplies to Wake Island, but it had been held up by bad weather. Indeed, almost half of the 209-ship Pacific Fleet was elsewhere: some en route to Midway Island, others off Johnston Island and one convoy near Samoa en route to Manila. Thirty ships were on the west coast of the mainland while another six were 'at sea'—meaning anywhere from Alaska to Peru.

In December 1941 radar was in its infancy as far as the US was concerned, although it was in use in Europe and played a large part in the Battle of Britain earlier in the year. The US had neither developed nor deployed radar to the same extent as its British allies, nor had it trained sufficient personnel in its use. There was not even a round-the-clock radar operation in Hawaii, even though US involvement in the war was by this stage inevitable.

There were six mobile search radar units on Oahu but, according to official sources, only one, located near Kohuku Point, was operating on the morning of 7 December. Its Sunday hours were 4 am to 7 am only. Its operators picked up some evidence of planes approaching about 6.45 am, but when this was reported to Fort Shaftner the information was either ignored, misinterpreted or was taken to indicate the presence of a flight of unarmed B-17s that was due to arrive from the mainland. But George Mooney, who now lives in Valley Springs, California, was one of five Signal Corps aircraft warning unit operators in Oahu that day, and he says his Westinghouse unit, at Kawailoa, was also working and picked up the Japanese planes. 'If only the top brass had listened to us . . . this terrible holocaust would never have happened', he swears. 'We had 45 to 50 minutes in which to take effective action. But no one would believe us. No one in authority was on duty—and that alone was very lax security at a time when war seemed inevitable.'

Apart from the radar, the Pentagon had already been warned by its intelligence services that a large part of the Japanese Navy was 'missing', yet it failed to organise any aerial reconnaissance of the seas north of the islands, which would have located a Japanese force. Even as the Japanese steamed south for Pearl Harbor, the Pentagon cosily believed that at the worst it was heading for the Philippines or Guam. But there were also other warnings that should have put Oahu on alert. At 3.42 am the USS *Condor*, a small converted minesweeper, spotted the periscope of a midget submarine less that four kilometres from the entrance buoy to Pearl Harbor. It notified the night patrol destroyer USS *Ward*, which could not find it. But no one took any action on the mainland. Three hours later, a navy Catalina spotted another midget submarine and dropped smoke. The *Ward* attacked and sank it with gunfire and depth charges. It sent a coded message at 6.45 am to the commandant of the 14th Naval District advising of the intercept and by 7 am the USS *Monaghan* had been sent to help.

An hour earlier, the first wave of 183 Japanese planes had left their ships 360 kilometres due north of Oahu: 49 high-level Nakajima B5N (Allied codename 'Kate') bombers, regarded as the best carrier-borne torpedo bomber in the world, each carrying one 1760 lb armour-piercing bomb; another 40 Kates each carrying one 1760 lb aerial torpedo; 51 Aichi D3A1 ('Val') dive-bombers with 1078 lbs of bombs mounted under their wings; and 43 Mitsubishi A6M (Allied codename 'Zeke' but almost always called 'Zero') fighters armed with machine-guns. They homed in on Oahu through a Honolulu radio station (which did not usually operate at night but was broadcasting soft music as a beacon to guide the incoming B-17s—a habit everyone knew about) and sighted the coastline at 7.40 am.

There they split, the horizontal bombers swinging out to the west over Kaena Point to come in at the mouth of Pearl Harbor, the torpedo bombers breaking away to drop down over the mountain range and hit the harbour from its northern shore, the fighters to attack Wheelers Field air base and the dive-bombers to follow the fighters but carry on to the harbour over Hickam Field, approaching it from the East. At 7.53 am Commander Mitsuo Fuchida sent out from his plane the code words *'Tora! Tora! Tora!'* (Tiger! Tiger! Tiger!), the prearranged signal indicating he had caught the whole of the US Pacific Fleet by surprise.

Not least in that category was the Commander-in-Chief of the Pacific Fleet, Admiral Husband E. Kimmel. It had taken almost an hour, because of switchboard congestion, for his subordinates to tell him about the sinking of the midget submarine, which should have alerted someone to the possibility that something was happening. He was still in his car en route to his office when the raid began.

Seaman James Foster was sitting in the toilet on board the *Arizona* when he heard the commotion outside. 'Men were running everywhere, but no one was saying anything', he recalls. 'I fought my way topside and did a hundred-yard dash to the boat deck, where Admiral [Isaac C.] Kidd and the Captain [Franklin Van Valkenburgh] were running for the bridge. I think the admiral gave me his last order. "Man your battle station", he shouted at me. I said "yes sir" and saluted.' Foster made 'a feeble attempt' to fire the gun but could not get it to work. Then his ears were deadened. The world erupted in a flash of light, and his comrades went sailing past him in the air and landed on a hatch. 'We got up and looked at each other', he says, 'then there was another explosion and I was into the oily waters of Pearl Harbor'.

Milhorn also failed to fire a shot from his anti-aircraft guns. After the untimely interruption of his talk with Tanner, he climbed 50 metres up to what he called the 'bird bath' where his gun was sited and managed to uncover it but not to load. 'There was a massive explosion. My clothes were ripped off me and I was blown into the handrail. My right kidney was torn loose and there were bits of metal sticking out all over my body.' Then he, too, went into the blazing water.

Coxswain Jim Forbes thought the planes coming in were from the *Independence* until they started dropping bombs. Manning his station in number three turret, he never fired a round. When the explosion destroyed the ship, he sank with it, some of the lucky men from the rear of the ship scrambling up through his turret to escape the wreckage already settling on the floor of Pearl Harbor. 'I was one of the last five men to leave the *Arizona* alive', he says. 'My watch, a non-waterproof one, stopped when I hit the water at 0845.' What all of them lived through was a seaman's nightmare—an armour-piercing bomb going through the deck and exploding in the forward magazine.

The first bombs had hit Ford Island 50 minutes earlier, at much the same time that the airfields at Wheeler, Hickam, Ewa and Kaneoha were attacked. A second wave of Japanese planes coming in over the east at 8.50 am sent horizontal bombers down the coastline and over Diamond Head, while dive-bombers broke off and went over the mountains to hit Hickam and Bellows Field. Of all the airfields on the island, only Haleiwa, which had a few training planes, escaped. In its wisdom, fearing sabotage more than attack, the military command on Oahu had taken planes out of dispersed strong points and lined them up in compact rows, with only three metres between wing tips, close to hangars where a minimum of guards could watch them.

For the Japanese pilots, trained to sort out single targets, it was like shooting rabbits in a pen. Their incendiary bullets would turn two or three planes at a time into fountains of fire which engulfed hangars and other planes. So much smoke rose from the first wave that those who followed could not even see planes to strafe. They hit the hangars and administration buildings instead. Within minutes of the first wave, many American fighters, bombers and patrol planes were destroyed or badly damaged. There was virtually nothing in which airmen could fly to drive off the attackers. By this time bomber pilots, each carrying charts drawn up by spies showing the exact location of most of the US warships, had already launched their attack against the eight battleships of the Pacific Fleet, the main target.

In the harbour, the ships in 'battleship row' were moored in tandem with one another. Torpedo bombers hit the outboard ones and the high-level bombers attacked the inboard ones from an altitude of 10 000 feet. The enemy planes then flew back to strafe the ships and survivors. One vessel they did not attack was the hospital ship USS *Solace*, clearly marked with red crosses. Her lifeboats sprang into action, ferrying the wounded from the stricken ships to shore hospitals and the *Solace*.

Moored outboard of the *Tennessee*, the USS *West Virginia* was hit by numerous torpedoes and bombs, knocking out her power, communications and anti-aircraft guns. Soon she was burning, but her crew remained at posts for ninety minutes, evacuating wounded, passing ammunition and firing still useful starboard guns. Other personnel initiated counter-flooding procedures, correcting a 28-degree list and allowing her gradually to sink upright without capsizing.

On the *West Virginia*, two officers and 103 enlisted men were eventually listed as killed or missing. But the tragedy did not end there. Unknown to the survivors, 70 men were trapped below deck and went down with her. When the *West Virginia* was placed in dry dock in Pearl Harbor in June 1942, workers discovered the bodies of three in a pump room. Chalked messages on the wall showed they had been alive in what became their tomb until the day before Christmas Eve, waiting for a rescue that never came.

The *West Virginia* protected the *Tennessee* inboard from the torpedoes, but she was also hit by two bombs in the first wave, although casualties were light. Hemmed in as she was by the sunken *West Virginia*, she could not move to carry the battle to the enemy.

Nearby, the USS *Oklahoma* was hit by three torpedoes in the first three minutes of the attack and began listing so heavily her commander ordered abandon ship. As she started to roll, two more torpedoes hit and bombs began to rain down. As men crawled over her now-exposed hull to escape into the flaming water, the Zeros came in to strafe them. The *Oklahoma* only stopped rolling when her masts stuck fast in the mud. Twenty officers and 395 enlisted men were killed in the brief battle and 32 were trapped inside the hull. They were rescued over the next 48 hours by workers who moved in with oxyacetylene torches at the height of the battle to cut holes through which they could escape.

The *Maryland*, inboard of the *Oklahoma*, was hit only by one armour-piercing bomb and one fragmentation bomb, which killed two officers and two men. She was one of the few of the great battleships able to fight back, her anti-aircraft gunners bringing down at least one Japanese plane.

The USS *Nevada*, berthed alone, was unrestricted. Her anti-aircraft batteries were firing within moments, shooting down perhaps two planes at the expense of only one hit from a torpedo, which struck well forward, leaving her power plant intact. She managed to get under way to the fury of the planes, which now concentrated on her. Five bombs wrecked the forward part of the ship and much of its superstructure, causing fires that burned through the navigation bridge and the charthouse deck. In the forward dynamo room, machinist Donald Ross forced his men to leave the area, which was choked with smoke and burning furiously. As the last one left, Ross went back and kept the room running by himself until he collapsed, blinded and soon unconscious. Dragged out and resuscitated, Ross went to the aft dynamo room to run that—and again collapsed. Pulled out again and recovered, he went back to the station and refused to leave until directly ordered by the Captain to abandon it. His courage, or stubbornness, earned Ross the Congressional Medal of Honour.

Meanwhile, the *Nevada* fought to get clear of the shallow waters of Pearl Harbor under her own steam, in normal times an impossibility because of the narrowness of the channel. She got only a few hundred yards before Admiral William Rea Furlong, worried she might be sunk and block the channel, ordered her to beach on the hard bottom at Waipio Point. Beach she did, but she kept on fighting.

The USS *California* was the last of the battleships to be hit. Flagship of Vice-Admiral William S. Pye, this dreadnought was less prepared than any of her sisters because she had been readying for a matériel inspection. Her tanks and voids were open and being vented, which meant her watertight integrity was poor. Most of her officers were ashore and the crew was slow in getting to general quarters. She was hit by two torpedoes at 0800 hours and immediately began listing to port. Then bombs struck the anti-aircraft ammunition magazine, killing 50 men outright and rupturing her bow plates. It took three days, but eventually the *California* sank into the mud of Pearl Harbor.

Meanwhile, other warships were also being hit—the *Vestal*, whose commanding officer was blown overboard but who swam back to his ship to keep on fighting; the target battleship *Utah*, sunk at her moorings; and the light cruiser *Raleigh*, hit by torpedoes and one bomb that went right through the ship and exploded on the harbour floor.

But nothing in this devastation compared to the USS *Arizona*. When the first wave came in, one torpedo passed in front of the *Vestal*, moored alongside her, and hit her in the bow but did little damage. Then the bombs started to fall. One armour-piercing bomb went through the forecastle and exploded in her forward magazine. The magazine erupted, literally ripping apart the front half of the ship, sending flames hundreds of feet into the air and in one searing instant killing hundreds of men, including Van Falkenburgh and Kidd. Other bombs hit the superstructure and another went down her stack. The *Arizona* sank in just nine minutes, trapping hundreds of men below decks and leaving the superstructure jutting out of the water, a mass of flames that spread to the waters around her. Seventy per cent of her complement died.

Standing on the shore at Liberty Landing, Galen Ballard could only stand and watch his shipmates die. He had been on leave at a friend's home in Honolulu, listening to Ink Spots records, when he decided instead to turn on the radio. The first thing he heard was an excited radio announcer shouting: 'The Japanese are attacking! This is no drill! Clear the streets! Seek shelter!' He grabbed his clothes and headed back to the ship but the *Arizona* was burning by the time he got to the landing. 'My home,' he says now, 'was in flames. The *Oklahoma* was capsized. The havoc everywhere was beyond comprehension. I could only stand and stare in shock.'

On Ford Island only a few yards from the ship, navy truck driver Dale Bradford was sent down to a muddy beach to help drag survivors out of the flames. 'You could hear the men screaming in there', he says. 'They tried to swim the 30 or 40 yards to the beach but the flames beat them back. The first men I saw looked like they were wearing spacesuits, so big were the blisters on their faces, arms and upper bodies.'

Of the 40 destroyer-type ships in Pearl Harbor, only three suffered severe damage and the Japanese paid little or no attention to the cruisers or repair ships at the docks and piers of the navy yard. But equally, since many were undergoing repairs they could not attack the Japanese. The Japanese also ignored the submarine base where the *Dolphin*, *Narwhal* and *Tautog* were moored. But most significantly, none of the priceless aircraft carriers was in port to be attacked.

With the smoke settling over Pearl Harbor and the very water burning, while men worked in the stench of charred flesh to rescue those they could, the Japanese turned their attention to the airfields. Hickam, beside the port, was strafed three times and eighteen of the 56 bombers were destroyed. Major Sara Entriken, a liaison officer with the US Army Nurse Corps, was watching from her window, shaken by the explosion on the *Arizona* as the planes began to attack. 'They flew so low I saw one pilot smiling at me', she says. 'By the time I got to the casualty room so many people were coming in it was obvious we could not handle them. We turned it into a first aid centre and sent the serious patients on to the Tripler General Hospital. The dead we just laid out in rows at the rear of the hospital to await removal.'

Wheeler Field, which mainly handled fighters, lost 40 of the 100 planes on the ground. Philip Rasmussen was one of six pilots who managed to take off. He shot down one Japanese bomber but was hit himself. 'There were more than 450 bullet holes in my plane', he remembers, 'but I made it back to Wheeler. Four of us did.'

The naval air station on Kanahoe Bay was home to Catalinas, Seagulls and Kingfishers. Most were destroyed where they stood within minutes, a backdrop to the carnage near them on the water. As they started bombing, Critchett, on the *Dewey*, was now aware this was no practice. 'They were hitting the seaplanes, blowing them into the sky, bits of them sailing over the island and landing behind us', he says. 'One of them knocked the ship's antenna off. All we had to shoot back with was a 12 mm gun and a .50 calibre but we did what we could.'

On shore, chief aviation ordnanceman John Finn jumped to a .50 calibre gun mounted on an instruction stand on a parking ramp. Hit repeatedly by the strafing planes, he kept on firing until ordered by an officer to get treatment for multiple bullet wounds. Even after that treatment he insisted on hobbling back to the station to help with arming planes. Finn was among fourteen men who won the Medal of Honour that day.

The Japanese planes vanished as suddenly as they had arrived. Only Commander Fuchida remained, flying over Pearl Harbor until 1000 hours to observe and photograph results, a difficult task because of the columns of smoke rising over the carnage. Fuchida was mentally preparing for a third strike as he flew back to the fleet. He wanted to attack the battleships that survived and the other warships he had noted unharmed, especially those in the dockyard area. He wanted to put the shore installations out of action, in particular the vast fuel tank farm. He reasoned that if he and his men could eliminate the tanks, the US would have no fuel for counteraction. But when he landed on the *Agaki*, he discovered that while Nagumo and his staff were delighted with what had been achieved, they had no intention of continuing the fight. All the planes that could return to the carriers had done so by 1214 hours. The withdrawal to Japanese waters had begun by 1300 hours.

On Oahu there was shock, disbelief, then crazy rumours. As the first radio messages went out over the island most people were in a state of shock. Then, before they could learn anything, Washington imposed blanket censorship. Within hours that had led to the worst type of rumours. In the next few hours the ships of the Pacific Fleet that could get to sea did so. The *Enterprise* put up planes to look for the Japanese but found nothing.

Salvage went on around the clock in Pearl Harbor. The search for survivors continued. Critchett on the *Dewey* recalls that at one stage as they steamed out of the harbour they had 300 people on board instead of their complement of 100. Like the others who got to sea, Critchett was not to return to harbour for ten days, hunting for the Japanese, for submarines, patrolling and waiting for the worst. By the time he got back to Pearl Harbor, divers had raised a sunken dry dock in which the USS *Shaw* had exploded. The *Cassin* and *Downes* were scrapped inside their dock and stripped before being rebuilt. The *Maryland* was ready to return to the war on 20 December. In due course, all the ships sunk or damaged at Pearl Harbor, with the exception of the *Oklahoma*, *Utah* and *Arizona*, returned to battle. The *Utah*, built in 1909, was already obsolete and raising her would have cost $4 million for the $280 000 she was worth as scrap. She sits today in Pearl Harbor on the opposite side of the island to the better known *Arizona*, like her, a national cemetery.

Of the major Japanese ships assigned to what they called Operation Hawaii, all were sunk before the war ended, four of the carriers at the Battle of Midway six months later on 5 June 1942. For all that, the Japanese victory was enormous. At a cost of only 29 aircraft—three fighters, one dive-bomber and five torpedo planes in the first wave, six fighters and fourteen dive-bombers in the second—they had destroyed 188 US aircraft of all types, sunk or damaged nineteen ships and left 2403 Americans either killed outright or mortally wounded, as well as 1178 injured. Pearl Harbor was arguably the worst defeat the US had suffered in its 200 years of history. It struck with so sharp a force that it left an indelible imprint on the American psyche.

President Roosevelt addressed a joint session of Congress on Monday 8 December to announce that Japanese forces had attacked Hong Kong, Guam, the Philippines, Wake and Midway. 'Yesterday, December 7, 1941—a date which will live in infamy—the United States of America was suddenly and deliberately attacked by naval and air forces of the Empire of Japan', Roosevelt began. 'No matter how long it may take us to overcome this premeditated invasion, the American people in their righteous might will win through to absolute victory.' Congress took 33 minutes to accept Roosevelt's address and vote the US into World War II. The count was 82–0 in the Senate and 388–1 in the House of Representatives. The US, united for the first time over a war, embarked on the struggle that would only end with the atomic bomb.

David Horner

Strategic and historical assessment[*]

THE Japanese attack on the US Pacific Fleet at Pearl Harbor on 7 December 1941 is perhaps the best known incident in modern military history. Just as the names Gallipoli and Kokoda mean more to Australians than their mere locations, so too, the name Pearl Harbor means more to Americans, and the world, than just the base of the US Pacific Fleet on the Hawaiian island of Oahu. It was not just the target of a surprise Japanese airborne attack; it marked a turning point in world history.

Before Pearl Harbor the United States stood aloof from world affairs. Although President Franklin Roosevelt had realised that the US had an obligation to assist Britain in its struggle against Nazi Germany, he faced an election at the end of 1940 and could not ignore the widespread popularity of the idea of isolationism in the country. Once he was re-elected he could begin to offer Britain more support, and by late 1941 the US Navy was conducting a secret war against Hitler's navy in the Atlantic. But he could not involve the United States further in the war without splitting the country.

Pearl Harbor changed America's perspective. On 8 December 1941 President Roosevelt began his speech to Congress with memorable words: 'Yesterday, December 7, 1941—a date which will live

---

[*] First published under the title 'Raid a strategic failure', in *The Australian Special Edition*, 7 December 1971.

16

in infamy—the United States of America was suddenly and deliberately attacked'. Thereafter, almost the whole of the United States supported the war effort. The country had been attacked treacherously, without warning, by a country which had planned the attack secretly and with the intent of doing as much damage as possible to the US ability to defend itself. The United States, along with the British Empire and its dominions, China and the Netherlands, was at war with Japan. A few days later Hitler declared war on the US, which then became a major participant in the Second World War.

It was the beginning of a transformation in the United States' role in international affairs. Out of the war grew the United Nations, the Western alliance, US possession of nuclear weapons, the Cold War and a continuing US political and military involvement around the world. Perhaps some other cataclysmic event might have propelled the US into this role, but it was Pearl Harbor that started the train of events.

The attack also marked the beginning of what has usually been called the Pacific War. In fact, Japan had been at war for several years, and the Japanese empire had been expanding for almost five decades. After defeating China in 1895 Japan had added Formosa (Taiwan) to its empire. It had defeated the Russian empire in 1905, thereby securing the Korean peninsula, and in 1931 had brought the northern Chinese state of Manchuria under its control. In 1937 it had invaded China, and in 1940, following the fall of France to Hitler's armies, Japanese forces had moved into Indo-China.

Pearl Harbor marked the acceleration of this expansion. Within a year, the boundary of the Japanese empire extended from the Southern Solomon Islands, through New Guinea, the Netherlands East Indies, the Philippines, Malaya, Thailand, and Burma and up to the border of India. It was one of the most rapid and astonishing advances in history. And it changed the political and social structure of these lands for ever.

However, as many Japanese leaders had foreseen, defeat for Japan was inevitable when it was faced with the industrial might of the US. Following the end of the war, Japanese society was transformed and it channelled its energy to gain economic rather than military power. Meanwhile, one way or another, the former colonies of Korea, the Philippines, Indo-China, Malaya, the Netherlands East Indies, India, Burma, and the Pacific islands received their independence. The outcome of war also led to victory for the communists in China. The structure of the Asia-Pacific region—one which is the most dynamic and fastest growing in the world—is a direct result of the Pacific War.

This, of course, is a view gained through benefit of hindsight. We now know, and it should have been obvious then, that when the United States severed financial and commercial relations with Japan and applied an oil embargo on that oil-dependent country, war was inevitable. Japan's only alternative was to withdraw from China, which would have meant a humiliating end to its territorial ambitions. To secure oil supplies from the Netherlands East Indies meant war with Britain, the Netherlands and probably the US. From that time it started planning for the Pearl Harbor attack.

Even though the Commander-in-Chief of the Imperial Combined Fleet, Admiral Yamamoto Isoroku, doubted whether it was possible to defeat the US, he knew that it was imperative to eliminate the threat from the US Pacific Fleet, and the attack was planned with great care and secrecy.

From a military perspective the Japanese attack was an outstanding tactical success. To that time there had been only one successful carrier-borne attack in history, that by antiquated British planes on the Italian base at Taranto in 1940. But as it turned out it was not the strategic victory that the Japanese had hoped for. In due course all the ships except the *Utah*, *Arizona* and *Oklahoma* were repaired and returned to service. And the Japanese failed to destroy the US Navy's extensive oil storage facilities, with a reserve of 4.5 million barrels. Had the oil and other essential dockyard facilities been destroyed, the US Navy would have been forced to retreat to the west coast of America, and would have found it far more difficult to carry the fight to the Japanese. Furthermore, while eight battleships had been put out of action, the carriers and heavy cruisers had escaped damage.

To achieve the maximum advantage the Japanese admirals might well have ordered another attack later in the day, and one of them asked Commander Fuchida what he thought should be the next targets. He replied that they should be the dockyards, the fuel tanks and any ships they encounted. But Admiral Nagumo went for safety first and headed for home, loath to remain near to Hawaii any longer than necessary, where he might come under attack from the

US aircraft carriers. The chance to inflict a crushing blow was lost. Even if planes from Admiral Halsey's US carriers had found the Japanese fleet, it is doubtful whether they could have caused much damage to the vastly superior force.

Ironically, the loss of the eight US battleships made a major contribution to the US victory later in the war. While the US Navy had been in the forefront of aircraft carrier development, there was still a widespread belief that the battleship was the most important naval vessel, that it could withstand an air attack, and that naval operations revolved around a major fleet engagement in which the battleship would be supreme. Aircraft carriers were useful for providing the fleet with air cover, perhaps also for attacking an opponent's fleet in conjunction with battleships, but they had little offensive role of their own. Without their battleships, the US admirals had to rethink their operational concepts, and the aircraft carrier had to play the leading role.

It would still take some months for these concepts to be developed, culminating in carrier raids on Japanese-held islands, and the carrier battles at Coral Sea in May and Midway in June 1942. But in these early campaigns it was a matter of necessity rather than philosophy which gave the carrier the principal role. During the Battle of the Coral Sea the US aircraft carrier *Yorktown* was badly damaged and limped back to Pearl Harbor. It went into dry dock and workmen sweated around the clock and had the carrier back at sea in three days, in time for the battle of Midway—an achievement that was possible only because the facilities had not been destroyed on 7 December.

In the long run the Japanese attack on Pearl Harbor failed in its purpose of crippling the US Pacific Fleet, but it was a tremendous blow to US military pride. The Commander of the US Pacific Fleet, Admiral Kimmel, was struck on the chest by a spent bullet while watching the attack from his office. 'It would have been merciful had it killed me', he admitted to a fellow officer. Kimmel, and the army commander on Hawaii, Major-General Short, were relieved of their commands. There were seven investigations—one presidential, three by the Navy and three by the Army—over the next four years to discover why the US was caught by surprise.

In September 1945 Congress set up a Joint Committee of Investigation and produced 39 volumes of testimony. The investigation revealed that the US had broken some of the Japanese codes and that information was available that might have indicated that the Japanese were going to attack Pearl Harbor. Blame was not apportioned to any individuals, but Admiral Kimmel and General Short believed that they had been made scapegoats for the errors of others,

In the ensuing years revisionist historians put forward the thesis that President Roosevelt either deliberately provoked the Japanese, or at least knew that they were going to attack Pearl Harbor, and did nothing, thereby ensuring that the US entered the war without firing the first shot. This view has not generally been accepted by historians. One of the most perceptive analysts of the incident, Roberta Wohlstetter, wrote in *Pearl Harbor, Warning and Decision* in 1962: 'We failed to anticipate Pearl Harbor not for want of the relevant materials but because of a plethora of irrelevant ones'.

This view is supported by perhaps the most comprehensive study of the raid, *At Dawn We Slept*, by Gordon Prange, published in 1981. Starting with his service in Japan in 1945 Prange researched the subject for 37 years and wrote a 12 000-page manuscript that fortunately was reduced to under 1000 pages by two of his students. Rather than discovering a Washington conspiracy, Prange found that 'the root trouble' was 'stark disbelief that such an attack was possible'.

For all his impressive research, Prange did not make use of recently released archives indicating the extent to which the Japanese codes had been broken. The conspiracy theory would not die, and in 1982 the respected historian John Toland published *Infamy*, suggesting that Roosevelt did indeed know that an attack was expected and that he allowed it to happen.

Toland's thesis has been severely criticised. It provides no proof, and resurrects much of the false evidence first presented at the end of the war. After further research, Prange's co-authors maintain in *Pearl Harbor: The Verdict of History* (1986) that the conclusions of their 1981 study were correct. Probably there was a concerted campaign by senior naval and army officers to cover-up their own incompetence, either for their own sakes or to maintain confidence in the higher command of the US armed forces.

One of the most convincing studies of the raid is by Rear Admiral Edwin Layton, who was the chief naval intelligence officer at Pearl Harbor throughout the war. In *'And I Was There'*, published in 1985, he argues that the intelligence debacle was caused by intraservice and interservice squabbles in Washington, and covered up by falsified evidence later. He concludes:

All the new evidence that has been gathered for this account shows beyond reasonable doubt that our leaders in Washington knew by the evening of 6 December that Japan would launch into war in a matter of hours rather than days. Not a shred of evidence has been uncovered from all the declassified intelligence files to suggest that anyone suspected that Pearl Harbor would be a target.

There is another theory behind the intelligence debacle, first hinted at by John Costello in *The Pacific War*, published in 1981, and argued in much greater depth by James Rushbridger and Eric Nave in *Betrayal at Pearl Harbor, How Churchill Lured Roosevelt into War*, published in 1991. Nave, who lived in Melbourne and died in 1993, was an Australian naval officer who worked for British naval intelligence breaking Japanese naval codes until he returned to Australia in early 1940.

According to this account, the British Far East Combined Bureau at Singapore had broken the Japanese JN-25 Fleet code, which Admiral Yamamoto used on 25 November when he signalled instructions to Vice-Admiral Nagumo at Tankan Bay to set sail and to prepare to refuel after eight days. This signal was intercepted by US and British intercept units, but apparently was not decoded by the US until after the war. Nave and Rushbridger claim that the British in Singapore decoded the signal in a matter of days and passed the information to London.

As well as relying on Nave's own knowledge, the account is supported by the evidence of a British code-breaker at Singapore, Commander Mortimer, who recalled both sending the information to London and the comments of one of the other staff in Singapore: 'With all the information we gave them. How could the Americans have been caught unprepared?'

The answer, according to Rushbridger and Nave, is that Churchill had not passed the information on to Roosevelt, as he wanted to ensure that the US entered the war, thereby saving Britain from defeat. The authors claim that there has been a concerted campaign to cover up these events, including the closing of the relevant intelligence files in Britain and Australia.

There are a host of unanswered questions. The account relies on the memories of two men, Nave and Mortimer, and is not supported by documentary evidence. The claims about Churchill are circumstantial. Even if the crucial message was decoded in time, was it understood in London and were the right conclusions drawn? As several reviewers of *Betrayal at Pearl Harbor* have commented in 1992, the case is not proved. Since then there have been even stronger criticisms of the book in learned journals. Another book, *Pearl Harbor: The Final Judgement*, by Henry Clausen and Bruce Lee, published in 1992, provides further evidence to disprove some of the claims in *Betrayal at Pearl Harbor*.

Despite the scores of books on Pearl Harbor, there are many researchers who believe that the full story has still to be told. That the event should hold the attention of historians is a mark not just of its intrinsic fascination and mystery, but also an indication of its importance in Pacific history.

Bryan Boswell

The Japanese master plan*

THE operations plans for the execution of Japan's war were complex and detailed. They were equally unorthodox and in the Western military minds of the day were considered frought with unacceptable dangers. It was to be a multifaceted onslaught involving simultaneous attacks on Pearl Harbor, Guam, Wake Island, Hong Kong, Malaya and the Philippines—strikes that would hit in every direction at once, totally contrary to the conventional military wisdom, which held that attacks on two fronts was the most balanced and effective plan to adopt.

But the Japanese battle plan took advantage of Japan's strengths—its wealth of seasoned ground forces, its proven capability to coordinate air, sea and land attacks, its experience in amphibious landings—and it would force each victim to concentrate on defence of its own territories rather than going to the aid of its allies.

With the Allies so weak, it was reasonable to expect a quick victory. The main point of attack was to be Pearl Harbor, which would neutralise the United States and secure one flank of Japan's assault by destroying the US Pacific Fleet, one of the three main threats. Japan's drive south would be protected on another flank by the coast of Asia and on the other by the non-aggression treaty with

---

* First published under the title, 'Tojo's master plan', in
  The Australian Special Edition, 7 December 1991.

Russia. The Chinese Army would be unable to help since it was already virtually cut off from the outside world.

With the attack on Pearl Harbor successfully executed, strong attacks, preliminaries to invasion, would be mounted against the Philippines and Malaya to destroy Allied air power there. There would be simultaneous air strikes at Hong Kong, Wake Island and Guam. Even while the Vals, Kates and Zeros were attacking Pearl Harbor, Japanese aircraft were waiting at airfields on Formosa to attack their targets. Under the plan, the Japanese Government expected to have control of Luzon in 50 days and the entire Philippines in three months. Meanwhile, nine infantry battalions supported by artillery and six squadrons of aircraft, 20 000 men in all, would move on Hong Kong.

West of Luzon in the Gulf of Siam, 22 ships would close in on the coasts of Malaya and Thailand to put ashore an army that would sweep the British from Singapore and advance right through to the borders of India and perhaps beyond. At 9 am on 7 December Malayan time, the convoys carrying the army assault on Malaya split up. One went north to the Kra Isthmus to await orders for the move on Burma, another to land troops for the attack on Singapore and the third to go ashore at Khota Bharu. At midnight the first elements reached their targets and shelling of the 8th Indian Brigade of Baluchs, Dogras and the Frontier Force Rifles—the northernmost outposts of what were in effect the defences of Singapore—began.

Japanese troops began to land at 1 am on 8 December but so fierce was the resistance that one Japanese commander actually asked for the assault to be abandoned. In rough seas with waves two metres high, many of the Japanese soldiers drowned while transferring to landing craft or trying to swim through the surf. Those who did land came under heavy machine-gun and mortar fire. But their officers ordered them to advance or die where they were. Three hours later the two central positions of the Dogras had been overwhelmed at a cost to the Japanese of 500 dead. The second and third waves of the Japanese came ashore on 8 December with their commander, Major-General Takumi, and that night the Indian brigade commander, Brigadier Key, was asking permission to withdraw his forces as far as Kuantan.

The residents of Singapore learned they were at war when bombs began exploding at 4 am on 8 December. The fighter control

24

operations room on the island had received a report that aircraft were approaching 225 kilometres out but they had been unable to raise anyone at the Civil Defence headquarters. So the lights of the city were all on, guiding the Japanese planes in. They stayed on throughout that first raid because no one could find the master switch at the power station to turn them off. Sixty-three people were killed and 133 injured in the raid but no one worried, especially after Air Chief Marshal Sir Robert Brooke-Popham issued an order of the day saying: 'We are ready. We have had plenty of warning and our preparations are made and tested. Japan has been drained for years by the exhausting claims of her wanton onslaught on China.' Despite the brave words it was the beginning of the end for Singapore, even if few would admit it. The Japanese had feared the attack on Pearl Harbor might compromise the strike on Malaya, but London was not even alerted. Word of the attack on Oahu did not reach Winston Churchill until almost three hours after the first bombs fell.

The other two landings in the north of Thailand were hampered by faulty execution of orders. Troops leaping ashore at Pattani beach, who had been personally picked by assault commander Major Shigeharu Asaeda, sank in the mud and drowned. Others took hours to reach the white sand, which Asaeda had not realised did not extend beyond the shoreline. Those landing were raked by Thai gunfire and many died. Meanwhile at Singora beach, the wave led by Colonel Tsuji intended to get ashore, seize Thai buses and use them to roll across the border into Malaya. He believed that an agent on shore had already persuaded the Thais not to interfere. He landed his men, but his agent was not there to greet him and he had to go into the town on his own and rouse the Japanese consulate by pounding on its gates. From there he went with his agent to persuade (or buy) the buses from the Thai police. It sounded fanciful—and so it transpired. Instead of cooperating, the Thais started firing and Tsuji's scheme of bussed glory vanished in the night. Nevertheless, the Japanese 15th Army under Lieutenant-General Iida, which had landed on the Kra Isthmus, was in Bangkok on 8 December and immediately became master of Thailand, controlling all airfields and railways.

In Manila on 7 December, five hours after Pearl Harbor, Major-General Lewis Brereton, commander of MacArthur's Far East

Air Force, asked for permission to attack the Japanese at Formosa with his Flying Fortresses. MacArthur said no, suggesting it would be the 'first overt act' of war, which conveniently ignored what had happened on Oahu. But if Brereton was frustrated, so were the Japanese, who should have been over Manila while he was still asleep. They had been held back by fog from their strikes at Clark airfield and its adjoining fighter bases. Some Japanese planes did get away early, but only managed to bomb unimportant targets far north of Manila. Then the fog lifted later that day and 196 Japanese naval planes swept out for targets on Luzon.

At 12.25, 27 new Mitsubishi high-level bombers with 27 more behind them dropped down on Clark airfield where, despite Pearl Harbor and all the warnings, every US plane was lined up, as author John Toland later wrote, 'like sitting ducks'. Yet despite ten minutes of ferocious bombing and strafing, only a handful of Flying Fortresses were damaged. Buildings blazed and dark palls of smoke hung over the oil dump, but the real targets had been missed. Then down came the Zeros. Still almost unopposed, they began strafing the parked planes. One by one, the B-17s and P-40Bs exploded and when the Zeros vanished this time all but three of the Flying Fortresses were destroyed and all of the fighter planes were on fire. In one blow the Japanese had destroyed MacArthur's Far East Air Force at virtually no cost to themselves. All of their bombers returned to Formosa and only seven of their fighters were lost.

In the space of a few hours Japan had crippled the US Pacific Fleet and the bulk of its Pacific area air force. Only one main naval force remained to oppose the Japanese in the whole theatre—the Royal Navy's Force Z, under Admiral 'Tom Thumb' Phillips, with the powerful *Prince of Wales* and *Repulse*, which the Japanese thought were locked in Singapore Harbour but which in fact were steaming north towards the Japanese convoys.

Meanwhile, the Japanese had also attacked Mindanao, Guam and Wake Island and were preparing to make their assault on the rest of South-East Asia. No attacks had been made on Dutch possessions, but already the Dutch were prepared for the war, seeing what had happened in Malaya. To many it seemed that Japan might well have bitten off more than it could chew and that the Allies could hold the storm. But in reality little was being done, or could be done, with the resources available to stem the tide that had begun to flow all over Asia on 7 December. It was only a matter of time.

David Day

The end of Australia's complacency*

EARLY on the morning of 7 December 1941, Pearl Harbor's status as a mere naval complex in the Pacific was undergoing a tragic metamorphosis. By morning's end, the pride of the United States Navy lay sunk or smouldering at anchorage in 'Battleship Row' at the hands of a new enemy, Japan. Although denounced as an act of treachery, Japan's entry into the war had been widely expected after diplomatic talks in Washington between the US and Japan had revealed an apparently unbridgeable gulf between the two Pacific powers. But few anticipated the manner of its entry, in striking suddenly against the core of US naval power. To most Australians it seemed madness for the Japanese to strike at the US and thereby provoke Washington into war. Japan's eventual defeat seemed certain and the threat to Australia slight.

Ever since the nineteenth century, Australians had feared the hoary spectre of an Asian invasion looming over the island continent. During the interwar period Britain's relative decline as a world power raised concerns about its ability to defend the Empire's distant dominions. These concerns had largely been allayed by the construction of the Singapore naval base, the so-called impregnable fortress whose brooding presence would preclude a Japanese invasion from threatening Australia. The Singapore base was barely complete

---

* First published under the title 'The nation's complacency rudely shattered', in *The Australian Special Edition*, 7 December 1991.

by the outbreak of war and still did not host a British fleet. With its naval forces concentrated against Germany and Italy, Britain relied on the symbolism of Singapore as a statement of British power and resolve while declining to reinforce this linchpin of the Empire with sufficient forces to ensure its inviolability. Rather than relying on the presence of a strong fleet at Singapore, Britain relied on its mixed garrison of British, Indian and Australian troops to withstand a siege for the months that it might take for a fleet to arrive from Europe. But it was unlikely that Japan would oblige by attacking Singapore unless British naval forces were tied down in Europe.

It was a conundrum that British planners preferred not to think about, for the possible outcomes were too painful to contemplate. With limited resources, Britain had been forced to make choices about its interests and priorities. It chose to concentrate its resources, first, on the defence of its homeland and the prosecution of the war against Germany and, second, on the defence of its interests in the Middle East and the Indian Ocean. Its empire in the Far East, including its two Pacific dominions of Australia and New Zealand, were as distant in its priorities as they were in nautical miles. The British Prime Minister, Winston Churchill, could justify the relative neglect of Australia with the confident assumption that Japan, even if it entered the war, lacked the capacity to invade Australia. Acting on this assumption, Churchill made repeated assurances that Britain would spring to Australia's defence in the event of a major threat developing, confident that his assurances would never be called on.

Despite serious misgivings, successive Australian governments accepted these assurances, preferring to rely upon their traditional imperial links rather than move towards a more self-reliant defence policy or to develop close defence links with the US. In the months before Pearl Harbor, as the Pacific edged closer to conflict, the Australian Government pressured Britain to make good its pledge to protect the dominion by basing a fleet at Singapore. Eventually, Churchill appeared to concede to Australian pressure, despatching to the Indian Ocean the modern battleship *Prince of Wales* and the cruiser *Repulse* as the first echelon of a larger British fleet to be based in 'eastern waters'.

Australia saw the move as a positive sign of British regard for the dominion's security when, in reality, it was no such thing. Not only did the two ships lack an aircraft carrier to provide air cover, but the other battleships destined to join the fleet in 1942 were four elderly vessels designed for fighting in the North Sea and disparagingly referred to by Churchill as 'floating coffins'. The ships were certainly sent east as a deterrent to Japan, but they were meant to deter Japan from entering the Indian Ocean and not to deter it from war *per se*.

It was only by a stroke of bad luck that the ships were at Singapore when Japan entered the war and, by an unfortunate succession of events, that they were caught off the coast of Malaya on 10 December 1941 by Japanese torpedo bombers and were quickly despatched. Rather than confronting the Japanese, Churchill had wanted the ships to withdraw to the safety of the Indian Ocean where they could protect India and the important reinforcement route along the east coast of Africa to the British bastion in the Middle East. Their sinking in the defence of Singapore embellished the myth that Britain accorded a high priority to the defence of Singapore and, by association, Australia.

In the months before Pearl Harbor, Australia had accepted the British assurances and sought to delay the onset of the expected Pacific War until the arrival of the British fleet in the Pacific. The system of imperial defence seemed to be working according to plan, shifting the forces of the Empire around the globe to meet threats as they arose. But it was a British plan that had the defence of British interests uppermost.

Although Australia's interests clearly lay in Britain not being defeated by Germany, it had even more vital interests of its own in not being defeated by Japan. In accordance with the imperial plan, Australia's best fighting men were scattered across the world. At the time of the attack on Pearl Harbor, three divisions of Australian troops were stationed in the Middle East and one in Singapore. Thousands of Australian airmen were based in Britain, engaged in the mass bombing of Germany, while thousands of its sailors were serving in the Mediterranean and elsewhere. Despite the deteriorating position in the Pacific, Australia continued to send reinforcements for its divisions in the Middle East and made no move to have them withdrawn homeward.

Australia continued to assume that the Japanese threat, if it came, would be a naval one limited to cruiser raids. In such circumstances, there was perhaps little point in withdrawing army divisions for

30

home defence. The idea of a Japanese invasion of Australia seemed far-fetched given the existence of Singapore and the strength of US Pacific forces. So the Australian reaction to Pearl Harbor was one of confidence and even relief. The nightmare situation of Japan declaring war on Britain without involving the US was averted. With both the US and British navies to protect her, Australia had little to fear. Or so it surmised. Because of wartime censorship, the extent of the damage to the US Pacific Fleet at Pearl Harbor was not known in Australia for some months. Neither were Australians aware that all the American aircraft carriers were saved from the carnage by being out on patrol.

It seemed sufficient that the US, after standing on the sidelines for so long, had at last been drawn into the now expanded conflict. It was inconceivable to most Australians that the combined forces of the British Empire, the US, China and the Netherlands could not defeat the Japanese. Unknown to Australia, the Allies would adopt a strategy that would place the security of the dominion in jeopardy.

The attack on Pearl Harbor had implications far wider than the expansive Pacific. It broadened the existing European War into a world war as the Axis powers of Germany, Italy and Japan confronted the Allied powers of the British Empire, the Soviet Union and now the US and China. At last Churchill could be assured that eventual victory would rest with the Allies. In a secret cable to the South African Prime Minister, Jan Smuts, Churchill expressed himself 'well content' with Pearl Harbor. He had staked the Empire on America's entry into the war against Germany and had encouraged a far from reluctant Roosevelt into a belligerent stance against Japanese expansion, always careful to ensure that Japan would not declare war against Britain alone.

Now, with Hitler's declaration of war against the US, everything fell into place in Churchill's grand plan. As he confided to his wife: 'The entry of the United States into the war is worth all the losses sustained in the East many times over'. And he was right, so far as the global picture and the ultimate result were concerned. But Australia could not be so sanguine that she would not be one of the losses, particularly after the shock sinking of the *Prince of Wales* and the *Repulse* just two days after Pearl Harbor. The Singapore base, which provided the very foundation of Australian defence, now lay open to Japanese naval siege.

Following these losses, which caused more alarm in Canberra than the attack on Pearl Harbor, Curtin called for the Russians to declare war on Japan and thereby draw Japanese forces away from their southward expansion. This was anathema to Churchill and Roosevelt, both of whom relied on the Russians to absorb German military strength before the planned Allied invasion of Europe. To deflect such calls, Churchill sallied forth to America to ensure that Roosevelt's first priority would remain the war in Europe. Churchill feared that the provocative nature of the Japanese attack on Pearl Harbor might incite the Americans to devote most of their war effort to the Pacific at the expense of the war against Germany.

According to a secret Anglo-American agreement that was reached early in 1941, in the event of Japanese entry into the war the Allies would fight a holding war in the Pacific until the defeat of Germany allowed them to swing their whole weight against the Japanese. Churchill was desperate to ensure that this agreement be followed by Roosevelt despite the dramatic and uncontemplated events at Pearl Harbor. In this he was successful, while also passing to the US the responsibility for the naval defence of Australia's eastern seaboard.

Although the Australian Government knew of the earlier agreement, it seems to have thought the accord had been overtaken by events. It was on such an optimistic assumption, and in the confident expectation that the system of imperial defence would ensure Australian security, that Canberra had greeted the attack on Pearl Harbor with relief. Australia's pugnacious Minister for External Affairs, Dr H.V. Evatt, had shared Churchill's exultation at the entry of the US into the war. No matter that war was now splashed across the vastness of the Pacific. The combined might of the US Pacific Fleet and the British naval base at Singapore would provide a formidable shield against an invasion of Australia.

As leader of the Labor Opposition during the 1930s, John Curtin had argued for Australian defence policy to have as its first priority the defence of the island continent. Only when this could be considered secure should Australia devote resources to the defence of the wider British Empire. These were radical notions at a time when many Australians still thought of Britain as 'home' and when their own sense of national identity was buried beneath a pervading sense of themselves as part of a British 'race'. His arguments had not been heeded by conservative politicians, or the national electorate.

Now, just two months after assuming office as the first Labor prime minister for a decade, Curtin was faced with extricating the nation from its own folly. Following Pearl Harbor, Curtin looked to London for the fulfilment of its historic promise to defend Australia. The key to the British response was the naval base at Singapore, often referred to as a 'fortress' by Churchill but in reality being no such thing. It was to harbour a fleet but had never done so; it was designed to withstand an enemy siege but was incapable of doing so; and it was promoted as securing Australia's defence when it was really designed to limit Japanese expansion to the Pacific.

Within weeks these shortcomings would become painfully apparent. By the end of December, as the seriousness of the Japanese challenge was becoming clearer, Curtin began to warn the Australian people that their very existence as a white nation was hanging in the balance. For the first time since 1788, the island continent faced the imminent prospect of a hostile invasion. 'All Australia is at stake in this war', Curtin wrote. The events of Pearl Harbor and their aftermath had finally convinced him Australia faced 'a powerful, ably-led and unbelievably courageous foe'. The Government's confident reaction to the attack on Pearl Harbor was fast being replaced with an almost hysterical conviction that Australia's historic fears of an Asian invasion might be realised. The dramatic events of 1942 would test the nation and its people as never before.

James Morrison

Curtin's alliance with the United States*

BARELY an hour after the first wave of bombers hit Pearl Harbor, the Australian Prime Minister, John Curtin, was woken in Melbourne to be told Japan was at war. It was 5.45 on Monday morning. For Curtin, just two months into office as leader of the first Labor government in nineteen years, the news could not have come at a worse time. Within hours, he made an address to the nation, telling Australians that Japan had 'struck like an assassin in the night' and that 'this is our darkest hour'. A week earlier, he had suffered the anguish of having to announce the sinking of HMAS *Sydney* and the loss of 645 men off the coast of Western Australia after an engagement with the German raider *Kormoran*. Now he had to prepare the nation not only for war but the very real prospect of invasion.

The former alcoholic, trade unionist and journalist, who had been reluctant to become prime minister and who, according to his biographer, Norman E. Lee, thought Robert Menzies was a better wartime leader than he, swung into action. The Prime Minister called an emergency meeting of Cabinet, cancelled all military leave, extended the partial mobilisation, ordered air-raid precautions and, in an attempt to mobilise the civilian population for the war effort,

---

* First published under the title 'Curtin's new alliance', in
  The Australian Special Edition, 7 December 1991.

declared 'no private citizen can now proceed on holiday. It cannot be allowed.'

Curtin said in his broadcast on 8 December 1941:

We are at war with Japan. As dawn broke this morning in places as far apart as Honolulu, Nauru, Ocean Island, Guam, Singapore and British Malaya, shells from Japanese aircraft and shots from Japanese military forces struck death to United States citizens and members of its defence forces, to the peaceful subjects of Great Britain and to our men in ships and on land. The Pacific Ocean was reddened with the blood of Japan's victims.

Melbourne and Sydney were blacked out. City buildings were sandbagged and protected by brick shields, public and private air-raid shelters were built and air-raid wardens went on duty every night. Five days later the order was given to evacuate women and children from Darwin. In Malaya up to 15 000 Australian troops—two brigades of the 8th Division and supporting troops—had been waiting for battle for up to a year. But they were not to see action until January 1942.

Just two days after Pearl Harbor, the Curtin Government was struck a second blow, this time with the news that the British battleship *Prince of Wales* and the older battle cruiser *Repulse* had been sunk by Japanese aircraft off the east coast of Malaya. Their sinking, by Japanese warplanes using captured or abandoned Allied air strips in Malaya, destroyed one of the mainstays of Australian defence strategy—that the might of the Royal Navy could successfully defend the nation in times of peril.

The US consul in Adelaide according to David Day in his chapter, 'Pearl Harbor to Nagasaki' in Carl Bridge's book *Munich to Nagasaki*, was reported as observing that public reaction to the news was 'the closest to actual panic' he had seen, with 'staid businessmen' being 'reduced almost to wringing their hands'. As the Japanese troops advanced rapidly down the peninsula toward Singapore in the path of a humiliating Allied retreat, Curtin found himself with his best troops scattered across the world. The battle-hardened 7th and 9th Divisions and the remnants of the 6th Division were in the Middle East, thousands of Australian airmen were based in Britain and thousands of our sailors were in the Mediterranean and elsewhere.

Prior to Pearl Harbor there had been a steady worsening of the situation in the Pacific, yet Australia continued to reinforce its Middle East units reassured by the British propaganda about the 'impregnability' of Singapore, which would block any Japanese advance. In reality 'fortress Singapore' proved anything but impregnable. Its fall on 15 February 1942 and the capture of more than 80 000 Allied soldiers, including 15 000 men of the Australian 8th Division, finally shattered what confidence remained back home. Four days later the cumulative shock that had overtaken the nation was intensified with the bombing of Darwin on 19 February when 188 Japanese bombers, dive-bombers and fighters (led by the same commanders as at Pearl Harbor) attacked, killing 243 and injuring nearly 400 people.

For the first time since white settlement, Australia faced the prospect of hostile invasion and, despite some Allied military briefing papers which doubted the prowess of the Japanese fighting machine, and the 'business-as-usual' attitude of the conservative Menzies and Fadden governments which had left industry hopelessly unprepared for war, Curtin harboured no illusions as to what was required of his people. In his Pearl Harbor address to the nation, Curtin said: 'This is our darkest hour. Let that be fully realised. Our efforts of the past two years must be as nothing compared with the efforts we must now put forward. I can give you the assurance that the Australian government is fully prepared.'

In fact the country was far from fully prepared. Its best troops were still in the Middle East and industrially things were not much better. Despite two years of war under Menzies, aircraft production had not really begun. It was under Curtin that Labor set out to put the nation on a war footing. But the difficulty the Labor leader had in convincing the country that the war was at its doorstep was illustrated by the dispute which developed when he tried to convince the unions and private industry to cancel the Christmas holidays. At one stage of the negotiations Curtin was moved to say: 'The nation has to present the spectacle of a country at war'. War, he added, did not take leave at Christmas time. In the end the holidays were limited to a maximum of three days.

The humble Curtin, unlike Menzies when he visited Churchill in London in 1941, did not fall under the spell of the British Prime Minister. After the bombing of Pearl Harbor and the destruction of the British Pacific defence strategy with the sinking of the *Prince of Wales* and the *Repulse*, Curtin wanted to bring home his troops from the Middle East to defend Australia. Churchill resisted, assuring Curtin in a cable he received on Christmas Day that British forces in Malaya would fall back slowly (they did not, it was a rout) and that he would do all he could to strengthen the defensive line from the Burmese capital of Rangoon to Darwin, seeking the cooperation of the Americans.

But Curtin knew that the situation was more serious in Malaya than Churchill painted. So it was that Curtin, knowing Britain was preoccupied with the northern hemisphere, wrote his famous look-to-America article for the Melbourne *Herald*, which was published on 27 December. In the article, which embittered Churchill towards Curtin for some years, Curtin said that Australia regarded the war with Japan not as a phase of the broader war but as a new war. The second part of the article was an attempt to make his people realise they faced invasion and to get the economy on to a war footing. 'We look for a solid and impregnable barrier of the democracies against the three Axis powers, and we refuse to accept the dictum that the Pacific struggle must be treated as a subordinate segment of the general conflict', it said. Curtin continued:

> The Australian government, therefore, regards the Pacific struggle as primarily one in which the US and Australia must have the fullest say in the democracies' fighting plan. Without any inhibitions of any kind, I make it quite clear that Australia looks to America, free of any pangs as to our traditional links or kinship with the United Kingdom. We know the problems that the United Kingdom faces. We know the constant threat of invasion. We know the dangers of dispersal of strength, but we know, too, that Australia can go and Britain can still hold on. We are, therefore, determined that Australia shall not go, and we shall exert all our energies towards the shaping of a plan, with the United States as its keystone, which will give to our country some confidence of being able to hold out until the tide of battle swings out against the enemy.

Churchill, and some Australian newspapers, were livid. Churchill thought that Curtin's request for aid would make a bad impression in American circles. As author Peter Charlton points out in *War Against Japan, 1941–42* (published in 1989), it did not. The Americans had been planning to use Australia as a country from which to launch a reinvasion of the Philippines, should its colony fall to the Japanese. Four days before Curtin's article, the first American convoy, originally bound for Manila, sailed up the Brisbane River.

In the end Curtin struck a deal with Churchill. Under the agreement, the 9th Division would remain in the Middle East, but the 6th and 7th would return home and Churchill would agree to the appointment of an American general as supreme allied commander in the South-West Pacific. The man Canberra had requested to lead the Allied forces in the South-West Pacific was General Douglas MacArthur, who had been trapped by the Japanese advance on the island of Corregidor, 50 kilometres from Manila. MacArthur had vowed he would die on The Rock with his men, but on the orders of the President, Franklin Roosevelt, escaped with his family from Corregidor in a motor torpedo boat squadron, promising, 'I shall return'.

MacArthur arrived in Australia on 17 March 1942. In Melbourne, where he was to take up his command, MacArthur was greeted as a hero when his train pulled in at Spencer Street railway station. He was later to address the Australian Parliament and tell a Government House dinner, 'we shall win, or we shall die'. When Curtin died on 5 July 1945, MacArthur wrote to Mrs Curtin saying her husband was 'one of the greatest of wartime statesmen, and the preservation of Australia from invasion will be his immemorial monument'.

Carl Bridge

The myth of the American alliance*

GROWING up in Sydney in the 1950s and 1960s, few Australians were not told the moral tale of the treacherous Japanese attack on Pearl Harbor, the fall of Singapore, the Japs teeming south to Australia and the US cavalry riding to our rescue in the form of General Douglas MacArthur. As a result of Britain's failure to defend us, Australia let go the apron strings of Mother England and became part of the empire of the US, the '51st State' that eventually went all the way with LBJ into Vietnam. We learnt, too, of how Bob Menzies sold pig iron to the Japanese for them to make the bombs that later rained on our soldiers, how he sent our troops to the Middle East leaving Australia defenceless, and how he planned to sacrifice most of Queensland to the enemy and retreat behind the infamous 'Brisbane Line'. Worse, the British Prime Minister, Winston Churchill, reputedly had wanted to abandon Australia to the Japs and win it back after he had dealt with Hitler.

Luckily, the tale continued, Churchill's accomplice, 'Pig Iron Bob', was ousted in the nick of time and the new leader, Labor's John Curtin, saw reality and made his famous statement that 'Australia looks to America free of any pangs as to her traditional links with the United Kingdom'. Whereupon old Uncle Sam rescued us. As one Labor MP said at the time: 'I'd rather be pushed

---

*   First published under the title 'Look to America, look to the myth', in *The Australian Special Edition*, 7 December 1991.

off the footpath by a drunken gob [US sailor] than be chased down Martin Place by a Jap with a bayonet'. So ended the British Empire in Australia.

But how true is the story? Could Menzies and Churchill have been so bad? Curtin and MacArthur so good? Did the British Empire in Australia end almost overnight with the Japanese thrust south? And how much of a US satellite did Australia become? A look at the wartime archives, both here and abroad, casts things in a very different light. Nationalist myth fades to be replaced by a more believable international history.

Australia, in 1939, had a population of only six million, with very small defence forces and an economy among the worst hit by the Depression. Our trade and defence were overwhelmingly dependent on Britain and we looked out on an increasingly hostile world. The US was still isolationist. Little wonder Menzies tried to appease Japan by selling them iron; or that our army could only contemplate defending the settled parts of the continent even if forces had not been sent abroad. The records show the Menzies Government had excellent cause to send a third of our forces to Europe and the Middle East: so that our Suez Canal trade lifeline was not severed and so our main defence guarantee, a British battle fleet to be sent to Singapore, was secure. Keeping the Australian Imperial Force (AIF) at home risked the annihilation of our trade and a possible British decision not to send the fleet. Most important, it was argued, if Britain fell, we were finished.

It is now clear that the US entered the war not only to save the world for democracy but to stop Germany and Japan from choking off her trade. The Great Depression of the 1930s had led nations to build high tariff walls to save their collapsing economies. Despite these barriers, the US had an enormous trade which in 1940–41 Hitler's Germany threatened to destroy. Similarly, Japan's planned Greater East Asian Co-prosperity Sphere would rule out US–Asian trade. The spectre of a trading collapse gradually drove the US from isolationism to war. By 1941 President Franklin Roosevelt said in private he was 'trailing his coat' in the Atlantic for an incident that would bring the US into the war against Hitler.

To rein in Japan, the US imposed oil, iron and financial embargoes. Roosevelt also initiated secret defence talks in Washington with the British (including the Australians), Chinese and Dutch in February 1941, more than ten months before Pearl Harbor. At these meetings it was decided that should Japan join the war on Germany's side, the US would soon be compelled to start 'shooting'. Germany would need to be defeated first and the bulk of the joint British–US effort would go in that direction. Consequently, a 'holding war' would need to be fought against Japan in the Pacific with the US necessarily shouldering the burden. It was anticipated that Hong Kong, the Philippines, Singapore and Java would fall, but the US Pacific Fleet and elements of the Royal Navy would protect Australia and New Zealand. In other words, Churchill (and Menzies) 'looked to America' to defend Australia well before Curtin did. Curtin's statement simply called in the bet.

Sentiment aside, the British and Americans had their own material reasons for wanting to hold Australia. Three Australian divisions were fighting Rommel in the desert, thousands of Australian airmen were engaged over Europe and Australian food and munitions production was a significant factor in the global war effort. Holding Australia would help defeat Germany. Further, if the US were to retake the Philippines and roll Japan back, Australia would be the key base.

Contrary to the folk legend, it was Churchill, not Curtin, who first recommended the return from the Middle East of the 6th and 7th Divisions to secure the Australian base, though Curtin did successfully oppose the diversion of some of those troops to Rangoon. What of the 9th Division? They, along with our airmen, kept fighting the Germans regardless of the outbreak of the Pacific War.

Pearl Harbor marked the beginning of the friendly invasion of Australia by the US. Between 1942 and 1944 almost a million GIs passed through Australia and the US pumped millions of dollars into the Australian economy. So profitable was this to Australia that as early as June 1942 Cabinet was considering plans to restrict military enlistments to keep up numbers in the civilian work force to service the Americans. Australia fed MacArthur's army and came out of the war with a positive account with the US. Britain lost a quarter of its wealth fighting the war and was enormously in debt to the US.

But we did not, as a result of all this, instantly become a client state of the US. In fact, the British came back. In 1945, Australia encouraged the British to send a fleet back to Singapore and two years later Chifley's Labor Government made a gift to Britain of £45 million so it could buy Australian primary products. The old prewar pattern of trading dependence on Britain was resurrected. None of this is surprising. The US then, as now, had no need of Australian wheat and other foodstuffs in peacetime, and little demand for our wool. Britain did. Further, once the Cold War had begun and the US had taken over from Britain as policeman of the world, the Americans were more interested in propping up the British and the Commonwealth economically so that they could be useful constables.

But what of ANZUS? It was signed in 1951. Didn't it mark the turning point, the real 'look to America'? Not really. The documents reveal that the Australian Foreign Minister, Percy Spender, had to threaten not to ratify the 'soft' peace treaty proposed by the US with Japan to secure an ANZUS which, with no standing army, was really a poor man's NATO. US global strategy left the British to defend the Malaysian corridor down to Australia well into the 1960s. And in 1961–62 ANZUS did not stop the US approving Indonesia's takeover of Dutch New Guinea (West Irian) right on our doorstep and against our wishes. British, not American, atomic bombs and rockets were tested at Woomera and Maralinga in the 1950s; Menzies supported British diplomacy against US wishes in the Suez crisis in 1956; and we fought beside British troops in the Malayan Emergency and Confrontation, right up to 1965.

When, then, did the British go and the Americans come in? Only in the mid-1960s did the US replace Britain as our main trading partner and foreign investor. In 1964, the first Australian US base, North West Cape, was opened, by which time the British had stopped nuclear tests in Australia. In 1965, Australia went into Vietnam with the US. For the first time ever we were at war without the British at our sides.

In the international context, what was actually happening was that the British economy was finally proving to be incapable of sustaining Britain's pretences as a global power. It began in 1956 when the US forced an ignominious British withdrawal in the Suez crisis by the simple expedient of threatening to pull the financial plug. This started a train of events in the 1960s which saw the first application for British entry into the European Community, the devaluation of the pound and the decision to withdraw all British forces from Asia by 1971. Britain cut and ran from Australian trade and Australian defence in the 1960s. They left us; we didn't leave them.

The US archives suggest we went into Vietnam as a result of our feeling that the British were about to leave us defenceless in the region and the West Irian episode showed that we needed to increase our ANZUS insurance premium if we wanted an unambiguous US commitment to our forward defence. We went into Vietnam out of ANZUS's weakness, not its strength. When LBJ visited Australia to help Harold Holt win the 1966 elections, it was said that when he gave Harold and Zara a lift on Air Force One he quipped that he was here because 'I like to come out and look my prime ministers over'. It was, as the *Auckland Star* remarked, rather like an emperor visiting his fiefdoms. Radicals were quick to pronounce Australia 'the 51st State'.

But appearance deceived. The US economy was faltering, as was its war effort in Vietnam. In 1969 the Guam Doctrine was promulgated, saying that the US would not again fight in a regional war, but would only help its allies if another superpower was involved. In 1971 the US was in deficit for only the second time in the century so Nixon announced a dollar float and plans were afoot to scale down the war. Ironically, the British withdrawal from Singapore happened within a couple of years of the US leaving Vietnam.

Pearl Harbor marked the beginning of a half-century of US world dominance. Washington's reaction to the attack was to exercise its economic muscle to move in militarily to guarantee its markets in Europe and Asia. Britain and Australia, as allies, were major bases in those operations, and their economies benefited from US investment during and after the war. Japan, its bid for superpower status thwarted in 1941–45, became Washington's offshore aircraft base in the Asian Cold War. It had had a big economic boost from the US in the 1950s, kick-started by the Korean War, which has enabled it today to mount a second challenge for superpower status.

Australia was Americanised, along with most of the globe after Pearl Harbor. But Australia's economy and defence were never as integrated into the US system as they were into Britain's. Only for a few brief years during World War II and the Vietnam war could we pretend to be an important cog in the US machine. Our economies were never complementary. When our usefulness ended, so did our influence. In 1941 and 1965 we were needed, in 1945 and 1971 we were not. Japan, with its need for primary resources, has proved to be the true economic heir to Britain. The stories of our youth were, to borrow a phrase from the late Manning Clark, great comforters to the Australian psyche. But in this case, no amount of nationalist myth-making will alter the unvarnished truths of international history.

2

The fall of Singapore

Peter Charlton

The retreat from Malaya*

O N the afternoon of 14 January 1942, about 1000 bicycle-riding Japanese troops, laughing and chattering away, rode between eight and six abreast across a wooden bridge over the Gemencheh Creek, about eleven kilometres west of the village of Gemas in the north of Johore State. The Japanese, who had not encountered any opposition for 60 kilometres, were dangerously overconfident. They were about to ride into an ambush. This was to be the first encounter between Australian troops and the Japanese in the Malayan retreat.

The site had been chosen by the commander of the Australian 8th Division, Major-General Gordon Bennett, following the fall of Kuala Lumpur on 11 January. The morale of the British troops was crumbling in the face of the Japanese onslaught. The Japanese attacks had a depressing similarity about them. The Japanese would attack, hold the troops in contact in the front and then work quickly around to the flanks, cutting off the British withdrawal and generally causing havoc. For Bennett, who had been put in charge of the defence of Johore and whose troops at that stage had yet to fight the enemy, the answer was simple. On 16 December 1941, he had written to the Australian Army headquarters in Melbourne: 'I have seen a total

---

★   First published under the title 'Bloody retreat from Malaya' in the *Weekend Australian Special Edition*, 15–16 February 1992.

absence of the offensive spirit [on the part of British and Indian troops], which after all is the one great remedy to the methods adopted by the Japanese. Counter attacks would be a stop to this penetration.'

The Australian 27th Brigade was to look after the Gemas area, and particularly the main trunk road running from the west towards Segamat, along which the Australian general knew the Japanese forces would have to come. The wooden bridge across the Gemencheh was an excellent position. The road twisted through dense jungle for about half a kilometre. A cutting, about 40 metres long and 3.5 metres high, ended about 60 metres from the bridge; on the other side of the creek, the road ran straight for about 250 metres, with no cover available on either side of the road. It was an ideal killing ground.

The commander of the 2/30th Battalion, Lieutenant-Colonel Frederick Galleghan, known as 'Black Jack' because of his part-West Indian origins, was a superb leader and a careful tactician. Put in charge of the ambush by Bennett, he realised that the site, although excellent in many ways, was not big enough for his entire battalion. It could only accommodate a company, so his company commanders drew from a hat for the honour. The draw went to Captain Des Duffy commanding B Company. Galleghan placed the rest of the battalion astride the road five kilometres behind and ready to face the shock of the inevitable Japanese flanking movements through the jungle. Even with Duffy's company, sections of troops were placed out wide again to prevent such action. In pouring rain on the night of 13 January, the infantry soldiers of the 2/30th Battalion moved into the carefully chosen positions. On the bridge, sappers from the 2/12th Field Company worked swiftly with explosives, preparing the old wooden structure for demolition.

At 4 pm on 14 January, the first Japanese troops appeared. Galleghan's troops, positioned close to the winding road, let them pass only metres away. Duffy let nearly 300 Japanese cyclists pass through the trap, leaving between 700 and 800 stuck in the killing ground. He then signalled to the engineers and the bridge was blown, hurling wooden debris, bicycles and men high into the air. The soldiers waiting in the ambush tossed grenades and poured machine-gun fire into the packed troops on the open road below. The Japanese had nowhere to go and nowhere to hide. Later, Duffy said: 'The entire 300 metres of road was thickly covered with dead and dying men—the result of the blast when the bridge was blown and the deadly fire of our Bren guns'. The ambush was over in less than twenty minutes and, apart from the Japanese who had been allowed to pass through, it was a complete success. Duffy's company dispersed and made their way back to the battalion position five kilometres to the west. Only one Australian soldier was killed in the action, probably the most successful ambush of World War II.

The triumph at Gemas led to unjustified optimism in Singapore, which was soon checked when the victory was quickly followed by a catastrophe on the Sungei (river) Muar. A key piece of the terrain was where only a ferry traversed the 500-metre-wide river. While the Japanese were to the north of the waterway, their final thrust to the causeway at Johore and then to Singapore would be frustrated. When the Japanese attacked on the morning of 15 January, the two Indian companies north of the river were quickly overrun. That night, despite heavy fire from the Australian gunners, the Japanese crossed the Muar using boats they had brought down the peninsula. By the end of that day they had overwhelmed the inexperienced and terrified Indian defenders on the southern banks.

With the Japanese across the Muar and landing further south of Batu Pahat, Bennett's main defensive positions at Johore were under threat. He was forced to commit two Australian battalions to the battle, the 2/19th and 2/29th. Late on the afternoon of 17 January, the 2/29th took the first Japanese assaults on the Muar road, forward of Bakri. Japanese patrols probed forward to determine the location of the Australian pits and then the whole position was raked by carefully directed mortar fire. All that night the Australians stayed in their pits, shaking from the accuracy of the Japanese mortar gunners.

During the night a battery of guns from the 2/4th Australian Anti-Tank Regiment came under heavy and accurate artillery and mortar fire. Then shortly after dawn, five Japanese tanks appeared on the road from Muar, heading directly for the battalion position to the rear. Positioned at each end of the cutting, the anti-tank gunners had good fields of fire but little cover. The gunners loaded and fired solid armour-piercing shells, but these had little impact on the lightly built tanks. The rounds simply went in one side and out the other. The Japanese continued to advance, three tanks reaching and then passing the forward Australian gun. Its commander, Lance-Sergeant C.W. Thornton, ordered his crew to ignore the other Japanese tanks still approaching their position, and to swing the gun around and fire into the rear of the tanks that passed. By that time the Australian gunners had switched to the more effective high explosive rounds. The gun troop commander, Lieutenant Ben Hackney, saw some of the Japanese tanks trapped inside the cutting attempting to turn and get away. He wrote later:

> But the Australain fire was too accurate . . . one by one they were smashed, set on fire and rendered useless. There came from the tanks sounds which resembled an Empire Day celebration as the ammunition within them burnt and cracked with loud bursts, and hissed, with every now and then a louder explosion as larger ammunition ignited.

In all, ten Japanese tanks were destroyed and a following infantry attack was beaten off.

Later that day the Japanese tried again and again, throwing themselves into assaults on the 2/29th's positions, each time being beaten off, but each time whittling down the defenders more and more. They slipped around the flanks of the Australians, using the jungle cover skilfully, and established a roadblock between the 2/29th and the 2/19th Battalion to the rear. The commander, Lieutenant-Colonel J.C. Robertson, went back through the jungle to try to establish links between the two Australian battalions, but Japanese fire from the roadblock seriously wounded him. Despite his injuries he managed to get back to within 100 metres of his battalion headquarters before being picked up by a Bren gun carrier, who had rushed to his rescue. Robertson, however, died of his wounds within an hour. The blow was felt by his entire battalion but still the Australians fought on, beating off probes from the south and the west. It seemed as if the Japanese were all around them, swarming through the jungle, cutting off all possible withdrawal routes.

Protection of the Australian flanks had been entrusted to the Indians, but these troops quickly lost their nerve and ran. The Australians were left on their own in the positions near Bakri, and the damage they inflicted on the Japanese advance, particularly on one whole division of the crack Imperial Guards, was substantial.

The Japanese commander, General Takumo Nishimura, called it 'serious and sanguinary'.

Command of the brigade now passed to Lieutenant-Colonel Charles Anderson, the commanding officer of the 2/19th Battalion, a survivor of World War I and a winner of the Military Cross. Ahead of him Anderson had a fighting withdrawal of about eight kilometres, by night, towards the bridge at Parit Sulong. Anderson's escape route ran through swampy areas, where movement off the road was virtually impossible for formed bodies of men. Here the Japanese had put ambushes and roadblocks. Before long, Anderson's weary men ran into Japanese troops dug in on a small rise at the side of the road. The forward company quickly moved to dislodge the Japanese from the position.

At first the Japanese troops were too strong and the company's attack slowed down, then stopped. Another company was brought in to reinforce the assault and together the Australians, singing 'Waltzing Matilda' charged in. They then forced the Japanese from their posts and quickly went wide and attacked them again from the rear. The action was successful and Anderson's force moved on, only to be halted by another roadblock not far on from the first. This time Anderson personally took charge of the operation to clear the route. Armed with hand grenades and a pistol, he led men around on the south side of the road while another group created a diversion on the north side. Moving quickly through the jungle, his eyes glinting behind the rounded spectacles, Anderson brought his men to the edge of the Japanese position. Pausing only to check his position, the Australian colonel threw the grenades and charged in firing his pistol. Another roadblock was cleared; the force moved on.

Now the roadblocks were closer together. Each time the Japanese fought desperately, each time the exhausted Australians summoned up enough energy to make one more effort. By now the ammunition was running low and Anderson was forced to put his men against the Japanese position with fixed bayonets. But after each clearing operation the casualties would mount. By nightfall on that terrible 20 January, Anderson's force had fought its way to the outskirts of the village of Parit Sulong, only to meet with the depressing news that the Japanese had beaten it there.

Anderson planned the attack on Parit Sulong at 11 am the

following day. For two hours, the Australians fought but could make no headway against the Japanese, who were well dug in. Some of the gunners fought in a wild frenzy with axes and shovels, but it was to no avail. British troops withdrawing on a parallel route were alerted to join the attack from the west, to divert the Japanese defenders and relieve some of the burden on the Australians. But that assault failed and Anderson was forced to pull his soldiers back.

The succession of struggles down the route had depleted the Diggers' already meagre supplies and they sent urgent messages to Bennett's headquarters requesting more ammunition. Anderson's staff officers could not be certain whether their plea had even been understood, because it had been couched in curious terms—their code books had been destroyed for security reasons before the withdrawal had begun. But when the reply from Bennett's head-quarters was received, it was crystal clear in its clarity: 'Look up at sparrowfart' (meaning supplies would be flown in at dawn). Day broke and light came quickly, as it does in the tropics. The Australians looked to the skies as instructed to see a couple of ancient Albacores, escorted by three equally ancient RAAF Buffaloes, lumbering along the axis of the road. One dumped much needed food and morphia to Anderson's beleaguered force, the other dropped bombs on the Japanese holding the bridge. But there was no ammunition.

The Australians were finished. Anderson was forced to take an agonising decision: to save the rest of his force he had to leave the wounded behind. Those of Anderson's weary soldiers who could move slipped away into the jungle to the north in an attempt to move around behind the Japanese. Later that night the Japanese captured the wounded Australians, bound them together with wire, doused them with petrol and then led them into the jungle where they were machine-gunned and set on fire. Meanwhile, Anderson and his men moved first to the north and then turned east, working through swamps and open ground. The Japanese, who saw them moving, mistook their intentions; they thought the Australians were about to mount a strong counterattack and hurriedly withdrew. In doing so they left a gap, about 400 metres wide. It was enough for Anderson's men to slip through and make their way to Yong Peng.

The British commander in Singapore, Lieutenant-General A. E.

Percival, said later that Anderson's effort during the battle of Muar was 'one of the epics of the Malayan campaign'. Yet despite Anderson's efforts, for which he was awarded a well-deserved Victoria Cross, Percival had no option other than to withdraw the remaining forces across the causeway linking Malaya to Singapore and hope to hold there.

Peter Charlton

The fall of the 'impregnable fortress'[*]

ABOUT 8 am on Saturday, 31 January 1942, the already nervous residents of Singapore were startled by a loud explosion from the north which rattled their windows and shook the furniture. Although the city had been systematically bombed for nearly two months, the latest blast was louder and more powerful than anything previously experienced. It was the detonation of the charges set in the causeway connecting the island of Singapore with the Malayan peninsula. More than 20 metres wide at the waterline and wider still at the base, the causeway had more than a tactical significance for the defenders of this now naked island. With the water rushing through the 20-metre gap left by the explosion, it seemed the umbilical cord linking the island with the mainland was severed for good.

In truth, the demolition's effects were more spectacular than realistic; it meant the Japanese would not be able to bicycle across the water gap. Then, no one really expected them to come that way in the first instance. If and when they came, it was thought they would cross the kilometre-wide Straits of Johore in a mass of boats and landing barges. It was clear the Japanese would press on to Singapore—for its fine harbour in the south of the island, for its

---

* First published under the title 'Humiliating fall of an "impregnable fortress" ', in the *Weekend Australian Special Edition*, 15–16 February 1992.

naval facilities in the north-east and because it would have been militarily impossible to leave the British, Indian and Australian troops on the island without exacting an unconditional surrender.

Singapore was the Gibraltar of Asia, and to the British the symbol of their prestige in Asia. The task of defending this symbol fell on the shoulders of the British Empire's troops. Among them, the Australians, still suffering from the withdrawals of the previous days, had been manning a bridgehead in the southern tip of Johore State. All through the night of 30–31 January they pulled back, out of their well-sited defensive positions and across the causeway. Most of the movement was by truck and anxious officers scanned the skies for any sign of the Japanese Air Force. Even with the cover of darkness, an attack from the air on such densely packed roads could have been catastrophic.

Fortunately for the withdrawing Australians, no attack came. From a vantage point near where the causeway came ashore on Singapore Island, Major-General Gordon Bennett watched the troop movements, dismayed by the actions and failures of the previous weeks. Later, the Australian general wrote he had never felt so 'sad and upset'. He added: 'Words fail me. Why? I thought I could hold Johore, but I assumed that British troops would have held their piece. This retreat seems fantastic. Fancy 550 miles [880 kilometres] in 55 days, chased by a Japanese army with no artillery.' Bennett was wrong on just one important point: the Japanese Army had yet to *employ* its artillery. His despair and disillusionment were shared by many others, but for the Australians and for some of the British troops these feelings were also tinged with a fine show of defiance. The Australians still wanted to come to grips with an enemy which, they believed fervently, they had met too late in the campaign.

In November 1939, Winston Churchill, yet to become British prime minister, had predicted the Japanese would need an army of at least 50 000 men, which would have had to be landed in marshes and jungles, to take 'Fortress Singapore'. Instead the Japanese had only 35 000 fighting on the Malayan mainland. They had lost only 2000 killed and 3000 wounded since the invasion on 7–8 December. And they had driven before them forces nearly twice their size numerically, in the process literally annihilating three of the seven Indian brigades, with their combined British and Indian battalion make-up.

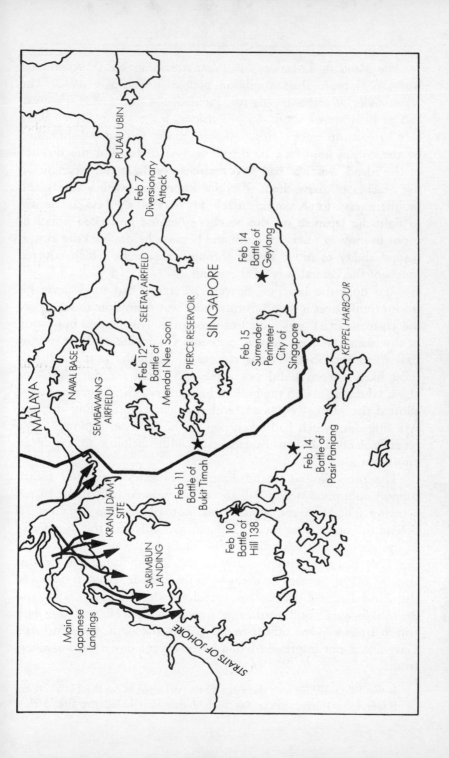

The island of Singapore, 40 kilometres long and 23 kilometres wide, held more than a million people in February 1942. The commander of forces in Malaya, Lieutenant-General A.E. Percival, had at his disposal about 85 000 troops, but at least 15 000 were base or garrison troops, unsuited for fighting and now demoralised by the conspicuous lack of British success so far. For the defence of the island, Percival had two real choices: fight the Japanese on the beaches or allow them to come ashore and, with a strong and mobile reserve force, counterattack. He decided the best course was to fight the Japanese on the beaches—because he lacked sufficient room to move a reserve around and because he doubted the British troops' ability to move swiftly through the jungle, which covered much of the central part of the island.

To hold the beaches, however, Percival had to disperse his troops thinly over a broad front. There was confusion about where the Japanese attack was most likely to come. During one inspection of the island, General Wavell, Supreme Commander of the South-East Asian and South Pacific regions, thought the north-west was most likely. Percival did not agree and opted for the north-east coast, where he placed the bulk of his artillery. The Australians were allotted the north-west coast, with Bennett commanding the two AIF brigades, which had taken part in the Malayan fighting, and a recently landed Indian Brigade, the 44th, helping to cover an enormous area.

The zone allotted to the Australian brigades with their Indian support comprised nearly half the entire western half of the island, a region split by rivers, which made communications difficult. To defend the north-west sector, Bennett had only half the number of troops allotted to the north-east; he allotted the causeway sector to the 27th Brigade, with the 2/30th and 2/26th battalions forward and the 2/29th in rear. To the west of this brigade, Bennett deployed the 22nd Brigade with all its battalions, the 2/18th, 2/19th and 2/20th forward. Still further west and south-west was the 44th Indian Brigade. One officer in the 2/20th Battalion, Captain Frank Gaven, was not impressed when he first went down to the water-front:

> It was like walking into the edge of the mangroves on the Hawkesbury River . . . I have never felt such desperation in all my life. I then

56

realised that forward defence was an impossible task. There were no defences or fortifications and no field of view of an enemy approach. It was a situation that would not offer the troops any glimmer of hope.

An officer in the neighbouring 2/19th Battalion thought his unit had been 'dumped in a scraggy waste of stunted rubber and tangled undergrowth, apparently miles from anywhere, our vision limited to the next rise and our means of movement confined to a few native foot tracks winding through the wilderness'.

Like his junior officers, Bennett realised the unsuitability of the terrain for the defence of the island. The battalion posts were hundreds of metres apart and the heavy vegetation and cover were perfect for the Japanese tactic of infiltration. Bennett realised the immense difficulties facing his troops and decided that offensive action was the only possible course of defence under such circumstances. The orders he issued for the defence included the requirements of heavy patrolling across the strait to the mainland. The signs of such an invasion were patently clear. One patrol reported gun emplacements dug every fifty metres for as far as they could see into the rubber plantations that reached right down to the Straits of Johore on the Malayan coastline. As well, the Japanese had set up huge kitchens to feed their soldiers before the invasion. This information was quickly relayed back to the battalion and through the Australian command structure, but was apparently discounted in Malayan Command Headquarters because of similar preparations opposite the north-east coast.

Because of Japan's absolute air superiority, all the Australians' defensive preparations had to be done by night. By early February, most of the island's aircraft had been withdrawn to the Netherlands East Indies and two of Singapore's three airfields were under Japanese observation and artillery fire. The defenders were left with virtually no air support. The Japanese, on the other hand, enjoyed not only air superiority but an observation balloon tethered near the Sultan of Johore's palace on the mainland. It gave excellent views of the island. Thanks to this superb observation, the Japanese were able to shell and bomb the Australian defenders with impunity, cutting communications, disrupting defence work and generally playing havoc. The defenders were not permitted to fire at either the observation balloon or at the palace, which was then occupied by the Japanese commanders. The reasoning was that the Malayan Command was preparing for a three-month stage. It was, therefore, thought necessary to ration ammunition.

Although the Japanese supply lines were hugely stretched by their rapid advance down the Malayan peninsula, they entertained no such similar thoughts. Instead, the Japanese commanders assembled a huge force of artillery and ammunition in preparation for the attack. Each of the 168 guns had between 500 and 1000 rounds to fire, and they began their barrage on 8 February, signalling the start of the invasion of Singapore Island, the so-called impregnable fortress. The weight of the Japanese artillery fire fell where they intended to launch their attack. This was not on the north-east sector where Percival had concentrated his artillery, but on the Australians in the west.

All that day, the artillery fire dropped with devastating accuracy, Lieutenant-Colonel A.L. Varley, commanding the 2/18th Battalion, noted in his diary that during four years' service in World War I, he had never experienced such concentrated shellfire over such a period. He wrote:

> On this occasion, 80 shells were counted falling in D Coy area in one minute. One platoon area had 67 in 10 minutes and this was typical of the whole area. Battalion HQ had 45 shells in seven minutes, half an hour's spell then another similar dose and so on throughout the whole area all day.

Nearby, Sergeant Tom Fardy, of the 2/20th Battalion, prepared for the worst after a few hours of such shelling. 'You're scared, then you become shit scared', he wrote. 'Then you decide you are going to take as many of the enemy with you, then you settle down and when the men see you settled it rubs off and everyone feels more settled.' In spite of the intensity of this artillery fire, which was reported to Percival's headquarters, no counter-battery from the heavier British artillery was ordered; the Australians had to rely on their own artillery. At one stage, the position was so critical the artillery liaison officer with the 2/20th Battalion said simply: 'Bring down fire everywhere'.

The British staff officers thought the Japanese artillery bombardment was the first of several days' preliminary shelling and that the Japanese attention would soon shift, either to the causeway area or to the north-east. The Australians would simply have to make do with their own resources. The accuracy of the Japanese fire resulted not just from the aerial observation, but also from their own patrolling. For the week since the Australians had crossed the causeway, Japanese patrols had operated in the thick vegetation of the island's coastline, avoiding detection by thinly spread Allied patrols and mapping each of the Australian defensive positions with accuracy. Still, despite the heavy and accurate shelling, Australian casualties were relatively light, thanks to the slit trenches which had been dug and the soft soil which absorbed the force of the explosions. But the shelling cut vital communications, the wire between defensive positions which allowed commanders to know what was going on to their front, their flanks and to the rear. Despite heroic efforts by the Australian signallers, the shellfire cut the wires as quickly as they could be repaired. The confusion was immense.

That night the Japanese attacked, crossing the Johore Strait in barges and boats, and landing first in the area held by the 2/20th Battalion. Nearby, an officer of the 2/4th Machine-Gun Battalion could see the landing barges dimly in the light given off by the burning oil tanks. He waited until they approached to within thirty metres of the foreshore, and then he ordered the Vickers machine-gunners to open up. The fire was devastating, tearing into the soft-sided barges. Quickly, the Japanese backed off and moved further west. The sheer weight of the Japanese numbers began to overwhelm the Australians. The machine-gunners had fired almost 10 000 rounds per gun when, out of ammunition and with the Japanese pressing against their flanks, their platoon commander ordered the guns be destroyed.

By dusk on 11 February, the defenders were pressed back into a shrinking perimeter around the city of Singapore itself. The strategic higher ground of Bukit Timah, and vast food and oil supplies there, had now fallen into Japanese hands. By 13 February, the end was apparent. The Japanese had captured much of the city's water supply. The available defensive troops were crammed into a tight perimeter and were short of ammunition, short of weapons, lacking any air cover and lacking the means of withdrawal from the island. On 15 February, Percival realised his stand was finally over, and a deputation of military and civilian leaders approached the Japanese front line along the Bukit Timah road. It reported back that Percival should prepare to meet his enemy counterpart to discuss surrender. Within hours, 130 000 Allied soldiers found themselves prisoners of war. Churchill's 'impregnable fortress' had crumbled in one of the most humiliating defeats of modern history.

James Morrison

The Tiger of Malaya*

LIEUTENANT-General Tomoyuki Yamashita was a big, heavy man, an officer of extensive experience as a commander but untested on the battlefield. His lack of battlefield experience was about all he had in common with the British commander in Malaya, Lieutenant-General A. E. Percival. The Japanese commander had headed the Japanese military missions to Italy and Germany between the wars and was one of his country's most respected military tacticians.

Percival, by contrast, was seen as an unassuming leader, an exceptional staff commander; tall with protruding teeth and a little moustache, his appearance was not unlike that of a rabbit. The war correspondent Ian Morrison thought Percival did not know how to deal with a group of men and had a mind that 'saw the difficulties to any scheme before it saw the possibilities. He was a negative person, with no vigour, no colour and no conviction. As a leader, he did not appeal either to the troops or to the general public', Morrison said.

Yamashita, however, was ambitious and aggressive, a gambler where Percival was cautious. Known at home as the 'Tiger of Malaya', his tactics of engaging the enemy in the front, outflanking

* First published under the title 'Tiger's bluff led to quick capitulation', in the *Weekend Australian Special Edition*, 15–16 September 1992.

him on both sides and then bringing in the reserves to cut off his retreat proved highly effective. Ironically, Percival was one of the few who correctly prophesied that a Japanese invasion force would capture airfields in Thailand and northern Malaya before attacking Singapore. Yamashita planned his final assault on Singapore knowing he was dangerously short of food, ammunition and weapons. He had eighteen tanks, his infantrymen were outnumbered three to one and they had rations of only 100 rounds a day. The dilemma he faced was that on the one hand a quick attack on Singapore could see him dragged into street fighting for the city with the prospect of running out of ammunition. On the other hand, if he delayed he would run the risk of the British being reinforced from the sea.

So Yamashita had gun emplacements built every fifty metres or so in the rubber plantations that ran all the way down to the Straits of Johore. During the bombardment of Singapore, which started on 8 February, he moved his guns around to create the impression of far greater firepower. Yamashita was later to admit his bluff:

> My attack on Singapore was a bluff that worked. I had 30,000 men and was outnumbered more than three to one. I knew if I had to fight long I would be beaten. That is why the surrender had to be at once. I was very frightened that the British would discover our numerical weakness and lack of supplies and force me into disastrous street fighting.

But despite his success, Yamashita was convinced the Japanese high command, headed by the then Prime Minister General Hideki Tojo, was plotting to have him assassinated. He believed, rightly, that Tojo was jealous of his popularity. Yamashita's fall from political grace came on 29 April 1942, when he addressed a parade in Singapore and referred to the people of Malaya and Singapore as Japan's 'subject people', at variance with the propaganda of Tokyo's 'co-prosperity sphere'. Tojo took his chance and ordered Yamashita transferred to a desk job in Manchuria. He was handed a poisoned chalice in October 1944 when he was ordered to lead the Four-teenth Area Army in the impossible task of crushing the Americans' counterattack in the Philippines. Yamashita surrendered to the Allies on Luzon Island. He was condemned for war crimes in the Philippines and was hanged on 23 February 1946.

James Morrison

Major-General
H. Gordon Bennett*

ABOUT 1 am on Monday, 16 February 1942, a junk slid out of Singapore harbour bound for Sumatra. It carried the commander of the 8th Division of the AIF, Major-General H. Gordon Bennett, two aides and eight British Malay Volunteer Force officers. Bennett—with only a map, torn out of a school atlas (with a scale of 160 kilometres to the centimetre) by one of his aides—was leaving behind him one of Britain's greatest military disasters, his 16 000 men and some would argue, his military reputation. He arrived in Sydney on 1 March to be met by his wife, daughter, well-wishers and photographers. The next day Bennett was praised for his 'gallantry' by the Prime Minister, John Curtin, who condoned his escape from Singapore. But his reception by the Chief of the General Staff, Lieutenant-General V. A. H. Sturdee, that morning at Victoria Barracks in Melbourne was chilly. Bennett, who had expected to be welcomed as a returning hero, said Sturdee turned his back on him after saying his escape had been 'ill-advised'.

Should Bennett have remained with his men? Was Bennett a competent divisional commander in Malaya? These two entwined questions have dogged military historians for the past fifty years and, in spite of a military court of inquiry, a royal commission and

---

* First published under the title 'Bennett's ambition the Achilles heel' in the *Weekend Australian Special Edition*, 15–16 September 1992.

countless books, have never been satisfactorily resolved. With the benefit of hindsight it could be argued that if Bennett had been a good divisional commander he had made the correct decision in returning home. If he had not been a good commander, it would have been best for him to remain with his men in captivity. Bennett had thought all officers above field rank would be separated from their men and sent for the war's duration to the relative comfort of Tokyo. He wanted to fight again and was not to know that it was not until six months after the surrender that senior officers were separated from their men. Furthermore, the impression lasts that Bennett escaped while ordering his men not to, although it was established as early as 1945 that he suppressed an order for them to take their chances after one of his brigade commanders said it could lead to a massacre of unarmed Australians by the Japanese.

On the one hand, Bennett is described as an inspirational leader—he was the only Allied general to show aggression during the Malayan campaign. On the other hand, A. B. Lodge writes in *The Fall of General Gordon Bennett* that he made four major errors during the campaign and his distrust of staff officers was such that it made his headquarters almost unworkable—a significant constraint on the competence of any commander? Lodge writes that Bennett probably reached his military ceiling as a fighting brigadier in World War I. His time out of the army between the wars meant that he was not practised in modern military tactics and he lacked the diplomacy to be part of an Allied force (he was a trenchant critic of Indian and British soldiers in Malaya and publicly described the British commander, Malayan forces, Lieutenant-General A. E. Percival, as weak).

But Bennett's record in Malaya was certainly no worse than any other commander and, many would argue, considerably better than most. His mistake probably was to have been so openly critical of others—who faced the same impossible position as he did—and to have been so convinced he was correct to ignore advice which conflicted with his own opinions. Bennett, the only general at that stage of the war to have fought the Japanese, believed he was fulfilling his patriotic duty in returning to Australia. He argued he brought back with him valuable information on Japanese tactics and, furthermore, exercised his obligation as a soldier to escape.

While many other officers escaped from Singapore, Bennett was the only one of general's rank to do so. It is argued Bennett's place was with his men. In view of the brutality with which the Japanese treated POWs, he could have used the weight of his rank as a major-general to stick up for their rights. Not only Sturdee, but nearly all the Australian generals, Blamey, Percival, his own chief of staff, many of his senior officers as well as other ranks who went into captivity, believed he should have stayed with his men. Lodge concludes that there could be little doubt the prospect of being deprived of promotion and further commands, of making up ground lost against his great rival, Blamey, and of eventually commanding the Australian Army 'provided at least as powerful a force as patriotism in driving him to leave Singapore'.

Supporters of Bennett point to the backing he received from his men, the front-line soldiers, the only verdict he really cared about. Bennett was cheered at the dockside by the hospital ships carrying the Changi survivors and led the 8th Division contingent on every ANZAC march until his death from a heart attack on 1 August 1962. But not all of Bennett's former troops were of the same opinion. Tony Newsom, an intelligence sergeant based at divisional headquarters and a Changi survivor, commented: 'After three and a half years, Hitler and the Emperor of Japan would have been cheered, too, if they'd been standing at the wharf'.

Christopher Dawson

'Black Jack' Galleghan*

BRIGADIER Sir Frederick Galleghan's first hat sported the red band of a telegram boy, as did his last cap, which rested on his coffin—that of a brigadier. 'Black Jack' Galleghan was one of the giants to stride out of World War II. Though he had yearned to earn his reputation as a fighting soldier, this was surpassed by his leadership and example as a prisoner of war in Singapore's infamous Changi prison. His calm and indomitable attitude towards his Japanese captors as Australian commandant of Changi was fundamental in maintaining morale among the Australian POWs. He inspired great love, especially among those who served under him in the 2/30th Battalion. He has been described as someone you either loved or hated: abrasive yet gentle, ferocious yet compassionate.

According to his biographer, Stan Arneil, Galleghan liked to say he had served Australia as a military officer for more than fifty years. It was true; his first pips as a second-lieutenant appeared on his shoulders in 1913 when he was a member of the cadet corps, which

---

* First published under the title 'Black Jack hero of Changi hell-hole', in the *Weekend Australian Special Edition*, 15–16 September 1992.

he had joined at school in 1909 at the age of twelve. One of his great disappointments was that he had not been commissioned in World War I. Instead he served as a front-line infantryman in the 34th Battalion, AIF, rising to the rank of sergeant. He was wounded twice.

'Cursing Black Jack was one of the best ways to get through the summer heat, in the sweat and dust of the hills and the long marches without water', wrote Arneil about the training around Tamworth in northern NSW in 1941. He continued:

> Imperceptibly, the troops realised that their unit was different and before they knew it the first glimpses of esprit de corps began to show. It was exactly what Galleghan had aimed for and the troops daily grew prouder of their unit. They grew fitter and fitter and revelled in it and they grew closer and closer together into a fighting team.

In Malaya in 1942, it was Galleghan's 2/30th Battalion that inflicted the biggest losses on the Japanese advances with the ambush at Gemas, in Malaya. Together with other Australians, Galleghan, who had been ordered into hospital, having lost his hearing, was devastated by Lieutenant-General A.E. Percival's capitulation in Singapore. He was, however, to lead his men on the long 25-kilometre march to Changi.

The Japanese guards held Galleghan in awe as they knew he had commanded the brigade at Gemas where many of their comrades had been killed. He remained unbending in his dealings with them. He refused to allow them into his quarters unless they were regimentally dressed and at one time he dressed down a detachment of Japanese guards. The Japanese took his reprimand to heart, borrowed his battalion tailor, restored their uniforms and boots and then asked Galleghan to inspect them. He was knighted in 1960 in recognition of his services to ex-servicemen and women and died eleven years later.

Sir David Griffin

A personal account*

To relate what happened on 15 February 1942 appeared at first glance to be a relatively easy assignment. For how could any of us fail to remember even the smallest detail of that most momentous day in our lives? Yet, it is by no means easy. Mercifully, perhaps, it has all started to fade. Memory has held the door but it has been steadily closing even on those historic days, and for me, at least, the best one could hope for would be to peer through the chink straining to catch a glimpse of another life, another age.

Many of my generation who were raised on Alice will remember the exchange in Through the Looking Glass. ' "The horror of that moment", the King went on, "I shall never, never forget." "You will though", the Queen said, "unless you make a memorandum of it." ' Some of us were in a position to make a memorandum of it and it seemed better for present purposes to reproduce it rather than to reconstruct it:

January 1942

The situation on the Malay peninsula even for those of us whose strategic knowledge is nil, obviously can scarcely be worse. Our artillery and infantry have been magnificent but without air support

---

* First published under the title 'Horrors—gone but not forgotten', in the Weekend Australian Special Edition, 15–16 February 1992.

they are having a rotten time. The successful ambush by the 30th Battalion at Gemas raised hopes but these were soon dashed by news of the disaster at Muar where the 19th and 29th had been over-whelmed and caught in a trap by a division of the Japanese Imperial Guards. My unit was sent up towards Muar with our vehicles to give any help we could to those who had managed to walk out. Of course it was raining—the campaign is being fought in almost incessant rain. We were clearing wounded from a tent and in the half light of the petrol lamps the long silver water drops flashed for an instant before vanishing into the surrounding blackness. The ground was awash with rivulets. Elsewhere the leaves from the rubber trees had been trampled into a thick mush. I asked nearly everyone if they had news of Charles [a friend]. Eventually I struck some chap from his company who told me we would not be seeing him any more. It made me feel terribly lonely all of a sudden. It was a most melancholy night.

Leaving the field of battle in the back of an army ambulance is an inglorious end to a military career. It is both undignified, unacceptable and disturbing but it had happened to me and there I was. As we swayed along the darkened jungle roads of Johore heading south it seemed a futile end to all the training and all the effort. To make matters worse Tony R. was in the ambulance with me. We had grown up together in the same class at Cranbrook and there he was lying deeply wounded in the opposite bunk below. It was a longish journey but finally we arrived at what before the war had been St Patrick's School for Girls at Katong on the eastern end of the island of Singapore. But now it was the 13th Australian General Hospital. A stretcher, an examination by an army surgeon—so merciful that later he became known as St Luke—an anaesthetic, an operation and a coming-to in what seemed to the fuddled patient to be a flashback to France in World War I.

Hollywood cameramen would pay thousands for this scene. The ward is in a Roman Catholic chapel. Gothic columns, yellow-glassed windows and elaborate Byzantine lighting arrangements. You can't see the floor, which is tiled, because of the beds. They are almost touching. The army sisters as they hurry up and down the narrow avenues brush the beds with their starched dresses. They are so brisk, so business-like, sympathetic yet impersonal. With their scarlet capes and white veils they have an air of comforting assurance.

February 1942

Well, it is just a week today since we became, so to speak, 'self-contained'. After the Argyll and Sutherland Highlanders, the last troops to cross, had marched over the causeway joining Malaya and Singapore with their bagpipes playing a regimental march there was a great explosion. It was the causeway being blown up and that was it. In desperate times the British certainly have a great sense of theatre. We are now an island entire unto ourselves.

Later

The expected storm is about to break. The big guns are firing across the Straits of Johore and the Japanese planes are coming over very high to drop bombs. Unless they happen to fall near you one takes very little notice of bombings. When they do, you hang on to yourself until it is all over—provided there is something of yourself apt to hang on to. When the sirens go the nurses perch steel helmets over their veils and call out 'Keep away from the windows boys'. One of them is very big and motherly. She tries hard to be severe but her eyes betray her with their twinkling. 'Oh, do keep away from the windows', she says at last. 'You know it is dangerous.' Then she hurries over to a window and has a peep herself.

Some of the raids are worth looking at, from this distance, provided you don't let yourself think of what it all means. There are men somewhere under those bombs, but you try and not let yourself think of that. Each morning squadrons of Japanese planes, 27 or 54, fly high over the city. When the bombs drop there is a great rolling rumble and the ground shakes. The most spectacular raid happened a few days ago, when the oil storage tanks were hit. The smoke rose up like a gigantic cumulus cloud with a thin grey edge. It looked stationary and solid. You could not help thinking of that bit in *On Our Selection* when the fire burns the cockatoo-fencing and Dave asks Dad if he doesn't think it is a fine sight. Fine sight it was, rising from the funeral pyre of all our hopes and aspirations. The end is coming; you can feel it.

There was an air of strain in the ward this morning. The nurses arrived as usual, but their joking was hard and forced. Everyone was restive, and the young chap who always lays on his stomach was crying terribly. He made us all nervy. The man beside me started muttering curses at him. After lunch we heard why the nurses had been strange. They had all been ordered home. They came in to say goodbye. All our friends, our only friends really.

The little South Australian girl came, then Nurse Enema and Tiny Mouse. Mouse has her veil off and I see with astonishment that she has grey hair and is quite old. They go to each bed and shake hands. We give them letters to post when they get to Sydney. It is awful, because the nurses are crying now. Just like leaving home and going to the war all over again. There have been battles with matron. The girls almost refuse to go. 'This is what we came for', Mouse says to me; 'to look after the boys'. She does not cry until she gets to the door, and then I see her crumple up and run out quickly.

The male orderlies have taken over. They try their best, but they have not the feminine touch. The doctors work about twenty hours a day. Wonderful people. The hospital keeps running somehow. The young chap on his stomach is in dreadful pain. They give him plenty of morphia. 'His wound is something awful', my orderly has just told me. 'You could put two fists into his back.'

The nights are the worst. When the sun sets, the blinds are pulled down and we spend the rest of the time gasping for air. The smell of sweat and the cloying stink of infection settles over everything. In vain the wounded smoke cigarettes. But that smell overpowers all others. We manage to sleep in spite of the heat and the roar of the guns.

Early this morning the young chap suddenly yelled out in a wild voice that went right through you: 'Christ, the pain—I tell you I can't stand it any more'. About nineteen minutes afterwards an orderly took him a cup of milk. He was still lying on his face, but this time he was dead.

There is a lot of speculation about the future. Will they machine gun the lot of us? They will certainly take all the beds and so on. Some of the walking patients are planning an escape by sampan. It is tremendously secret, so, of course, everyone knows about it. Even if I could walk I don't think my courage would be up to trying it.

We are keeping our spirits up with optimistic talk, 'They won't leave us here. There will probably be a breakthrough along the Katong road and they will pull us out. There are two hospital ships in the harbour ready for the wounded.' But that big tower of smoke is out there like the genie in the Arabian Nights and there does not seem much chance of coaxing it back into its bottle.

The noise from Singapore is deafening. Warfare for the soldier is largely a question of noise. One sort is 'ours', the other sort 'theirs'. We hear them all. The Jap planes have a distinctive note, a drone with a rise and fall, high-pitched but heavy. Our planes probably make a noise, too, but we don't hear them. There aren't any left to hear.

A few nights ago we all woke up in the midst of a shattering boom which rocked the building. My first impression was that the Moon had resigned its satelliteship and returned to Earth. They told us later the magazines at Changi had been blown by the sappers as our troops pulled out. The most distressing noises come from the ack-ack. The big fellows are not so bad, but the little Bofors fire with a cracking snap which makes the flesh tug at your stitches.

It is Sunday. We are reminded of it by one of the padres who comes in with a white garment flung over his shirt and shorts. He carries a suitcase and seems to be setting up some communion things. We talk about books occasionally.

Singapore is quite hidden by smoke. We are lucky not to be there.

Well, it has happened. All over. I should say about six o'clock this evening. And the silly thing was that none of us really realised what had happened. The noise got worse all day until it was practically continuous. The troops smoked cigarettes one after the other and tried to think of anything rather than the war.

Then, before we were aware of it, everything seemed very still. It was puzzling. In a quarter of an hour or so a man with horribly broken legs trussed up in a contraption of ropes and pulleys called out: 'The bloody guns have stopped, boys!' Then we knew. It was quiet—quiet for the first time for weeks. The Singapore show is finished.

An orderly comes in and lets up all the blinds, then turns on all the electric lights. We blink at them. Can lights have ever been as bright before? Scores of voices called out 'Is she all over, mate?' 'What's the idea of the lights?' A shell-shocked man without a leg screams out 'Put down those bloody blinds!'

Conversation which had been lagging all day burst out. We have to talk. Regrets, speculations, indignation and relief. If it had to come, best to come soon. Every minute saved probably means one less blanket with its lifeless contents being carried past our door. Everywhere there is an overwhelming sensation of relief. This seems to swallow up everything. Probably it is different if you are in there throwing your rifle away. If there is anyone left to throw it away. Most of us can't sleep tonight. There is too much to think about. Fancy being a prisoner of war! Really one yourself.

The padre has just been here. My friend of the books. He has a pretty good slant on this. 'It's my big chance', he says. 'Lots of the lads will be wanting some help.' He is a monk, I think, in ordinary times. He means it, that is the remarkable thing!

3

Singapore—an assessment

David Horner

Australia's responsibility*

'THE worst disaster in British military history', was how the British Prime Minister, Winston Churchill, described the surrender of Singapore to Japanese forces on 15 February 1942. After landing at Kota Bharu on the north-east coast of Malaya on the morning of 8 December 1941, the Japanese Army had advanced down the peninsula defeating British, Indian and Australian forces on the way, and on 8 February had crossed the Straits of Johore to attack Singapore. Two days later Churchill wrote: 'It will be a lasting disgrace if we are defeated by an army of clever gangsters many times inferior in numbers to our men'. It took a Japanese army of about 60 000 men one week of fighting to force the island's garrison of about 85 000 Empire troops to surrender. It *was* a disgrace, and historians have sought to find the reasons why.

The reasons are many. Fighting Hitler's Germany in Europe and the Middle East, Britain gave the defence of Malaya a low priority, despatching poorly trained troops and obsolescent aircraft. Then when Germany attacked the Soviet Union in June 1941 Britain sent valuable planes and munitions to help the Soviets rather than reinforce the Far East. Yet the attack on the Soviet Union meant that the Japanese were free to move south in the Pacific.

★   First published under the title 'Blame for disaster has to be shared',
    in the *Weekend Australian Special Edition*, 15–16 September 1992.

Britain failed adequately to assess the level of the Japanese threat, and with an element of racism assumed that their forces would be superior to those of Japan. Meanwhile, the British forces in Malaya basked in a peacetime-like atmosphere. Ignorance, indolence and arrogance redoubled on each other, leading to what in retrospect was inevitable defeat. Through it all shone the Australians. Duped by the British into believing that Singapore was an impregnable fortress, they had nevertheless sent forces to Malaya which fought bravely beside less competent British and Indian units. Singapore was a disgrace to British arms, but not for Australia. At least this is the image that many Australian accounts would have us believe.

There is an element of truth in this picture. But to what extent should Australia share the blame for the debacle in Malaya and the fall of Singapore? The first question concerns the reason why it was important to hold Singapore. After the First World War Australian military leaders considered the threat from Japan, and concluded that Australia needed a large army for home defence. This assessment did not suit British planners who wanted Australia to contribute to the Empire's naval forces and to be ready to provide an expedition-ary force, and they persuaded the Australian Government to go along with what became known as the Singapore strategy. Britain built a naval base at Singapore to which their main fleet would be sent if Japan moved south, and Australia would not therefore need a large army or home defence.

Senior Australian Army officers were critical of this strategy, arguing that Japan would only move south when Britain was occupied with an enemy in Europe, and that Australia had to develop home defences. The Australian Government, however, sought advice from Britain, which claimed that it had the ability to carry out its promises. With financial problems, the Australian Government preferred to put what few funds it had into the Royal Australian Navy rather than into the Army.

Since the Australian Government failed adequately to challenge Britain over the Singapore strategy during the 1920s and 1930s, it thereby became a collaborator in the eventual disaster. This is not to suggest that the Australian Government was always satisfied with Britain's explanations. As early as the 1923 Imperial Conference the Australian Prime Minister, Stanley Bruce, said that while he was not clear as to how Singapore could be protected, 'I am clear on this point, that apparently it can be done'. When the Australian Minister for Defence, Sir Archdale Parkhill, challenged the British at the 1937 Imperial Conference, they were less than honest with their assurances. Some historians have argued that in these financially straitened times Australia had no option but to gamble on the Singapore strategy, but it was a gamble based on trust rather than knowledge. As an Australian historian, Neil Primrose, put it, 'in failing to appreciate that Australia was ultimately of only marginal significance in the scale of British priorities, Australian leaders and their advisers deserved the obfuscations which were practised upon them'.

The next question concerns the assessment of the Japanese threat. Japan's recent history gave evidence of their intentions. They had defeated China in 1895 and Russia in 1905, and in 1931 had moved into Manchuria. In 1937 they had begun another war with China, and in 1939 had fought a small war with the Soviet Union. Yet Britain tended to play down the extent of the Japanese threat and was disparaging of Japanese military capability. Until 1940 Australia had no diplomatic representation in Japan, nor in any other country except for Britain, and had little capacity for independently assessing the international situation.

Once war broke out in Europe in 1939 the British Government wanted Australian assistance and persuaded themselves that Japan would not be willing to take on the British Empire. The Australian Government, under R. G. Menzies, was caught between the assessments of its own Army staff, who thought that Japan posed a threat, and those from London. Perhaps Australia had no real option but to send the divisions of the Australian Imperial Force (AIF) to the Middle East in early 1940. But it underlined the need for Australia to have its own means of gathering military intelligence.

Even without this capacity Australian intelligence staff had a more realistic assessment than the British. For example, in December 1940 the British Commander-in-Chief in Malaya, Air Chief Marshal Sir Robert Brooke-Popham, visited Hong Kong and saw some Japanese soldiers at the Chinese frontier. He wrote that he could not believe that 'they would form an intelligent fighting force'. The following October he told Australian Cabinet Ministers that 'Japan had superiority in number but not in quality' of aircraft. Yet a few days earlier an RAAF memorandum had noted that the Japanese Zero fighter had a performance far beyond that of the Buffalo aircraft flown by the RAF and RAAF in Malaya. And the officers of the 8th Australian Division in Malaya were disturbed by the optimistic British assessments. One recalled a British officer telling him, 'The Japanese Army is a bubble waiting to be pricked'.

When in October 1940 senior Australian military officers attended a conference in Singapore and learned that the defences of Malaya were alarmingly weak, the Australian Government agreed to send the 22nd Brigade of the 8th Division as a temporary measure while the British prepared to send Indian forces there. Meanwhile, Menzies planned to visit London to press for additional British troops, planes and ships be sent to the Far East. The 22nd Brigade set sail in February 1941.

In June 1941, soon after Menzies returned from London, the Australian Government decided to send the 27th Brigade of the 8th Division to Malaya. By now it was clear that the 8th Division was not going to be relieved by Indian troops, and might have to fight in Malaya. But the 8th Division would lack its third brigade and the normal support troops normally allocated to a division. It is true that Australia was short of trained soldiers, but it is a cardinal rule that a nation should only send balanced forces to fight overseas. If they are not balanced the commander lacks freedom to manoeuvre his force or has to rely to a great extent on other allied forces.

This was the problem faced by the commander of the 8th Division, Major-General Henry Gordon Bennett. For a position requiring not only military competence, but tact and diplomacy, his was an unfortunate appointment. A militia soldier with an outstanding record from the First World War, Bennett had an inflated opinion of his own ability. He might have been right in his estimate of some of the British commanders in Malaya, but by openly criticising them he made it difficult to work smoothly with them. Furthermore, he clashed with his own senior commanders and staff officers. Thus in selecting Bennett as the commander of the AIF in Malaya, and in not giving him his full division and support troops, the Australian Chiefs of Staff made the task of the AIF in Malaya even more difficult.

Given these difficulties, could the 8th Division have performed better during the fighting in Malaya and Singapore? When the Japanese landed in northern Malaya on 8 December the two brigades of the 8th Division were preparing to defend Johore at the southern end of the peninsula. The division was not committed to operations for another five weeks, and in the meantime the RAAF's two Buffalo and two Hudson Squadrons suffered heavy losses against the superior Japanese Air Force. During this time the 8th Division had the advantage of continuing its training and learning from the experience of the unfortunate British and Indian troops who were suffering a series of defeats and withdrawals. Bennett was quick to criticise the performance of these other troops and spoke confidently of how the Australians would deal with the Japanese.

There was some justification for Bennett's concern about the lack of training of some Indian units and the ability of several senior British officers. The British Army commander in Malaya, Lieutenant-General A. E. Percival, had been a clever staff officer, and in this capacity had drawn up plans for the defence of Malaya. But he lacked the personality and leadership to be an effective commander. Later he was to prevent the building of defences on the north coast of Singapore for fear of upsetting the local population!

At the beginning of January Bennett had the 22nd Brigade on the east coast of Johore and the 27th Brigade in northern Johore facing the likely line of Japanese attack down the west coast. Earlier he had rightly insisted to Percival that his Australian force should not be split up. But now, when Percival decided to put Bennett in charge of Westforce, which included the 27th Brigade and several British and Indian Brigades, the 22nd Brigade remained on the east coast.

Bennett therefore faced the coming battles with an unsatisfactory command arrangement, in which he planned to fight the main battle with one Australian brigade, using the other brigades as support troops. He expected the Japanese to come down the centre of the peninsula and he sited the 27th Brigade there, while along the west coast he placed the ill-equipped and ill-trained 45th Indian Brigade, which had just arrived from India.

Initially the fighting went well, and on 14 January the 2/30th Australian Battalion conducted a brilliant ambush of an advancing Japanese battalion near the town of Gemas. The Australians caught the Japanese on bicycles as they crossed a bridge, killing several hundred for relatively slight Australian losses. It was the biggest set-back suffered by the Japanese during the campaign.

But the Japanese then attacked along the coast at Muar River, and Bennett had to send the 2/19th and 2/29th Battalions to assist the 45th Indian Brigade. The 2/19th Battalion came from the 22nd Brigade on the east coast. Soon the two Australian battalions found themselves conducting a desperate rear guard action, until the Japanese moved a force across their withdrawal route. The Australians fought with determination and courage, epitomised by the award of the Victoria Cross to the commanding officer of the 2/19th Battalion, Lieutenant-Colonel Charles Anderson. When a relieving attack by an Indian Brigade failed, Anderson had to order the men of the two battalions to make their way independently through swamp and deep jungle back to Allied lines. Only 400 men of the two battalions made it. The wounded who were left behind were slaughtered by the Japanese.

The Japanese advance could not be halted, and at the end of the month the British Empire troops marched across the causeway to the island of Singapore to await the final assault. Individually, the Australians had fought well, evidence of the hard training insisted upon by Bennett. But they had not been able to show their full worth. They had not fought as a concentrated force. Like the other British and Indian units, their equipment was not suited to the jungle. And despite his confidence, Bennett had failed to appreciate the rapid Japanese movement along the coast.

Earlier in the campaign Bennett had implored the Australian Government to send additional forces to Malaya. Percival too had asked the British Government for reinforcements, and in late January some of these started to arrive. The British 18th Division, which arrived at the end of January, was soft after the long voyage from Britain, was not trained or equipped for jungle warfare, and lacked transport and supporting arms. The Indian brigades and reinforcements which arrived during January had not completed their training.

But the Australian reinforcements, who landed on 25 January, were in little better shape. The 2/4th Machine-Gun Battalion was a good unit, but 1907 other reinforcements turned out to be a liability rather than an asset. Some had not had seven days of serious training in Australia, and many had never fired a rifle. The selection of these reinforcements reflects poorly on Army Headquarters in Melbourne. As the Australian official historian pointed out, there were 16 600 trained reinforcements in the Middle East, while sufficient volunteers could have been found among the 87 000 militiamen on full-time duty in Australia.

The incompetent decision to send ill-prepared reinforcements focuses attention on the Australian Government's attitude at this time. In mid-January Britain had seriously considered the possibility of evacuating Singapore. When they learned of this, the Australian Government accused Britain of an 'inexcusable betrayal' and said that the fortress should hold out. The British had already come to the same conclusion, but the incident shows that the Australian Chiefs of Staff had failed to follow through to a logical conclusion their claims that without adequate reinforcements the British Empire forces in Malaya and Singapore would be defeated. There was almost certainly an 'inexcusable betrayal' but that fact should not have clouded the judgment of the Australians. The militarily sound decision would have been not to send reinforcements if they could not alter the outcome.

The two Australian brigades in the north-west of the island bore the brunt of the Japanese assault on Singapore on 8 February. Historians have argued about whether Percival should have prepared his defences better, pointing out that the bulk of his forces were in the eastern sector. From an Australian perspective, criticism has been levelled at the premature withdrawal of the 27th Brigade during the Japanese attack. As Brett Lodge has shown in his detailed study, *The Fall of General Gordon Bennett*, published in 1986, his conduct of operations on the island was not without fault.

None of this should overshadow the achievements of the men themselves. It is difficult to be certain of the figures of casualties in the campaign, but the Australian official history says that 1789 Australians were killed, 1306 wounded and a further 14 972 were captured. The prisoners suffered terribly and over a third died in captivity. The total number of British Empire forces killed varies between 8000 quoted by the British official history and 15 000 by the Japanese. The Australians numbered about 13 per cent of the total force and between 12 and 22 per cent of the Allied force killed were Australian. Total Japanese battle casualties were nearly 10 000.

Undoubtedly, blame for the fall of Singapore rests with Britain's failure to take the defence of Malaya seriously. But although Australia had argued belatedly during 1941 for additional air and naval forces, it cannot be completely absolved of blame. Australia had accepted the Singapore strategy, it had not developed a capacity for making independent assessments of international affairs or potential enemies' capabilities, and it had chosen to accept British leadership in strategic affairs.

These shortcomings led to other failures. Australia had insufficient trained troops to send a balanced force to Malaya, and the forces that were sent were not properly equipped for war. They were commanded by a general who despite a splendid First World War record lacked tact, caused disharmony in his own division, and whose command in battle was less sure than he would have liked people to believe.

Both during and after the campaign some Australian officers were quick to criticise the performance of their British and Indian allies. The British responded with counterclaims. The Australians who fought in Malaya had no more to be ashamed of than their allies, and they were the only defenders to earn respect from the Japanese for their fighting qualities. But the Australian Government and its senior military advisers had to accept their share of responsibility for the disaster.

Gregory Pemberton

Towards a new-found Australian sovereignty*

THE fall of Singapore, and not the blood-soaked battlefields of Gallipoli, may well mark the birthplace of Australian independence. At Gallipoli, Australians were acting at the behest of Britain in an ill-conceived and ill-executed invasion of another belligerent. In the Pacific War that followed the attack on Pearl Harbor and the Japanese invasion of the Malayan peninsula, Australia faced a genuine threat to its own security. And, while not without some stumbles, Australians for the first time united behind their Government to meet the challenge. Not only did the nation effectively mobilise to fight the Pacific War, and its forces performed creditably on most occasions, but the Government acquired the ability to think for itself and make its own decisions, even if it meant disagreeing with its traditional overlords in London and their sympathisers in Australia.

More suprising is the fact that this new-found independence was forged not on the battlefields of Malaya or Singapore, but in an unprepossessing public service building, known as East Block, in Canberra. It was there in the dark days that followed the Japanese attack on Pearl Harbor that the then Prime Minister, John Curtin, realised Australia would have to stand on its own. The short-term

---

* First published under the title 'Out of crisis a new-found sovereignty', in the *Weekend Australian Special Edition*, 15–16 February 1992.

success of Japan's devastating raid on the US Pacific Fleet opened the gateway for the subsequent Japanese drive southwards into the European colonies of South-East Asia and of the South Pacific. Australia was virtually incapable of mounting any serious self-defence effort to meet this threat, essentially because since Gallipoli it had been integrated into an imperial defence strategy.

In particular, Australia was vulnerable because it had accepted with little dissent the illusion of security known as the 'Singapore strategy'. The strategy had been developed following the 1923 Imperial Conference to counter the rise of Japanese power in the Pacific. Essentially it involved the development of Singapore as a defended naval base that would host a substantial British fleet should Japan threaten an advance.

The theory was fine but from the very start there were always grave doubts as to whether Britain would be able or even willing to take the steps necessary to implement the Singapore strategy. In Westminster, development of Singapore's defences was never allocated a high priority. As early as 1923, the then Australian Prime Minister, Stanley Bruce, opined wistfully: 'While I am not quite as clear as I should like to be as to how the protection of Singapore is to be assured, I am clear on this point, that apparently it can be done'. But it was never done. Australia's leaders were aware there were serious doubts as to whether London would, or could, despatch an adequate fleet to Singapore if the Japanese threatened while Britain was engaged in Europe. British military planners had always based their plans on two contradictory assumptions: that Britain would send a fleet when Britain was engaged solely in a war against Japan; and that Japan would strike against Singapore only when Britain was otherwise engaged, thus revealing a fatal flaw in the Singapore strategy. And while it may be a myth that the guns of Singapore were fixed, it is undeniably true that the minds of Australia's conservative leaders were. For they cannot entirely excuse themselves from their failure to act on Britain's very inaction.

Australia's willingness to contribute to imperial defence interests ahead of its own was based on this illusion, nurtured by London and culpably believed by Canberra. While it is true, right up to the Japanese attack, that British officials, including Winston Churchill, deliberately misled Australia as to the viability of the Singapore strategy, there was sufficient information available for them to have seen the truth. Instead, wilful ignorance prevailed. As leaders of the nation, they always knew there were deficiencies in Singapore's defences and the unlikelihood of a fleet being despatched but they did not take adequate steps to move the British to action or adopt an alternative defence strategy.

Labor was only briefly in office in the interwar period but no Australian government would have spent much more on a self-reliant Australian defence policy than was actually spent on imperial defence. This acceptance of the Singapore strategy fatally compromised our defence policy. Air power, which may have had the potential to enable an underpopulated nation such as Australia to ensure its security, was never developed fully, largely because of the Singapore strategy. Nor was Britain keen to see Australia develop its own aircraft industry with US help because of the threat to its motor vehicle market. Instead, imperial defence called for the financial emphasis to be placed on the navy. This also meant a 'blue water' fleet for integration into the Royal Navy around the globe rather than vessels for Australia's coastal defence.

When war came to Europe, unquestioning belief in Singapore as a bastion against Japanese invasion again contributed to the nation's defensive weakness. On the shallow basis of the security Singapore offered against Japan, the Menzies Government immediately joined Britain in the war and despatched its best manpower resources to the Middle East. Once there, the memories of Gallipoli were revived as Australian troops were soon involved—with Menzies' acquiescence—in another Churchill-inspired disaster, this time in Greece. The RAN was dispersed around the globe with the Royal Navy. The RAAF was converted into a glorified training depot for the RAF under the Empire Air Training Scheme, thereby preventing it from developing as a combat force.

As the Far Eastern crisis grew more ominous, Britain proposed, for its own reason, that some Australian forces should be returned from the Middle East to reinforce the Far East. Arthur Fadden, who had replaced Menzies as Prime Minister, also began to press in October 1941 for the withdrawal of Australian forces from Tobruk.

The Labor Party had opposed the original commitment of the forces to the Middle East and in 1941 some Labor members were still calling for a withdrawal. When Labor won government, it ushered in a greater degree of independence from Britain. It declared war against Japan retrospectively one day before Britain's declaration.

Although Prime Minister Curtin agreed to keeping the divisions in the Middle East, he urged Churchill of the need to reinforce Singapore. Churchill was largely unconcerned about Singapore as he was primarily interested in a Middle East victory. Indeed, Churchill welcomed the Japanese attack on Pearl Harbor because it brought the US into the war. He was soon in Washington agreeing with President Roosevelt that the Allies should concentrate their efforts against Germany, not Japan—an agreement directly counter to Australian interests.

As Japan's drive southwards towards Australia continued, Curtin began to act as one would expect of a national leader rather than an imperial stooge. On Christmas Day 1941, with frantic calls coming from Singapore urging the need for reinforcements, Curtin relayed a message to Churchill in Washington: 'Please understand that the stage of gentle suggestion has now passed. Continuous overstatements by British Far East Commands as to degree of preparedness have produced a very serious effect on public opinion. This is the gravest type of emergency.' Two days later, concerned by Churchill's lack of positive response, Curtin published his famous call that Australia 'looks to America, free of any pangs as to our traditional links or kinship with the United Kingdom'.

Conservative historians have sought to play down the significance of this implicit criticism of Westminster and have preferred to cite the supposedly poor impression it made on Roosevelt. (Their sources—Churchill and the wife of prominent Liberal R.G. Casey—are hardly impeccable.) The point conservative historians cannot see, or wish to obscure, is that in Australia's hour of need, Britain exposed the fact that the whole foundation of imperial defence—and thus the traditional relationship with Britain—was that the British interests would always be placed above the interests of any one dominion. Churchill completely failed to appreciate the Australian point of view. He complained to Curtin of the 'mood of panic' being shown and offered paternalistically to salve popular anxieties by broadcasting to the Australian people. At a time when Australia wanted reinforcements to hold the line against the Japanese, who were rapidly advancing down the Malayan peninsula towards

Singapore, Churchill only offered words—and even began to consider a withdrawal from Singapore.

The Australian Government insisted that Singapore had to be held. Whatever the military wisdom of Australia's stand, it was certainly understandable given years of British propaganda that Singapore was not only impregnable but essential to Australia's security because it was to host the expected main Royal Navy fleet. The increasingly bitter cables passing between Canberra and London culminated in one amended by Dr H. V. Evatt, Australia's then Minister for External Affairs, that the evacuation of Singapore would be an 'inexcusable betrayal'. Menzies disassociated himself from this strongly worded cable but the Government's viewpoint was in accordance with its own military advice.

All was in vain, however, and Singapore surrendered in what was one of the greatest disasters in British military history. With the loss of Singapore, the Australian Government desired that its troops from the Middle East should return directly to Australia. This was in accordance with its military advice and was underlined on 19 February when Darwin was bombed for the first time.

In London, however, Churchill had other ideas. He decided to divert at least one Australian division to Rangoon to help protect imperial interests in Burma. He was supported by both Bruce, then High Commissioner in London, and former Country Party leader Earle Page, Australia's representative on the London-based Pacific War Council and the British War Cabinet. Indeed, Page possibly initiated the idea. The Australian Advisory War Council immediately reaffirmed its original decision to bring troops home despite the objections of some non-Labor members. Incredibly Page, 'staggered' by Curtin's refusal, even tried to deflect the Government's policy on this issue and held off passing Curtin's cable to Churchill in the hope that Canberra would soon change its mind. Even when Evatt twice again cabled that Australia's decision was unchanged, Page still pressed for Australia to agree. Finally, Curtin settled the matter on 20 February when he reaffirmed the original policy.

Or so he thought. Unknown to Canberra, Churchill had meanwhile taken the extraordinary step of diverting the returning Australian convoy northwards towards Burma and away from Australia. Without mentioning this indefensible usurpation of Australian sovereignty, he cabled Curtin ten minutes later asking him to accept such a diversion. He also called on Roosevelt to add his voice in support of this coup—which the President duly did. Despite this pressure, on 21 February the Australian War Cabinet stood firm.

But Churchill still had one last card. The fleet carrying the Australian troops no longer had the fuel to reach Australia direct because of the earlier diversion. So the British Prime Minister despatched a final cable which appalled even Bruce who described it as 'arrogant and offensive'. It began: 'We could not contemplate that you would refuse our request and that of the President of the United States for the diversion of the leading division to save the situation in Burma'. He explained that because Australia's agreement had been presumed, the convoy had already been diverted north-wards and the time now needed for refuelling would 'give a few days for the situation to develop and for you to review the position should you wish to do so'. Both Bruce and Page caved in under this pressure and asked that, for the sake of preventing a 'crisis' in Anglo-Australian relations and the Allied cause, Canberra should accept Churchill's high-handed action.

John Burton, Evatt's private secretary (who was later appointed Secretary of the Department of External Affairs in March 1947) still recalls the tense atmosphere in the Defence Department's Canberra headquarters in East Block when Churchill's cable arrived. Australian ministers were so confounded by the enormity of the decision to countermand such a pointed 'request' from Churchill that they were not able to offer a decision. Even the usually ebullient Evatt claimed he was too ill to offer the final advice. The decision was left to Curtin alone to make.

Curtin, who had only just left hospital, also could not make such a momentous decision lightly. Rather than reply immediately, he left the building alone and disappeared into the night. Later, with the time ticking away to the 23 February deadline for the Australian reply, Burton and other government officials waited anxiously in East Block for Curtin to return to dictate the cable. As the appointed hour approached they became concerned with Curtin's prolonged absence. His rooms at the Hotel Canberra were searched in vain. Next, notices were placed in Canberra's two cinemas at Civic and Manuka asking whether the Prime Minister was 'in the house'. There was no response. Then, with only minutes to go, the Prime Minister entered East Block with a grim resolve etched on his face.

That resolve had come to him only gradually as he walked around the lower slopes of the Majura hills, his path illuminated only by the light flashing on the summit of Mount Ainslie. Once in the room, he gruffly called for a stenographer, whereupon he dictated his reply to Churchill:

> Australia's outer defences are now quickly vanishing and our vulnerability is completely exposed. Now you contemplate using the AIF to save Burma. All this has been done, as in Greece, without adequate air support. We feel a primary obligation to save Australia not only for itself but to preserve it as a base for the development of the war against Japan. In the circumstances it is quite impossible to reverse a decision which we made with the utmost care and which we have affirmed and reaffirmed.

No longer in any mood for the 'restraint' Bruce had urged for the sake of smooth relations, Curtin forthrightly accused Churchill of treating Australia's approval of this diversion as 'merely a matter of form' and thereby increasing the 'physical dangers' to the convoy. Fearful of the possible loss of the convoy to submarine attack, Curtin then pronounced that 'the responsibility of the consequences of such a diversion rests upon you'.

At last, Churchill accepted Australia's decision, adding tersely: 'Of course, I take full responsibility for my action'. The great question remaining, however, was whether Britain would henceforth be prepared to let Australia take responsibility for its actions. After this, Britain could never again take Australian subservience for granted, at least while nationalists like Curtin held the reins of power in Canberra.

If Australia had submitted to Churchill's wishes, even more Australians would have ended up in Japanese POW camps and valuable troops would not have been available for the victorious campaign in New Guinea. Australia was not being selfish. It allowed some of these troops to be diverted to Ceylon, in order to assuage Churchill, where they contributed little and did not reach the Pacific in time for the successful defence of Port Moresby.

This concession shows that even for Curtin the imperial ties still held strongly but they had been stretched so far over Burma that Britain could never again revive the imperial relationship in its paternalistic form. After the war, the Labor Government was wary of again being drawn into Britain's plans for the defence of its empire, including yet another commitment to the Middle East. For that it attracted much criticism from the press and elsewhere. Finally, after Labor's electoral defeat in 1949, the Menzies Government returned Australia to the path of imperial defence, which in an indirect way led down the long, slippery road to Vietnam.

David Horner

Wavell's secret report*

IN January 1993 a secret report by General Sir Archibald Wavell, the British commander in the Far East in early 1942, was released at the Public Record Office in London. Completed on 1 June 1942, the report accused the soldiers of the 8th Australian Division of cowardice, looting, rape, murder and disobeying orders, and concluded that the 'Australians are held responsible' for the fall of Singapore on 15 February 1942. The report was withheld from the Australian Government by the British Prime Minister, Winston Churchill, and was suppressed again in 1973, when it would normally have been released under the 30-year rule.

It might be easy to dismiss these claims as 'a lot of rot' as Mr Ron Maston, a survivor of the campaign, said in *The Australian* in January 1993. Most veterans of the campaign saw none of the incidents described in Wavell's report, and rightly they see it as a serious slur on their reputations.

The broad claim that the Australians were responsible for the fall of Singapore is palpable nonsense. Singapore was lost through the years of neglect in the 1930s—through faulty British strategy which relied on sending the main fleet while the garrison held out against attack—and through the failure to take the defence of Malaya

---

* First published under the title 'Singapore slings', in the *Weekend Australian*, 16–17 January 1993.

92

seriously. All this is well known. If Australia has any share in the blame it is because of its excessive readiness to believe the promises made by Britain before the war that Singapore could be held.

Nevertheless, there are sufficient grains of truth in Wavell's report to warrant a detailed examination of his claims. This is not the first time that the stories of Australian ill-discipline have been revealed. In 1979, while researching for my book *High Command*, I came across many of the stories mentioned in Wavell's report, plus some stories not mentioned. For example, the War Diary of Headquarters, Malaya Command on 10 February 1942 quotes a report from Major-General H. Gordon Bennett, the commander of the 8th Division, that about 600 Australian troops had 'been picked up in the last three days and have returned to their units and will be used in the attack'. The following day the War Diary reported 200 unarmed Australians attempting to force their way onto evacuation craft. When the 8th Division duty officer was informed he stated that the Military Police were dealing with the matter. A British admiral wrote on 12 February that the Australians were 'rushing the sampans'.

Mr G. W. Seabridge, the editor of the *Straits Times*, wrote at the time that although the Australians had fought well on the offensive they were 'totally unsuitable for fighting on the retreat . . . There were desertions. Men seen in Singapore town . . . were heard to boast that they had come "down the line" because they were fed up with being plastered . . . There were cases of looting and rape.'

Evidence for this lack of discipline is found not just in British records. Files in the Australian War Memorial show that on 12 February 1942 about 200 Australians boarded the *Empire Star* in Singapore harbour. Major-General Charles Lloyd, the senior Australian officer at Wavell's headquarters in Java, met the ship when it docked at Batavia (Jakarta) two days later and found the forecastle held by the Australians. The Master of the ship said they had stormed the gangway at the last moment before departure from Singapore. The men claimed that it was 'a bugger's muddle in Singapore, and they had had it'. Lloyd arranged for the men to be taken off to gaol. Later Brigadier Blackburn, commanding an Australian brigade on Java, offered to take the deserters into his force, hoping that he could improve their morale and training. Unfortunately they proved a bad influence in their new units. This incident is mentioned in less detail in the Australian official history, *The Japanese Thrust*, by Lionel Wigmore, published in 1957.

Soon after the fall of Singapore reports about the Australians continued to circulate in Ceylon and India. Lieutenant-Colonel Ashmore of Headquarters, Malaya Command reported that he 'saw five Australian soldiers, naked except for a pair of dirty shorts, no boots or socks, lying and sprawling in the gutter of one of the main thoroughfares leading west from Singapore on February 10th. They had their rifles and were drinking from bottles.' Major Westall of the Royal Marines stated that on 11 February 'the waterfront of Singapore was a mass of demoralized troops looking for any means of leaving the island. I should say at least 80 per cent of them were Australians, the remainder British and Indian.' Australian officers were trying to get the men to return to their units.

However, not all British officers held these views. Lieutenant-Colonel I. M. Stewart, the commanding officer of the Argyll and Sutherland Highlanders, wrote:

> The AIF to my knowledge fought very well indeed. We were actually under command of the Australian Division in the fighting on the island. It is true that a number straggled down into the town, and did make an early get away, but this equally applies to British troops . . . Admittedly a bad Australian is the worst thing ever, but a good one to my mind, is the best!'

These British comments must be seen in perspective. Even before the beginning of the campaign the Australian commander, the egotistical Major-General Gordon Bennett, had been intensely critical of both the British commanders and the British and Indian soldiers. He asserted that once the Australians got into action they would show the British how to fight. He had to wait until mid-January before his men joined the battle in the southern Malayan state of Johore. After a spectacularly successful ambush at Gemas, two Australian battalions were cut off in the battle of Muar. The Australians fought with great gallantry, and Lieutenant-Colonel Charles Anderson was awarded the Victoria Cross after leading the remnants of the battalions to safety.

During the battle Bennett, according to a British liaison officer who prepared a report for Headquarters, Malaya Command, told the British high command that his two battalions 'might be lost through indolence or inefficiency of [British] staff', and that he intended to make a full report. He added that if the two battalions were lost 'all Australia would know the reason'. After the battle a British staff officer admitted that 'British and Australian troops were as sulphuric acid is to water'.

It was not just Bennett who was critical. His chief administrative staff officer, Colonel J. R. Broadbent, described the British organisation on 28 January 1942 as 'punk'. As a result, some British officers sought every opportunity to find fault with the Australians. General Pownall, Wavell's chief of staff, wrote on 13 February that 'not even the Australians, for all that they started so cock-a-hoop and critical of others, put up a good showing in the end'. A staff officer from HQ Malaya Command commented that he did not 'realise to the full extent to which the AIF had been blowing [their] own trumpets (without justification) till they were seen at closer quarters on the Island'.

Senior British officers were critical of Bennett's handling of the fighting on Singapore Island and were even more critical when he escaped from the Island at the time of the surrender. Major Maurice Austin, an Australian officer at Wavell's headquarters on Java, recalled the cold attitude of the British officers there when it was learnt that Bennett had left Singapore.

Despite the circulation of these unfavourable stories, that might have been the end of the recriminations had it not been for Bennett's report of the campaign which, in April 1942, was forwarded both to the War Office and to Wavell in New Delhi where he was now Commander-in-Chief, India.

Even before the report arrived, the British High Commissioner in Canberra, Sir Ronald Cross, warned London that Bennett was 'unreliable and untrustworthy', and that he had given the impression in the press that only the Australian troops had consistently fought with success.

In fact Bennett's report went much further. It criticised the British higher command as well as British officers and the British and Indian troops. He spoke of a 'retreat complex' suffered by troops and officers alike, and said that the prime cause of the defeat was the low morale of the Indians.

Wavell immediately put a staff officer, Major H. P. Thomas, to work on a detailed examination of Bennett's report. Thomas not only pointed out the errors of fact in it, but went on to collect information of the poor performance of the Australians. It was this information which formed the basis of Wavell's report and provided the corroborative evidence. Thomas concluded that the Australians had begun the campaign very well, but their morale and discipline had deteriorated towards the end. He pointed out that the Australians in Singapore were the only troops in the entire campaign to come under sustained artillery fire.

Wavell's official account of the events in the campaign was completed in July 1942 and his shorter dispatch was finished in August. Both these documents were forwarded to Australia but they included little comment on the Australians.

The next critical account came after the end of the war, in 1946, when Lieutenant-General A. E. Percival, who had commanded Malaya Command, was released from captivity and submitted his report. He dealt squarely with some of the contentious issues, and said that many of the 2000 Australian reinforcements who had arrived towards the end of January 1942 had had only a few weeks' training and lacked discipline. In response, the Chief of the General Staff of the Australian Army had to admit that this was the case, but claimed that 'events moved so rapidly and disastrously that it was not possible to create an organisation for training the reinforcements'.

The crucial paragraph in Percival's report needs to be read in full:

The plan for the forward troops [i.e. AIF] to fall back to battalion perimeter positions was contrary to the policy laid down by Headquarters Malaya Command and, in my opinion, involved an operation which was too difficult in the middle of a night battle which was being fought fiercely at close quarters. As a result of it there was much confusion and disorganisation, groups of men becoming detached and lost in the close country. Some were collected and taken back to the Base Depot where they were refitted and reorganised. Others made their way to Singapore Town. The 22 Australian Infantry Brigade, however, did not cease to exist—on the contrary it continued to fight well later on . . . it would be very wrong to judge the performance of the AIF by these stragglers. The action of these men must be judged in relation to existing conditions. They were not long-service soldiers and discipline was not deep-rooted. They had volunteered for service and had been sent to Malaya to defend the Naval Base. The Naval Base was no longer of any use but Australia, their homeland, was being threatened. Many of them belonged to units which, after heavy casualties on the mainland, had been reorganised but had had no time to regain their full fighting efficiency. They had fought well throughout a long night against heavy odds and were exhausted. This is the true picture and should be judged on its merits. Active and effective measures were quickly taken by Headquarters, Malaya Command and by Headquarters AIF to deal with the situation by means of reinforced stragglers' posts and officer's patrols in the town area.

The Australian Chief of the General Staff considered that the statement was factually correct and that Percival had made every effort to depict the situation as accurately and as fairly as possible.

The Australian Army also sought the opinion of Major-General C. A. Callaghan, who had taken command of the division when Bennett had escaped. Callaghan thought that Percival's report was 'a perfectly fair and accurate summary of the operations'. Indeed he thought that Percival had 'very generously glossed' over two instances when Australian operations were open to criticism. These were the deployment orders give to the 45th Indian Brigade under Bennett's command at Muar—which some believe left the brigade open to attack—and the precipitate withdrawal of the 27th Australian Brigade from the causeway area on Singapore Island on 10 February. Both the British and Australian official historians later criticised the withdrawal of the 27th Brigade.

Callaghan admitted that there was a certain amount of truth in the reports of Australian deserters in Singapore town, and he added that this 'temporary lapse of the Australian on the island and the criticism it has invoked has caused me a lot of uneasiness'. Callaghan was 'grateful to Gen. Percival for presenting this episode in a way that, while admitting that something of the sort did take place previous criticism is rebuked and the fighting reputation of the Australian in Malaya left unsullied'.

Colonel J. H. Thyer, who had been Bennett's chief of staff, agreed with this assessment. By the end of the campaign Thyer was on extremely bad terms with Bennett, a militia officer who was suspicious of regular officers such as Thyer. Not only was Thyer very critical of Bennett, but he added that the 'fact must be faced

. . . that the AIF did not measure up to the task required of it in a heart-breaking withdrawal. Ultimately, the morale deteriorated, and in the last stages only two thirds *at most* of those fit to fight were manning the final perimeter.' Thyer wrote that these remarks applied equally to the British troops, while he thought the Indian troops were not first-class.

The Malayan campaign volume of the Australian official histories was the only one in which the responsible government minister, Sir Wilfrid Kent Hughes, a friend of Bennett's, tried to influence the outcome. The contentious matter revolved around the performance of Bennett and his subordinate commanders, particularly Brigadier Taylor of the 22nd Brigade, on Singapore Island. The official historian resisted the interference of the Minister and tried to be even-handed. Bennett thought that the final version whitewashed Thyer and Taylor, while Thyer commented that 'the watering down and other modifications do not worry me. The discerning person will read between the lines.'

In his book *The Fall of General Gordon Bennett*, Brett Lodge demonstrates persuasively that there were definite shortcomings in Bennett's command in Malaya and Singapore. The confusion in the Australian force can be attributed directly to Bennett's egotism, prejudices and tactlessness. But this in no way absolves the senior British commanders of their blunders. Percival never had a firm grip on the campaign, and many British and Indian units were poorly trained.

Despite Bennett's mistakes the Australian soldiers fought exceptionally well. The 8th Division was never complete. One of its three brigades was not sent to Malaya and, despite a directive from the Australian Government, Bennett allowed his force to become split up. Nevertheless, at Gemas they mounted a highly effective ambush that took heavy toll of the advancing Japanese. In the withdrawal down the peninsula their units sustained heavy casualties and had to be reformed for the battle on Singapore. There the Australians bore the full brunt of the Japanese attack.

The statistics speak for themselves. The Australians formed 13 per cent of the total Empire force but suffered perhaps 20 per cent of the casualties. Out of a strength of almost 18 500, the 8th Division lost 1789 killed and 1306 wounded in barely four weeks of fighting.

Incidents such as those described in Wavell's report must be seen in context. Perhaps, after presiding over defeats in Greece, Crete, Libya, Malaya and Burma, Wavell had lost his own sense of perspective.

There are explanations for some of the claims. In many cases, stragglers had become separated from their units in the confused fighting and were not deserters. Units such as X and Y Battalions were thrown together with spare men and reinforcements. Naturally they lacked cohesion. The claims of rape have not been sustained. The Australians were not the only ones to wear the popular slouch hat, and there may have been cases of mistaken identity.

Wavell's claim that an Australian battalion went missing needs more evidence. Perhaps it refers to an attack by the Jats Indian Battalion on 11 February that was not supported by the Australian Special Reserve Battalion. In fact the attack had been cancelled by the Indian brigade commander and the order had failed to reach the Jats.

It would be a grave injustice if the actions of a very small number of Australians soldiers were to detract from the determination, devotion and courage of the majority of the 8th Division in Malaya and Singapore. Equally, the loss of lives and suffering endured by the men of the 8th Division would be even more tragic if the weaknesses in Australian as well as British command, organisation, training and equipment were to be glossed over. It is through facing past errors squarely that we ensure that they never happen again.

4

After the fall—the POW experience

Gary Hughes

Dignity and horror in the POW camps*

THERE is an inevitable silence that is shared by those Australians who were POWs under the Japanese during World War II—a point at which words run out. It has nothing to do with any reluctance to talk about their experiences. Rather, it is a frustrated silence that comes from a language incapable of conveying the enormity of the horror, suffering, despair, human misery and sheer waste of young life. Mere words are literally not enough.

On 15 February 1942, Singapore was signed away and some 15 000 Australians became POWs, many of them without being given the chance to fire a shot in anger. Some had only been in the army for weeks or months. Many had no training. 'We never had a chance to fight', recalls Mr Jack Flannery, who was with the 4th Reserve Motor Transport Company when the supposedly impregnable island fortress fell. Mr Walter Sheldon, who was also with the 4th Transport, still recalls what he sees as the ineptitude of the British high command.

The feeling of being cheated of the chance to fight for their country, of being wasted at a time when Australia was threatened, made the suffering all the harder to endure. But perhaps worst of all was that for many years to come, due to the surrender and the

---

* First published under the title 'Dignity outlives the horror', in the *Weekend Australian Special Edition* 15–16 February 1992.

lack of comprehension back home of the ordeal that followed, these men and women were considered part of a defeated army, their contribution and suffering largely unappreciated, if not ignored.

There were many Australians, however, who did get the chance to fight in those initial months. Apart from those who fought the delaying action against the Japanese down the Malay peninsula, there were another 7000 Australians scattered across the islands lying in the path of the Japanese advance. 'We were put on those islands simply as tokens to divert Japanese attention and get them to commit more troops than necessary to capture them', says former Labor federal Cabinet minister, Mr Tom Uren, who was captured on Timor. On Timor, 1000 Australians faced a 24 000–strong Japanese invasion force. In four days of fighting, the Australians suffered 40 per cent casualties.

There were 22 000 Australian men and women taken prisoner by the Japanese. Only 14000 survived to return to Australia, a death rate of 36 per cent compared with the overall rate among Australian servicemen and women of 3 per cent in World War II. After their return home they continued to die at four times the rate of other veterans until 1959 because of the physical abuse they had suffered. The death rate among their rapidly dwindling number is still 20 per cent higher than among others who served. According to the most recent figures, only 5485 are still alive.

The cold statistics are just as meaningless as names such as Hell Fire Pass, 55 Kilo Camp, 105 Kilo Camp, Three Pagodas Pass, Hintok, Kinsayok, Songkurai or Wampo for those who were not there. Those names are dotted along the 420-kilometre Burma–Thailand railway, built by the Japanese using forced labour to form a supply line from Thailand to the Japanese Army in Burma. Tens of thousands died of starvation, disease, exhaustion and at the hands of the brutal Japanese and Korean guards and were buried in makeshift graves along the track or cremated on funeral pyres to stop the spread of cholera. Some 12 000 Australian POWs were forced to work in Thailand and Burma, along with about 50 000 other Allied POWs and 250 000 Asian labourers.

In recent years, a growing number of former POWs have written of their experiences on the railway, including the legendary surgeon Sir Edward 'Weary' Dunlop. But those who were there say that even the chilling visions conjured up by the authors understate the truth. 'How can you describe it?' says Mr Uren, who was with D Force under Sir Edward and after the railway was finished went to work in Japan.

The jungle camps were makeshift at best. Food was scarce, with supply lines stretched. Rice was the staple diet, with maggot-infested meat or fish a much anticipated treat. The maggots were cooked and eaten as well to provide protein. The work demanded by the Japanese, especially during the dreaded 'speedos' when prisoners were forced to work around the clock to complete the railway, would have been exhausting for fit men on a good diet. For the POWs it was, in all too many cases, a death sentence. Added to that was the sadism and brutality of the guards. 'They were not only cruel, they were animals,' says Mr Flannery. 'The Japanese engineers were very barbaric, very cruel', says Mr Uren. 'It was a sadism and barbarism that was impossible to understand.'

But it was disease that took the heaviest toll on the starving POWs. Dysentery, malaria, beri-beri and—most feared of all— cholera. Jungle ulcers, which started from any small wound, spread rapidly eating away at living flesh. Sharpened spoons were used to clean out the infected ulcers and in the worst cases limbs were amputated without anaesthetic. Yet despite the indescribable conditions, the Australians generally fared better than other POWs, largely because of mateship.

Throughout his parliamentary career and since his retirement, Mr Uren has battled for a better deal for the ex-POWs from government. He argues that those who suffered at the hands of the Japanese are a special group and deserving of special consideration, including easier access to pensions and free nursing home care, whether suffering from a war-related disability or not.

Silvia Dropulic

Sister Vivian Bullwinkel's memories*

From the days of Florence Nightingale, wars have had their heroines in the guise of women dedicated to nursing the shattered remnants of men sent back from the front. In Singapore, the Australian nurses described themselves as 'just an ordinary bunch of women'. They proved to be something more than that. As the Japanese pressed their attack on Singapore, concerned Australian medical officers attempted to evacuate their female nursing staff from the island. Despite being under air and artillery bombardment day and night, the nurses were reluctant to leave their charges but senior officers, fearful of atrocities being committed against the women, insisted they accompany the seriously wounded. On 11 February 59 nurses left Singapore aboard the *Empire Star*, which although frequently bombed, managed to reach Australia.

A day later the remaining 65 nurses and about 300 civilian passengers boarded the *Vyner Brooke*. Late in the afternoon of 14 February, the *Vyner Brooke* was attacked and sunk by Japanese bombers in the Banka Straits off the coast of Sumatra. Two of the nurses were killed immediately, nine were last seen drifting off in a life raft while the others reached land on Banka Island. Sister Vivian Bullwinkel (now Vivien Stratham) clung to the side of a life

---

* First published under the title 'War Heroine "not bitter" ', in the *Weekend Australian Special Edition*, 15–16 February 1992.

raft which landed at Radji beach. Soon 22 nurses and other passengers from the *Vyner Brooke* were joined by twenty British soldiers who had survived the sinking of another boat in the Banka Straits.

After discussing their plight, the survivors decided that with so many wounded and children, they should surrender. An officer from the *Vyner Brooke* left to walk into the town of Mantok and report to the Japanese. Another group of civilian women and children, under the care of a Chinese doctor, also set off for Mantok and captivity.

At mid-morning on 16 February, the ship's officer returned with a Japanese officer and a troop of fifteen soldiers. The men were immediately ordered up and marched off around the point where they were shot and bayoneted. 'There were 22 of us and one civilian', Sister Bullwinkel recalls from her home in suburban Perth:

> We were left there on the beach with the wounded. We were all sitting down and we were ordered up and then told to march into the sea, which we did. When we got to about waist level they started machine gunning us from behind. I got a bullet through me but for some reason or other it didn't strike anything terribly vital. I was amazed to find myself still alive because I'd always thought that when you were shot, you were shot. To then find yourself still alive is quite surprising. I became scared, I thought, if they see me moving they'll know I'm still alive and I don't think I can go through all that again. So I just lay in the water and the waves brought me onto the beach again. Eventually I pulled myself together, went down to the beach, and I was just about to have a drink when from behind me a voice said: 'Where have you been, nurse?'.

It was one of the Englishmen, Private Kingsley, who had been lying on a stretcher when the Japanese arrived and had been bayoneted. All Sister Bullwinkel knew of Kingsley was that he was married and from Yorkshire and that it was his thirty-ninth birthday in a few days' time.

In search of food, the Australian nurse, whose ambition in life had been to become a sports mistress, walked to a village and asked some Indonesians for help. 'The men wouldn't have anything to do with me, saying I should give myself up', Sister Bullwinkel said. 'The thing I'll always remember all of my life is that as I was leaving the village two of the women came to the edge of the village and called out to me. I went back to them and they gave me rice, pineapple and dried fish. It was a gesture I'll never forget—that two women of another nationality who couldn't speak English were brave enough to defy their men and give me some food.'

For ten days, Sister Bullwinkel kept Kingsley alive until they decided they would have to give themselves up. But they agreed it would not be until Kingsley had celebrated his birthday in freedom. The two were captured. Kingsley died in captivity but Sister Bullwinkel survived. She recalls some other experiences:

> It was not very pleasant. We lived amongst rats, filth. We had no water, very little food and no medical supplies. You could never get away on your own, even to go to the toilet or to wash or shower and if you went outside you had 600 other people with you. That was one of the difficult things to adjust to—never being on your own, you only had 24 inches by six feet on a bench to live on. We had to dig our own graves and bury our own people. There was a lot of face slapping but the worst treatment that we got was that we were stood out in the sun because they felt we weren't doing as we were told. The civilians suffered more than we did, I think it's because we made no attempt to talk to the Japanese or have anything to do with them.

Sister Bullwinkel lived under these conditions until September 1945 when word was out that the war was over. Not long afterwards the Australian Government arranged to bring the prisoners back home. Just 24 of the original *Vyner Brooke* passengers would survive the war. 'We were told that the Emperor was sorry and that the war had gone on enough and he had decided it should finish', Sister Bullwinkel said. 'So they were never beaten in their own minds. It was the Emperor who called a halt to the war.'

Sister Bullwinkel, who went on to become Matron of the Fairfield Infectious Diseases Hospital in Melbourne and who holds a Florence Nightingale Medal, said the experiences did not make her bitter. If anything they made her appreciate the simpler things in life such as being able to shower alone and have personal items such as a comb or a cake of soap. Sister Bullwinkel, who has been to Singapore many times over the years, is going back to Singapore for the fiftieth anniversary. 'These days of course you can't relate to anything prewar', she said. 'There's nothing there to even remind you of what Singapore was like before the war. I love Singapore.'

Les Hoffman

A newspaper correspondent in Singapore*

My earliest memory is of a vast sea of upturned, expectant faces. I was peering between the rails from the deck of a liner, tugging at my aunt's skirt and asking excitedly: 'Which is him?' The scene was Singapore. The year, 1946. Like thousands of children aged three or four all over the world, I was about to meet my father for the first time. Then the memory gets slightly vague. I can't remember our actual meeting, nor what he looked like. I can't even remember my mother being there—yet she was, for it was she who brought me back to Singapore.

For her, everything had gone full circle. It had started in January 1942, in the frantic final days of a besieged Singapore, when she fled on one of the last ships to depart, overloaded with refugees. Ironically, it was the liner *The Empress of Japan*. My mother was six months' pregnant. Four years and one month later she returned— with me in tow. I was meeting a father I had never known; she was returning to a husband she had believed was dead, a belief so strong that at my birth she gave me his names, Leslie Clive, and a lifetime of explaining the confusion.

I have vague memories of the following few years, of houses and schools, faces, incidents and accidents. History flew over my

---

*   First published under the title 'Daddy, what did you do in the war?', in the *Weekend Australian Special Edition*, 15–16 February 1992.

young head. It was not until my teens that I probably even realised there had been a war so large it had encompassed all the world. It was not that I was uninterested, it was just that I was growing up in a world too busy repairing itself. At the age of seven I was in boarding school in Perth. Like hundreds of other children I travelled to Perth each February and returned each December. Singapore and Malaya—as it was then—were in the midst of the 'communist emergency', with daily tales of terrorists, ambushes and murder. There was no time to talk about The War. That was then; this was a new crisis. Anyway, it was not a subject you easily broached with Dad. The snippits I prised free were sparingly delivered.

E. M. Glover, who was managing editor of the *Malayan Tribune*, wrote in his book, *In 70 Days*, about the fall of Singapore:

> Leslie Hoffman formerly night editor of the *Tribune*, was one of the hundreds of unfortunate men and women who suffered at the hands of Kempei Tai [the Japanese military police]. He survived repeated beatings, torture and solitary confinement. How much he suffered will probably never be known, for Leslie Hoffman is not the type of man to give details about such matters.

My mother was talked into fleeing Singapore because Dad, as a senior journalist with the *Tribune*, had been writing anti-Japanese articles as the war progressed down the Malay peninsula. His scathing attacks on the 'yellow peril' were written in the hope of stirring resistance to the invaders. Singapore, after all, was impregnable.

It was only when the bombs began to fall and thousands died and the only aircraft in the sky wore the badge of a blood-red sun that the realisation dawned that the British Empire was not so invincible. All those big guns in Singapore were useless. Every last one of them pointed in the wrong direction—out to sea. Capitulation was untenable, but it happened.

With my mother gone and no one to worry about but himself, my father moved in with his brother and their father, a widower. He had to. The home he and Mum had established in the three years before the start of the war was ransacked by looters in the hectic final days before the island city's fall. With the Japanese in control, there was no newspaper to write for. It was wiser for him to keep as low a profile as possible. But it was only a question of time before the new rulers connected Leslie Hoffman with the disparaging articles written about them. In fact, several people from the *Tribune* were taken away, never to be seen again.

Despite early atrocities, and what happened later, there was a certain laxness in the running of internment camps during the last part of 1942 and into early 1943. The administration of the camps was largely left to the internees; they had to find their own blankets, medical supplies and comforts. The Japanese made no effort to take away their money—and some internees had plenty. Three or four broken-down trucks were repaired and used by the internees to drive into the city, with a Japanese guard, to collect camp supplies.

By February 1943 there were 3000 men and 400 women and children in the Changi internment camp. An early edict from the Japanese was that all radios on the island had to be brought in to have their short-wave bands removed. For those in the internment camps to have a short-wave radio was akin to spying. Like many of the people on the 'outside', Dad regarded his radio as the only way for him to know what was going on. He and his brother carefully built a radio into a padded footrest in his father's living room. When they needed it, all they had to do was plug it in. Listening to the radio had an added danger—across the road from my grandfather's house, Japanese officers had commandeered a mansion as their mess.

After the radio began operating, my father went back to being a reporter—but of a different kind. He had no newspaper to write for but there was news to be passed around of friends and relations who had escaped the island. Radio Australia and Radio India had daily broadcasts of messages from the refugees to those they had left behind. Dad was one of dozens on the island who listened, wrote down the messages, which were being repeated over and over again, and passed them on. Soon a network was built up. Messages were passed from one person to the next. Each person only knew from whom they received the messages and to whom they passed them on.

Nearly twelve months after I was born in India, Dad heard the news on Radio India. Much later, when I was fifteen, my grandfather told me of the party they had to celebrate the news. The only alcohol they could get was Indian coconut toddy, a near-lethal brew which was still fermenting when it was drunk. Two glasses were enough to give anyone the courage to take on the entire

Japanese Army. And during the course of that celebration they almost did. The singing and revelry did not please the Japanese officers in the mess across the road. Repeated commands to 'shut up' achieved little—until a salvo of bullets led to the party hurriedly adjourning to a cousin's house two streets away. My grandfather greeted my scepticism of the story by showing me the bullet holes in the woodwork of his front verandah.

By July 1943 the Japanese had tightened their control of Changi internment camp. According to the official record of subsequent war crimes trials, the internees had succeeded in tapping the telephone between the camp and the city. From what they heard, it was obvious that something was about to happen. It was only later that they discovered that the Kempei Tai had been brought to Singapore and plans were being made to raid the camp. The military police believed—quite correctly, as it turned out—that the camp commandant and the guards were being bribed.

Then, in September, six Japanese oil tankers were blown up in Singapore harbour. While the internees believed it was the work of guerilla saboteurs operating from the jungle on the Malayan mainland, the Japanese strongly suspected that even if it was not actually arranged from the internment camp, the internees were heavily involved in the planning of the attack. No one on the island thought of the true explanation—that a raiding party from Australia, led by Captain John Lyon, using an Indonesian fishing boat, the *Krait* (now on display at Darling Harbour), had pulled off one of the most daring and successful raids of World War II.

But the event did have its effect on the internees; it was the signal for the Kempei Tai to start a reign of terror which was to become known as the 'double tenth'. It was the tenth day of the tenth month that the military police launched their raids, first on Changi, then on selected homes and offices across the island. Internees were kept standing on the parade ground all day as the camp was turned upside down. Radios, money and messages were found and selected suspected ringleaders were taken away. The YMCA buildings in Stamford Road were the headquarters of the Kempei Tai. The people of Singapore would walk miles out of their way to avoid passing too near to the place, which echoed with the screams of men and women being tortured at all hours of the day and night.

111

And still the raids continued. No one knew when the Kempei Tai would turn up—or where. My father was picked up in one of the earliest raids. Interrogation started immediately, in my grandfather's house. My father soon realised resistance was pointless, so he took pleasure in informing his interrogator that he was sitting on the offending radio inside the footstool. But it did not stop the beatings. The Kempei Tai would not go to court without a confession from their victims. When my father woke up to this he confessed to listening to the radio illegally. This was better than admitting to spying, which could have resulted in the death penalty. It took the military police quite some time to accept that he was not going to admit to being a spy. In the end, he was given a five-year sentence and thrown into Outram Prison, the civil gaol.

In late August 1945, he watched from his tiny cell window as British troops liberated the general hospital across the road from the prison. Hours later, they opened the prison gates and all the inmates were released. Despite everything, including beri-beri and other illnesses, Leslie Hoffman had survived. At one stage he had shared a cell with a director of the *Strait Times*, who gave him a job to start 'when the war ended'. The day after his release, Dad reported to the *Strait Times* office and started work.

Almost forty years later, I bought a house in Sydney from a retired British Army officer who had served in Singapore in the 1970s. About six months later, he rang to ask if I had been in Singapore during the war. He had, he explained, been having dinner with a Mr Hebditch who had got excited when he mentioned selling his house to a chap from Singapore called Leslie Hoffman. It transpired that Edward Hebditch had been looking for Leslie Hoffman since the end of the war. He had been languishing in Outram Prison when Dad was thrown into his cell after being sentenced. After introducing themselves, my father said: 'Oh, I heard on the radio that your family arrived in Durban and are all safe'. They were still safe and well in South Africa when the war ended.

Mr Hebditch and my father only shared Cell 19 for a few weeks. Mr Hebditch came down with dysentery and was moved to hospital in early 1944. He was then moved to another internment camp until the liberation in 1945. He and Dad enjoyed a long telephone conversation before Mr Hebditch flew back to England. Two years later, when Dad died, they still hadn't been able to meet up again.

There are two groups of survivors from that war: those who will never forgive the Japanese for what happened, and those who are ready to forgive and forget. My father was in the latter group. I once asked him to explain his feelings. He knew the people who had tortured him—as a reporter he had covered the 1945 Double Tenth trial of interrogators at which, of the 21 accused, seven were acquitted, seven were gaoled and eight were sentenced to death. He said: 'I saw the ones who tortured me stand trial. They are dead. They were individuals, not a people.' For him the score had been settled.

Gary Hughes

The Changi spy network*

IT took Stan Bryant-Smith fifty years to decide finally to tell the largely untold story of the spies in Changi. Throughout the three and a half years that Japan occupied Malaya and Singapore, Australian prisoners of war organised and ran an intelligence network that supplied the Allies with information about Japanese forces. The network was based at Changi prison camp and Changi gaol in Singapore. Through local communist Chinese guerillas it kept up a flow of intelligence information to the Allies' South-East Asian command headquarters in India.

Mr Bryant-Smith is the last surviving member of the four-man team that operated the secret network. He has decided to speak out now so there will be some record of the work of the unit, which has remained unrecognised until now. 'It has never been acknowledged and those of us involved never talked about it because if you were in intelligence you didn't talk of such things, even after the war', said Mr Bryant-Smith, in Singapore for the fiftieth anniversary of the surrender of the strategic island fortress to the Japanese. 'But people should know that we didn't just sit around and do nothing as POWs. We were still fighting the Japs every way we could. We got information out as often as we could without ever knowing if it was getting through. It was only after the war we found out that

---

* First published under the title 'Singapore death camp spy breaks 50-year silence', in the *Weekend Australian*, 15–16 February

114

in fact most of it did get through and just how useful it was', Mr Bryant-Smith, now 77 of Penrith in NSW, said.

At night, the then Sergeant Bryant-Smith would slip through the barbed-wire fence surrounding Changi prison and the camp outside the walls and creep past Japanese guards to reach a small nearby Malayan village. In the village he linked with an underground unit of communist Chinese guerillas, based there specifically to receive information from the prisoners. The guerilla group would then use runners to take the information across the island to the Malayan peninsula, where other communist units had radios air-dropped to them by the Brits.

On one occasion late in the war, POWs working on the Singapore wharves learned that four huge storage sheds—or godowns as they were known—were packed with Japanese artillery ordnance. The Australian prisoners passed the information on to Mr Bryant-Smith's unit and that night word was sent to the Chinese guerillas. 'The very next day American bombers came over and dropped incendiaries on godown numbers 8, 12, 14 and 15 where the ordnance was stored', Mr Bryant-Smith said.

Mr Bryant-Smith, now treasurer of the Eighth Division Association and a member of the government liaison committee that helped plan the fiftieth anniversary celebrations, served with the 2/29 Battalion. He, along with other Australian units, faced the full brunt of the attack by the crack Japanese Imperial Guards on Singapore in the days leading up to the surrender. He said that on two occasions the Australians turned back the Japanese attack after fierce fighting and he believes they could have been driven off the island. But on each occasion the British high command ordered the Australians to withdraw. In the final days the Australians gathered at Kranji, now the site of the Allied War Cemetery on Singapore Island, ready to make a final stand. 'We hadn't had supplies of water or ammunition for three days but we were prepared to make a stand and fight and die there', he said, 'but the British surrendered'.

In early 1943 Mr Bryant-Smith was one of 3500 Australians sent to work on the Burma–Thailand railway with F Force, one of the slave labour work gangs. They were forced to march more than 300 kilometres into the rugged jungle on the Thai–Burma border, where they spent the next eight months working in appalling conditions on a starvation diet. Disease took an horrendous toll as did the beatings. Forty-four per cent of those in F Force died on the railway.

Christopher Dawson

Keeping track of the POWs*

WHILE the war against Japan raged in the Pacific, the fate and whereabouts of the Australians captured by the Japanese remained virtually unknown. Throughout the war the Japanese Government refused to comply with the terms of the International Convention concerning prisoners of war on the basis that it had never ratified the pact. Only when the first letters from Australian POWs arrived in the country via the Red Cross was the fate of many soldiers able to be determined. The Chief Censor arranged for the examination of the letters, which numbered in the thousands, in a bid to determine the whereabouts of the writer and other casualty information. 'The casualty category of the writer was changed from "Missing" to "Missing believed Prisoner of War" or "Missing believed Deceased", according to the evidence recorded', Captain L.I. Parker, author of a History of Central Army Records during World War II, says.

The place of internment of any individual soldier was largely impossible to determine and although reports were received of the Japanese moving prisoners, the extent of these movements and who was being moved was not known. The problem in compiling records for the Army was that there was virtually no authenticated

*   First published under the title 'The tragic search for POWs', in the *Weekend Australian Special Edition*, 15–16 February 1992.

information about soldiers missing in operations against the Japanese or those believed to have been captured. All efforts to gain information through the appropriate channels of communication were fruitless.

In March 1943 the Japanese determined to take propaganda advantage of Australia's anxiety about her lost legions. It started a series of radio broadcasts which included names of several prisoners with messages for next of kin, relatives or friends and statements praising the Japanese. In Australia, attempts were made to communicate with Australian prisoners via short-wave radio broadcasts.

In order to help recovery teams in their search, rolls of Australian Military Forces' prisoners and those missing in campaigns against the Japanese were made up to 30 June 1944—by theatre of operations in which personnel were serving; by units; and by POW locations as recorded at the date of the roll's compilation. A great deal of information was gained at recovery camps and transmitted to Australia. So rapid was the recovery and movement to Australia of POWs by sea and air that much of the interrogation had to be completed after the arrival of personnel in Australia.

Between September and November 1945, Australian Army headquarters' staff received, verified, collated and transmitted to next of kin or to the appropriate authority information concerning the recovery or death of more than 20 000 Australians and 30 000 Allied personnel. The work was carried out 24 hours a day by three shifts of eight hours.

5

Under threat of invasion

James Morrison

Preparing to resist invasion*

THE day after the fall of Singapore the words of the Labor Prime Minister John Curtin may well have given rise to fears that sport, betting and beer drinking would be banned. Describing the surrender as Australia's Dunkirk, Curtin said hours previously devoted to sport and leisure should be given to the duties of war and hinted that a ban on organised sport would be considered by Cabinet. 'Whatever criticism it may evoke, I tell this nation that as things stand today in Australia, brains and brawn are better than either bets or beer', Curtin said. 'Brains and brawn are demanded in every war job. We have to pep up war production. We have to organise the unstinted and unflagging resistance which will enable us not to become a people governed by others.'

With almost 17 000 men of the 8th Division of the AIF in Japanese hands in Singapore. Curtin—a former alcoholic—was unable to sleep for worry that Australian troops returning unescorted from the Middle East could be sunk in the Indian Ocean. At Forsyth Park, in the Sydney harbourside suburb of Neutral Bay, a group of women armed with only dummy rifles and hand grenades stormed a 'machine-gun nest'. The oldest participant, Mrs M. Bryson, 55,

---

* First published under the title 'Brains and brawn, not betting and beer, needed for victory', in the *Weekend Australian Special Edition*, 15–16 February 1992.

120

said: 'I hope I never see a Jap, but if I do he will come off second best'. Another to take part in the exercise, Miss E. Weller, said 'Australia is as much my country as any man's. I want to be trained to defend my land. I hate fascists and God help the first Jap I see.'

In Canberra a deputation of women led by Mrs Jessie Street (the wife and mother of later Chief Justices of NSW) had been told by the Minister for the Army, Frank Forde, that there would not be enough rifles to arm a women's army, and the Minister for Munitions said the country had left itself short of arms after it had rushed all its reserve rifle stocks to Britain after Dunkirk. A squadron of Australian Spitfire pilots in Britain said they wanted to come home to help defend their country; having missed the Battle of Britain they felt they had nothing to do.

A doctor at Lithgow, a town just beyond NSW's Blue Mountains, warned that if an influenza epidemic were to hit the State, half the staff employed at the city's small arms factory could be laid up sick. The doctor said this was because of sweatshop working conditions at the factory and the long hours the men worked. Meetings of coalminers, who had been striking over retirement provisions in their pension schemes, voted to return to work, with a miners' leader saying: 'We have to protect the government and give all that is necessary to conduct the war and protect Australia'. The previous week the country had experienced its first nationwide blackout and a Sydney fashion designer known as Madame P. Pellier said dozens of ideas for 'brown-out' fashions were being used by dress designers for the coming autumn and winter fashions. The House of Peapes was selling 'air-conditioned' woollen suits for £4 10s and David Jones and Farmers were holding their annual summer sales.

A future Labor prime minister, who was to lead Australia out of another war almost thirty years later, Mr Gough Whitlam, then a third-year law student at the University of Sydney and a member of the RAAF Reserve, had announced his engagement to Margaret Elaine Dovey.

On the Sydney Stock Exchange, the market indicator of ordinary shares dropped to 98.57 points, down from the Saturday close of 100.58, and for the first time since 1934, the base year for the indicator, it had fallen below 100. The shares of the beer giant Tooths fell 2/6 to 38/9 and had fallen 8 shillings since the announcement of the Federal Government's economic plan the week before. Dealers said the market had largely accounted for the surrender, and was probably influenced more by the uncertainty surrounding its own future.

The week before, the War Cabinet in Canberra had announced a wide-ranging series of measures designed to put the economy on a war footing. Under the proposal, wages and prices were to be pegged and the Commonwealth Bank was to control interest rates. All investment, except that 'obviously' intended for war production, was prohibited without government permission. It was the planned prohibition of speculative investment which had dampened markets, and it was thought the activity of the market would be restricted to the trading of government bonds. Two days after the surrender, Curtin launched the Liberty War Loan intended to raise £35 million, and within days of the issue it was half filled.

On the same day of the surrender, the Japanese invaded south-west Sumatra and the fear of invasion, compounded by the bombing of Darwin on 19 February, spread. Within weeks road and railway signs were removed, and an unofficial guerilla army, the People's Army (of which the women at Forsyth Park were members) grew with 1000 members in one Sydney suburb alone. Women filled men's jobs in increasing numbers, became factory workers, tram conductors and railway porters. By the middle of the year the Australian Women's Land Army was recruiting female agricultural workers.

In many ways the Australian population had been gradually prepared for the surrender. Only two weeks before, the Army had sent a memorandum to Canberra stressing the importance of defending the industrial and population centres in Port Kembla, Sydney, Newcastle and Lithgow, as well as Brisbane, which was to have a large American base, and Melbourne, where military headquarters were located. This was to be known as 'the Brisbane Line'. Although no politician had the courage to touch such a proposal which would have abandoned the rest of the country to the Japanese and was later dumped by the supreme commander of the South-West Pacific, General Douglas MacArthur, rumours of it filtered out and in the weeks following the surrender civilians started to evacuate the northern parts of the country.

Curtin had been advised two months previously by the Australian representative in Singapore that the island could not be held unless there were huge reinforcements, and that as things stood its fall was 'only a matter of weeks'. By 16 January the *Sydney Morning Herald*, in an editorial calling for reinforcements for Singapore, posed the question: 'Is the Singapore base to prove to democracy in the south-west Pacific what the Maginot Line proved to France—a delusion and a snare?' Of the surrender, Tokyo radio said the passing of the British stronghold into Japanese hands had put Japan 'in a position to control the fate of India and Australia'. Curtin said: 'Dunkirk's fall initiated the Battle for Britain; Singapore's fall opens the Battle for Australia'.

Gregory Pemberton

The arrival and role of General MacArthur*

IT was a sunny Saturday morning at 9.50 am on 21 March 1942, when General Douglas MacArthur's luxurious carriage, provided courtesy of the South Australian Railways Commissioner, pulled into Spencer Street Station in Melbourne. MacArthur, 62, had completed a journey of retreat from the Philippines. He had lost fourteen kilograms during the previous three months of siege, escape and retreat. He was not having a good war. Now his fate was being tied to that of Australia, the base for the counterattack.

In Adelaide, MacArthur had defiantly (if also defensively) told Australian reporters that he had been ordered to leave the Philippines for Australia in order to organise 'the American offensive against Japan, a primary object of which is the relief of The Philippines. I came through and I shall return . . .' Washington objected to the hint of megalomania conveyed by MacArthur's insistence on using the first person singular, but the General was not to be swayed. This short sentence passed into history as one of the most famous sayings of World War II. For bitter American soldiers left in the Philippines, however, it became the basis for sardonic humour. On appropriate occasions they would pronounce: 'I am going to the latrine, but I shall return'.

---

* First published under the title 'Australia's darkest hour: the truth behind the MacArthur myth', in the *Weekend Australian*, 28–29 March 1992.

124

MacArthur arrived in the darkest days of White Australia. Hong Kong and Singapore had surrendered, Darwin had been bombed, Australian garrisons on Rabaul and Ambon had been overcome. The Japanese were soon to land in northern New Guinea. The Prime Minister, John Curtin, had made his momentous decision of 23 February 1942 to override the British Prime Minister, Winston Churchill, and insist that Australia's experienced troops return home directly from the Middle East and not be squandered in any more futile imperial disasters.

Only one day before, the President of the United States, Franklin Roosevelt, had made a decision of almost equal moment in Australian history—he ordered MacArthur, as commander of American forces in the Philippines, to leave his besieged garrison for Australia. His mission was to organise an Allied force for the reconquest of the South Pacific. Macarthur had left Corregidor in Manila Bay with his family and a small personal staff on a dangerous journey in small patrol boats to Mindanao, from where they continued in B-17 bombers. Eluding Japanese fighters, they landed on 17 March at a remote airfield 80 kilometres from Darwin because the town itself was again under air attack. Apparently oblivious to Australia's geography and transport system (or lack of it), MacArthur wanted to drive to the nearest railway station (Alice Springs). However, he was wisely advised to put up with another flight instead. He was thrown to the aircraft floor as they hastily took off just ahead of Japanese fighters.

In the meantime, Curtin had been informed of his arrival and was asked by Roosevelt to accept the nomination of MacArthur as Supreme Commander of all Allied Forces in the South-West Pacific. He agreed without hesitation. The headline in the *New York Times* on 18 March read: 'MacArthur in Australia as Allied Commander— Move Hailed as Foreshadowing Turn of the Tide'.

As MacArthur sat on wooden seats and travelled the slow 1600 kilometres from Alice Springs to Adelaide by aged train, he only then began to realise the magnitude of the task before him. He would never, however, reveal such doubts in public. That was not the MacArthur style. Instead, he would blame others for failing him. From Australia, MacArthur crazily ordered the besieged Corregidor garrison to counterattack the Japanese. He raged against the final capitulation and worked privately to prevent General Wainwright, the man he had left in charge, being awarded the Congressional Medal of Honour.

From a chair on the observation platform at Spencer Street, MacArthur saw a crowd of between 5000 and 6000 curious onlookers, held in check by 50 Victorian policemen. The commander of US Army forces in Australia had scoured the American support units in Melbourne to provide a white-helmeted honour guard of some 260 troops. There was no band—MacArthur had sent word he did not want one. Formally attired Australian officials and dignitaries, who gathered on the station's platform to greet the General, found him to be dressed casually in a ribbonless bush jacket, well-worn khaki drill and non-regulation checked socks. He wore none of his 26 decorations (thirteen of them for bravery). According to one American observer present, the General 'looked like business'.

This was precisely the impression remembered by one excited young Australian woman at the time, Mary Petherick (later Waters), a 22-year-old medical researcher at the Baker Institute, Alfred Hospital. Accompanied by her father, the Reverend Ernest Petherick and her younger sister, she stood near where Bourke Street joins Spencer Street. Her father had taken his daughters along, telling them it was important to be present at moments of great historical significance such as the arrival of this American general who would 'save Australia'.

Yet despite the undeniable instances of panic in some parts of northern Australia at this stage of the war, it would be incorrect to assume there was widespread terror among the Australian people as a whole, especially in the more southern parts of Australia. In a poll taken in April 1942, albeit just after MacArthur's arrival, only 54 per cent believed Australia was threatened by invasion. The press treatment of MacArthur's arrival was far from hysterical; in fact, it was relatively subdued. His safe arrival caused as much relief in the US as it did in Australia.

Mary Waters recalls that her Melbourne acquaintances were certainly aware of the dangers but were not terrified. She ascribes this partly to the lack of detailed information. They all knew that 'the bastions of Hong Kong and Singapore' had fallen, but their impression of events in Darwin was that a 'few bombs' had fallen outside the city, causing only a few casualties. The general public had not yet been informed of the disaster at Rabaul. Nevertheless, there was a palpable feeling of relief among her friends and generally among the population when MacArthur arrived: 'You all felt a lot safer because he was here'. The feeling was that, with MacArthur's arrival, 'the Americans meant business'.

Like most Australians, Mary Waters had not known of MacArthur before the war but by the time he arrived in Melbourne, he had acquired a 'great name'. She suspected he was adept at ensuring that he got good press coverage for himself. He certainly had a sense of the theatrical and of historical drama. Leaving the train at Spencer Street, and after sending his wife and child ahead of him, he was drawn irresistibly to the ABC microphone provided. He had his address already prepared on a crumpled piece of paper, telling his listeners that he was proud to have served with Australian soldiers in World War I and to be their comrade once more. He then chided Washington, saying that success in modern war depended on receiving sufficient troops and material to meet the known strength of the enemy. 'No general can make something out of nothing. My success or failure will depend primarily upon the resources which the respective governments place at my disposal. In any event, I shall do my best. I shall keep the soldiers' faith', he said.

Observers on his staff in Melbourne, who generally hated him, noted that behind the public facade of bravado, MacArthur swung in and out of moods of despair and recrimination against his 'enemies' in Washington. Mary Waters's suspicion that MacArthur was adept at PR was correct. His conduct in the Philippines immediately before his departure has attracted much subsequent criticism, not least of all for accepting a $US500 000 gift from the President of the Philippines and for implicitly supporting the idea of a separate peace between the Philippines and Japan.

Initially, MacArthur had seemed paralysed by the Japanese assault and failed to act decisively. He was partly responsible for the success of Japan's air strikes there, and his refusal to visit the front more than once had earned the bitter epithet of 'Dugout Doug' among the GIs. But press and radio accounts of the five-month defence of Bataan and Corregidor, however, made him a national hero, although these actions did not greatly affect Japan's war plans. The right-wing press saw in him a weapon with which to attack Roosevelt's New Deal policies.

MacArthur's headquarters released 140 press statements in a three-month period, many drafted by MacArthur himself, which referred only to the General. According to a recent biography by Michael Schaller: 'Singlehandedly, it seemed, he parried enemy thrusts and frustrated Tokyo's entire war plan. Neither fellow officers nor frontline troops received much credit for anything. MacArthur, or his public relations officers, were so determined to stress the positive that their releases frequently reported victories in imaginary battles.' Roosevelt thought MacArthur's actions in the Philippines were more 'criminal' than heroic and awarded him the Congressional Medal of Honour only under great political pressure. One Roosevelt official joked that, in Australia, Macarthur was the 'right man in the right place'—that is, 'thousands of miles away from American newspapers'. In Australia and the New Guinea campaign, MacArthur would prove equally adept at managing his PR image even at, or especially at, the expense of his allies.

There is no doubt the Labor Government in Australia was both pleased and relieved to have MacArthur in the country. Deputy Prime Minister Frank Forde, who had greeted the general at the station, believed he was the man to advise the Government 'along the right lines'. Curtin's government soon suspected correctly that the Anglo-US leadership had adopted a 'beat Hitler first' policy that relegated the Pacific War, and therefore Australia's defence, to second priority. So it correctly saw in MacArthur a natural ally, if only of temporary expedience, whose desire to promote his own career by a campaign to retake the Philippines coincided with Australia's desire to see a greater military effort made in the South Pacific. He certainly contributed more than Dr H. V. Evatt, the External Affairs Minister, towards gaining the resources necessary to take the offensive.

Although the Western hemisphere retained its first priority, US planners did proceed with their scheme to develop Australia as a base for the war against Japan. By March, about 80 000 American troops had been sent over with an additional 20 000 scheduled to arrive by the end of the year. It is arguable that without MacArthur's great influence, the US might have relied more exclusively on a naval thrust through the central Pacific and relegated the South Pacific to an even lower rank in the order of global importance.

Much has been made of the extent to which the Labor leadership actually abdicated national responsibility to MacArthur. According to MacArthur's British Liaison Officer, the General said 'Curtin indicated to him that Australia was ready to shift over to us away from the British Empire . . . his quotation is probably extravagant, but he—MacArthur—had previously told me that Curtin and co more or less offered him the country on a platter'. Such judgments by British officials need to be treated with caution. British officials were automatically predisposed to be critical of Labor governments, especially in the dominions. They were also extremely sensitive to the US challenge to Britain's influence in its dominions. The British High Commissioner, Sir Ronald Cross, actually had proposed an economic and financial squeeze on Australia to keep it in line. The Dominion Secretary rejected this idea but agreed there was a tendency for some dominions to swing away from the Empire—'a rot which started in Australia'.

The British paranoia was fed by the hysteria of conservative Australian leaders. W.M. (Billy) Hughes, then leader of the United Australia Party, had cabled Churchill: 'Some of his [Curtin's] ministers are extremists and anti-British . . . Curtin is at best cool towards Britain. Under influence of Caucus and leagues. May pump for America as against Britain. The press, almost solidly behind government, feeds people daily with insidious pro-American propaganda . . . Empire needs a victory.'

According to John Burton, private secretary to Evatt, there is no doubt that Curtin, Evatt and other Labor ministers fell under MacArthur's spell. Burton recalls that Curtin was not a forceful personality but a cautious conciliator. He struck up a close relationship with MacArthur and often dealt directly with him. He took his chief strategic counsel from the General, often bypassing Australia's army commander, General Thomas Blamey, and the chiefs of staff (two of whom, courtesy of the previous government, were in any case British officers). Despite being Commander of Allied Land Forces, Blamey could not get past the cabal of US staff officers surrounding MacArthur.

Placed under the American Commander of Allied Air Forces, the RAAF all but lost its separate identity. At one point, Curtin told reporters he was 'subject, in effect, to a form of direction by a representative of another government'. It appears there was little choice for the Australian Government in these dangerous days. The abject failure of imperial defence, in which conservative leaders had so complacently acquiesced, had placed Australia in such a vulnerable predicament that there was little choice but to accommodate the needs of MacArthur and the Americans. Inevitably, MacArthur's influence trespassed into Australian political matters. He convinced Curtin in 1943 to bend, if not break, Labor Party principle and legislate for Australian conscripts to be sent on operations outside Australia.

He was on less secure ground in 1943 when he publicly accused the Australian Government of having a 'defensive' outlook in 1942 and took credit for the decision to take the offensive against Japan in New Guinea. Australia's General Iven Mackay dismissed this claim as 'a piece of skite'. On the basis of its advice, the Australian Cabinet had resolved on such a course even before MacArthur arrived. No doubt his presence and his stirring address to a joint session of Parliament in April 1942 buttressed morale. But from his distant headquarters in Brisbane, MacArthur underestimated Japanese strength in New Guinea and the difficulties of the task facing Allied forces there. He blamed US commanders and Australian units for failing to achieve rapid victories. When success did arrive, he was upset that the US Commander, General Eichelberger, was upstaging him publicly. Following complaints from Australian commanders, Curtin had to ask MacArthur to allow greater news coverage of Australia's part in military operations.

Despite the outstanding performance by Australian forces on the Kokoda Track, at Milne Bay and at Buna, MacArthur relegated them to the unglamorous and dangerous backwater of defeating the 90 000 Japanese troops remaining in New Guinea and the surrounding islands as he pressed on to his date with destiny and fame (and, possibly, the Republican presidential nomination) in the Philippines. In downplaying the significance of Australia's military achievements in New Guinea, MacArthur was merely replicating the pattern established during the prior period of imperial defence.

Nothing helps reinforce the notion that you are reliant entirely upon the protection of a 'great and powerful friend' than suppressing or ignoring past instances when the country was able to demonstrate a fair degree of self-reliance and independent achievement.

In Australia, the imperial legacy is preserved in Anzac Day and other icons of our military history. The new dependent relationship

Above Fire erupts from the bow of the destroyer USS *Shaw* as it takes a direct hit. *Below* Sailors clear away debris on the USS *Yorktown* after the ship received a direct hit from a Japanese bomb. (*USA Armed Forces Ships F309 and F248*)

President Franklin Roosevelt. He described 7 December 1941, when the Japanese attacked Pearl Harbor, as 'a date which will live in infamy'.

Australian anti-tank troops fire at advancing Japanese tanks during the Battle of Muar, January 1942. (*Australian War Memorial AWM 011302*)

The USS *Pennsylvania*, which escaped serious damage in the attack on Pearl Harbor, was in drydock behind the destroyer USS *Cassin* which was severely damaged and rolled into the destroyer USS *Downes*. (*USA Armed Forces F222*)

Above Smoke billows over Singapore Island from a fire at the Naval Base. *Below* Elated Japanese troops on the Singapore waterfront, 16 February 1942, after the surrender of the British forces. (*Australian War Memorial AWM 012447 and AWM 127905*)

Gordon Bennett . . . remembered as the general who left his troops. (*Australian War Memorial AWM 11303/8*)

Vivien (Bullwinkle) Stratham . . . her horrific experiences, she says, have left her with a greater appreciation of the simpler things in life.

Right The works of Murray Griffin depict the life-sapping work expected of the POWs. (Murray Griffin: *Bridge Work, Thailand Railway*, pen and brush and brown ink over pencil, heightened with white, 51.4 × 35.6 cms, *Australian War Memorial AWM 25107*)
Below Personnel of 'C' Company, 2/29th Australian Infantry Battalion, in their hut at the rear of Changi Gaol. (*Western Australian Army F105*)

Above Former POWs from 8 Division demonstrate conditions in their Changi cell in September 1945. *Below* 'Retreads', members of the Volunteer Defence Corps, erect barbed-wire entanglements on a beach as a defence against Japanese invasion. (*Australian War Memorial AWM 116462 and AWM 45123*)

MacArthur and Curtin: according to the US general, the Australian prime minister had 'offered him the country on a platter'. (*Australian War Memorial AWM 072967*)

The aircraft carrier USS *Lexington* on fire during the battle of the Coral Sea. Many of the crew can be seen abandoning ship. (*Australian War Memorial AWM 157901*)

with the US is legitimised by the celebration of the Battle of the Coral Sea and other memorials to America's 'saving' of Australia during the Pacific War. Given Prime Minister Paul Keating's recent evocative attack on the nature of the old imperial relationship, it is time he also called for a reassessment of the nature of our relationship with the US. He could begin by undoing some of the self-serving public relations work of MacArthur and drawing the nation's attention to the scale of their own soldiers' achievements in New Guinea.

Carl Bridge and Paul Burns

The Brisbane Line*

IN traditional Labor demonology, the darkest deed attributed to Robert Menzies was his wartime government's alleged plan to retreat behind the infamous Brisbane Line in the event of a Japanese invasion. The man who sold pig iron to the Japanese before the war so they could make bombs to drop on us was said to have decided to leave all of northern Australia and its civilian population to the enemy's mercy without firing a shot and to form a Vichy-style collaborationist government in the south. The plan was 'discovered' in late 1942 by the rambunctious Eddie Ward, member for East Sydney and Minister for Labour and National Service in the Curtin Government. Ward then used it conveniently to discredit the conservatives in the 1943 federal elections, which Labor won by a landslide. Afterwards a royal commission was held into allegations that the vital document was missing from official files and the commissioner reported in the negative. Rumours have persisted ever since. What is the truth about the Brisbane Line?

Between the wars the Army evolved a strategy for defending Australia that was based on the reasonable assumption that any enemy would attempt to destroy the major industrial area from Newcastle to Wollongong. If this area was lost, Australia would lose

---

* First published under the title 'Brisbane line was Labor bogy', in the *Weekend Australian Special Edition*, 2–3 May 1992.

the capacity to make war effectively. Consequently, the industrial heartland had priority in army defence planning. A 1936 Defence paper spelled this out: 'The occupation of a portion of northern Australia would not vitally affect the bulk of the Australian people who reside in the southern and eastern portions of the continent'. There was no Japanese rampart, like the French Maginot Line, to be manned against a Japanese landward advance. Rather, there was a notional line defining an area within which troops were to be concentrated in readiness to rush out to meet any Japanese landings in force within range of the key industrial heartland. This was the plan General MacArthur would later rather misleadingly brand the Brisbane Line.

Both Labor and the conservative prewar governments were primarily reliant on the strength of the British Navy and on the supposed invulnerability of its Singapore base. Should enemy transport ships get through the naval shield it was expected they would attack with no more than three divisions, about 60 000 men. After war broke out in Europe, Menzies committed eventually three AIF divisions to the Middle East and later one to Malaya. Home defence in the air was weakened by sending the bulk of the RAAF to fight in the skies over Europe. The Navy sailed for the Mediterranean. These commitments were made on the understanding that the Australian forces would return home if war broke out in the Far East. In the meantime, the continent was to be defended by its 250 000 ill-equipped and mostly untrained militia.

In 1940, an Allied conference revealed Singapore's vulnerability and Menzies rushed to London in an attempt to persuade the British to look to the defence of Malaya, provide a fleet at Singapore and contribute to Australia's air defence requirements. But Churchill was adamant that there was no danger from Japan. And if there was, he was sure the US would come to Australia's aid. From September 1940, Curtin and his Labor shadow Cabinet had a hand in defence policy decisions through the Advisory War Council. They knew about the deficiencies in equipment and trained men affecting home defence planning. They accepted the equipment shortages—they knew Menzies was trying to right them; and they broadly agreed with the strategy for continental defence as one of concentrating the main force in the vital south-east industrial areas.

Under Menzies, plans for evacuation, which were primarily a

State responsibility, were formative only. There was little intention to defend the far north. Plans for the defence of Darwin were based on the assumption that Darwin would be lost to the enemy. On 10 June 1941, on the eve of the Japanese move into Indo-China, Cabinet directed the armed services to draw up joint operational plans to meet specific forms of attack on Australia and to institute machinery for combined operational planning in each State. These guidelines were given to Cabinet in late August. They accepted the strategy of concentrating the main military force in the vital south-east industrial area. When it took office in early October the Curtin Labor Government kept this vital strategy.

The Japanese move south led Australia, Britain and the US to freeze Japanese assets. The Government now needed to be seen doing something significant for the defence of the continent. It responded by despatching AIF brigades to Malaya and Darwin, and calling up 35 000 men for full-time duty in the home forces, some of whom went to Rabaul and Thursday Island. It also appointed a general to be charged solely with organising the defence of Australia. Menzies chose Sir Iven Mackay, well known to the public because of his victories with the 6th Division in North Africa. Mackay's exact standing in the home command structure in relation to the Chief of the General Staff, Vernon Sturdee, had not been clarified before Labor came to office.

One thing, however, was clear to the Curtin Government even before the outbreak of the Pacific war. With the limited resources available for home defence it was not possible to defend the whole of Australia. It did not have sufficient trained men. Nor did it have the equipment or the infrastructure: no tanks, few modern aircraft and no strategic railways into tropical Australia. Defences had to be concentrated in the vital areas of Brisbane, Newcastle, Sydney, Port Kembla and in Western Australia, around Fremantle. Left undefended or ill-defended were towns in Queensland north of Brisbane, Darwin and north-west Australia. Until Singapore was about to fall in February 1942, this strategy was accepted without demur by politicians on all sides.

On 4 February 1942, Mackay wrote a memorandum for Frank Forde, the Labor deputy leader, Minister for the Army and member for the north Queensland seat of Capricornia, repeating the Labor Cabinet's accepted strategy: 'It may be necessary to submit to the occupation of certain Australian areas by the enemy should local resistance be overcome', mainly in north Queensland because of a lack of troops. Curtin was in hospital when Mackay's memorandum was put to Cabinet. Forde, as deputy leader, realised that if he approved the Mackay proposal and this became known 'he would immediatley lose . . . his seat'. Influenced by such overtly political considerations and against all military logic—despite the fall of Singapore on 15 February and the bombing of Darwin on 19 February—Forde and his Cabinet colleagues now asserted baldly that the strategy must be to defend the whole of Australia.

Forde himself was in such a panic that he asked Sturdee whether garrisons at Port Moresby and Thursday Island should be withdrawn to the mainland. But Sturdee left the Cabinet in no doubt that the Mackay memorandum was the only realistic home defence plan. Forde then sought from the Chiefs of Staff an appreciation of the defence of Australia that would take into account the 50 000 American troops due in April and the two Australian divisions returning from the Middle East. Mackay had realistically left these factors out of his appreciation. He realised that in early February there were few US troops in Australia to rely on, that even when they did arrive it would be several months before the raw conscripts would be sufficiently trained to be of any use, and the AIF would need to be re-equipped. His headquarters saw Forde's instruction as politically motivated and militarily unsound. Mackay and his staff then conducted a military exercise based on the assumption that the ports most vital for the war effort were from Brisbane to Melbourne. If the enemy landed elsewhere 'we must get back later what he has seized while still holding the vital ports'.

By 27 February the Army had a new appreciation for Cabinet, which took the Americans into account. This appreciation, however, reiterated that the only viable strategy was to concentrate on the defence of the vital south-east industrial region. Given the available forces, Townsville, Darwin and Fremantle were all still at risk. The American factor would eventually alter this equation, but it would take time.

Not until 18 March was the Deputy Chief of the General Staff, Rowell, called to defend the appreciation before the Cabinet and the Advisory War Council. Politicians of all parties were adamant that both Darwin and Port Moresby were to be defended to the fullest possible extent. They also wanted forces moved from southern parts of Australia (for example, Victoria) to northern areas (such as southern Queensland). The Advisory War Council instruction, with its example of southern Queensland, was deliberately vague. While it left the way open for politicians on both sides to claim there was a plan to defend the north, the crucial emphasis on the defence of the vital south-east industrial areas still stood.

The realistic military appreciations panicked Cabinet. Forde sought a new commander-in-chief to replace Sturdee. His choice was Gordon Bennett, who had escaped in controversial circumstances from Singapore before its surrender. Forde was attracted by Bennett's determination that 'the Japanese must be fought to the death in New Guinea and not permitted to set foot on Australian soil'. The general ultimately chosen by the War Council, however, was the more politically sophisticated Thomas Blamey, Deputy Commander-in-Chief, Middle East.

Evacuation policy was a bone of contention between the Commonwealth and the States. On 12 December 1941, women and children were compulsorily evacuated from Darwin. In all States there was a public clamour for large-scale evacuation. This was discouraged by the Army. At a special conference the premiers were asked not to encourage wives to participate in wholesale evacuation to country areas as this would interfere with the productive effort of the men. But the State ministers agitated for federal funds for just such an evacuation from dangerous areas. For the Commonwealth, evacuation had, extraordinary as it may seem to the non-military mind, the lowest priority of all civil defence matters. Evacuation of the civilian population was deemed to be neither feasible nor desirable because it would disrupt military movements. Moving industry inland on any worthwhile scale was also impractical. Despite this, Queensland still went ahead with an evacuation census and in early 1942 evacuated more than 10 000 women and children inland.

Not until 4 February did all the premiers agree there should be no wholesale evacuation of civilians. In Western Australia the refusal of the GOC Western Command to send troops any further north than the Moore River, 105 kilometres north of Perth, after the bombing of Derby, Broome and Wyndham led the West Australian Labor Party to complain directly to Curtin. Curtin, a West Australian, did not tell his State colleagues that the Army had advised him that 'it would not be possible to provide adequate defence for the north-west'. Cabinet looked also to implement a scorched-earth policy. Little was done, however, in either Queensland or Western Australia because there was a shortage of army officers to do the planning. Ironically, denial of resources planning was much further advanced in NSW and Victoria, where sufficient officers were concentrated. There detailed instructions existed for the destruction of military installations, fuel facilities, radio and telegraph communications, roads, bridges, wharves, mines, railways and other facilities of use to the Japanese. Thus, paradoxically, the south could be demolished while the more vulnerable north could not.

When Blamey was appointed he accepted the necessity of the strategy to concentrate defence on the vital south-east industrial areas. He knew that much of the north and north-west could not be adequately defended. So he supported the strategy. Politically deft, he gave Mackay command of the Second Army, which was responsible for the defence of NSW, Victoria and South Australia, but not Queensland, since Mackay had gravely upset the politicians with his suggestions that part of the north of that State might have to be abandoned to the enemy.

General MacArthur, who had arrived in Australia from the Philippines on 17 March, did not, as he later claimed, immediately abandon what he called the Brisbane Line. From March to June 1942, while major naval battles raged to the north, culminating in the Coral Sea and at Midway, MacArthur still operated on the assumption that the land defence of Australia would take place in north-east Queensland. He believed the region was a Japanese objective but initially he did not have the trained troops to prevent them from landing. If the worst came to the worst, Darwin and Port Moresby would be abandoned to the enemy and a scorched-earth policy implemented. About 400 guerillas, among them trained local Aborigines, were to cause as much disruption as possible behind enemy lines. Not until July 1942 did MacArthur look to the defence of Australia in New Guinea. But as late as June, Blamey was still adhering to the policy of defending only the Perth–Fremantle region in the west. He told Bennett, who had taken command of III Corps there, not to defend the north-west.

The Japanese advance on Kokoda in July refuelled fears of

invasion. By then scorched-earth policies were finalised. Queensland and Western Australia were now designated as the States where those policies were most likely to be implemented. This created the correct impression that in extreme circumstances those States were to be sacrificed.

There was no Brisbane Line. Instead, there were three factors, all misunderstood, that contributed to the Brisbane Line fantasy: priority of defence for the vital south-east; the Government's policy of non-evacuation of civilians; and the scorched-earth policy. All these were in fact Labor Party policies with which the Opposition agreed. Amazingly, they were still in place at the time of the 1943 elections. These plans taken together provide the groundwork for Ward's mistaken claims about the existence of a Brisbane Line. The actual vital-areas policy and related scorched-earth plans were more a Curtin policy than a Menzies policy. Little wonder that when the fiery Ward made his allegations against Menzies, Curtin was distinctly uneasy. Curtin allowed Ward to run with the issue for its advantageous electoral mileage. But Curtin knew the only plan that resembled Ward's fevered fantasies had been contemplated under Menzies but had become operational under Labor. So much for the myth that Curtin saved Australia, although he certainly won the 1943 election.

6

The Battle of the Coral Sea

Tom Frame

The strategic setting*

MAY 1942 marked a turning point in the national histories of Australia and the United States. To Australia, facing the prospect of a hostile invasion for the first time in its European history, the Japanese southward thrust through Asia and the Pacific after Pearl Harbor seemed unstoppable. Within three weeks of the surprise Japanese attack, the war front was less than 1600 kilometres from Darwin, Hong Kong had fallen, the battleship HMS *Prince of Wales* and the battlecruiser HMS *Repulse* had been sunk, and Thailand, Malaya and the Philippines had been invaded. Singapore had been taken and with it the 8th Division of the Second Australian Imperial Force. The Dutch East Indies was next to fall, the Japanese landed on New Guinea and New Britain, Darwin was bombed and the war came to Australia. There was a sense of despondency among the Allies as Japan had achieved its objectives with devastating efficiency.

The Commander-in-Chief of the Imperial Combined Fleet, Admiral Yamamoto Isoroku, recognising that the Japanese Navy had to bring the US Navy to a decisive engagement and destroy its naval air power, planned an attack on the key US naval base at Midway Island. Admiral Yamamoto's plan was codenamed 'MI'.

---

* First published under the title 'Strategic triumph turned tide of war', in *The Australian Special Edition*, 2–3 May 1992.

The victory he envisaged at Midway would secure command of the seas for Japan and allow it to consolidate its gains. But before this plan was executed at Midway, New Guinea needed to be cleared completely of Allied forces and Port Moresby captured. This latter plan, codenamed 'MO', would be executed simultaneously with an attack on the Solomon Islands to enhance the Japanese position in the South-West Pacific. Although the Japanese carrier strength available for MO was limited to *Shokaku* (Soaring Crane) and *Zuikaku* (Happy Crane) and the light carrier *Shoho*, Admiral Yamamoto was confident that the element of surprise he had enjoyed at Pearl Harbor would be sufficient to ensure that MO would be likewise successful. This was also preferred to a cross-country march from the nouthern coast of New Guinea, which the Japanese already held.

Two important points need to be made in relation to MO. The first is that Japan expected to succeed. Second, the Japanese had not yet intended to occupy Australia. An assessment prepared by the Japanese Imperial General Staff in 1942 explained the reasons:

> If the invasion is attempted, the Australians, in view of their national character, would resist to the end. Also, because the geographic conditions of Australia present numerous difficulties in a military sense, it is apparent that a military venture in that country would be a difficult one. To alter the plan already in force and to employ a force larger than the one employed in the southern area since the outbreak of the war, to suddenly invade Australia which lies 4000 nautical miles away would be a reckless adventure and is beyond Japan's ability.

It is for this reason that Japan sought to capture New Caledonia, Fiji and Samoa and to establish a seaplane base in the Louisiade Archipelago—240 kilometres south-east of the 'tail' of New Guinea. The fact that the Japanese did not intend to invade Australia is immaterial to any overall assessment of the strategic significance of the plan. Australia was a focus for shipping across the two ocean basins, the Indian and Pacific, on either side of the continent. Japan could achieve its ends, severing sea communications to the north of Australia, without conquering continental territory.

For the first time in the war, good fortune was with the Allies. Having broken the Japanese naval communications codes and anticipating a possible thrust towards Port Moresby and Australia, two Allied carrier task forces and a cruiser striking force were concentrated in the Coral Sea–New Hebrides area. It was now the Allies who enjoyed the element of surprise while the Japanese relied on intelligence, which reported that only the carrier *Saratoga* was able to mount a counterattack. In fact, *Saratoga* was completing a refit at Puget Sound, 12 480 kilometres from Noumea.

On 3 May 1942, the Allies received intelligence that the Japanese were landing at Tulagi Harbor in the Solomon Islands. Meanwhile, the Japanese covering group, under Rear Admiral Goto, and the support force, commanded by Rear Admiral Marushiuge, sailed for the Jomard Passage and entry into the Coral Sea. In company with the Port Moresby invasion group commanded by Rear Admiral Kajoike, the whole group would subsequently alter course to the west and start the offensive against Port Moresby. If *Saratoga* did attempt to offer resistance, the two carriers of Vice-Admiral Takagi's carrier striking force would converge on the US carrier and launch an attack with fighter aircraft. Vice-Admiral Shigeyoshi Inoue commanded the Japanese forces from his flagship, the cruiser *Kashima*, which was in Rabaul. At the time of the Coral Sea battle, he was simultaneously in command of the Japanese 4th Fleet and the South Seas Force.

There is no doubt that Admiral Inoue was a brilliant administrator and staff officer, but his ability to exercise command at sea was considered suspect. Taking command of the 4th Fleet based at Truk, Admiral Inoue was given the task of capturing Guam and Wake Islands in conjunction with the attack on Pearl Harbor. The former was weakly defended so it was essentially a formality. However, the latter had been strengthened during 1941. When Admiral Inoue encountered firmer resistance than he expected, his ships retired to the west and could have been destroyed while returning to Kwajalein. With the support of forces returning from Pearl Harbor, Admiral Inoue was finally successful. However, his invasion fleet had been the only force that had not achieved its initial objective. In April 1942, Admiral Inoue transferred his base from Truk to Rabaul in preparation for MO, during which he would exercise overall command.

Opposing Admiral Inoue in the Coral Sea was Rear Admiral Frank Fletcher USN, the commander of Allied Task Force 17. Admiral Fletcher had considerable naval sea-going experience by the time of this command. After commanding the unsuccessful expedition to relieve US forces striving to retain possession of Wake Island in December 1941, Admiral Fletcher's command was reorganised as Task Force 17 with his flag flying from the aircraft carrier *Yorktown*.

On the morning of 4 May 1942, Task Force 17, consisting of the US carrier *Yorktown*, heavy cruisers *Astoria*, *Chester* and *Portland* and six destroyers, was within 160 kilometres of the Japanese invasion force when planes from the *Yorktown* attacked Tulagi and Gavutu Harbor. One Japanese destroyer was sunk and another badly damaged. Five enemy landing craft were sent to the bottom, a minelayer was damaged and several aircraft were shot down. On 6 May, when news of an advancing Japanese naval force was received, the Allied ships were reorganised into three groups: an attack group, a support group, which included HMAS *Australia* and *Hobart* commanded by the Australian-born Rear Admiral John Crace, and an air group based on the carriers *Yorktown* and *Lexington*.

On the morning of 8 May, scout aircraft from the attack group located a large Japanese force based on three carriers, which appeared bound for Port Moresby. Ninety-two planes from the US carriers were launched and succeeded in destroying the Japanese carrier *Shoho*. In response, Japanese carrier aircraft from the *Zuikaku* and *Shokaku* attacked and sank the tanker *Neosho* and the destroyer *Sims*, the former being mistaken for a US light carrier which had been detached to the south. A lull in the action followed while each carrier force tried to locate the other. There were several aerial clashes but neither side's carrier aircraft could locate the surface forces.

In the early morning of 7 May, Japanese land-based air forces concentrated their efforts on the Allied support force, commanded by Admiral Crace, which was deployed to intercept the Port Moresby invasion force in the Jomard Passage. Three Japanese bombing and torpedo attacks were sustained by Admiral Crace's force, attacks that would otherwise have been mounted on the more highly valued Allied carrier force. The Japanese operational plan was in disarray by the end of 7 May. Having received reports of Admiral Crace's force and the existence of two carrier battle groups in the Coral Sea, Admiral Inoue ordered the Port Moresby invasion group to turn back for the Jomard Passage until the US carrier strength had been neutralised. Japanese emphasis was now turned to finding and destroying the US carriers.

Early the next morning, 8 May, air patrols for both sides simultaneously located the surface forces and the battle reached its crucial stage. Allied planes mounted a fierce attack on the *Shokaku* and inflicted severe damage, while the battle-stricken *Lexington* was abandoned after leaks of aviation fuel put her in immediate danger of explosion. The Japanese had lost considerably more carrier fighter aircraft and Admiral Inoue was unwilling to risk his carriers further. He was also unwilling to send the invasion force through the Jomard Passage in the face of Admiral Crace's force and the likelihood of attack from Allied land-based aircraft. Because of the heavy losses sustained by both sides, the Allies and the Japanese withdrew the main part of their forces.

As the invasion force returned to Rabaul, with the *Shoho* sunk, the *Shokaku* damaged and the *Zuikaky* withdrawn to the south, Admiral Yamamoto was left with no choice but to confirm Admiral Inoue's effective cancellation of Operation MO. Had Admiral Yamamoto ordered the invasion force to turn again towards Port Moresby, it arguably stood a very good chance of reaching its destination. With the *Lexington* sunk and the *Yorktown* bound for Noumea, the likely Allied air resistance would have been a fraction of that expected on 6 May.

The battle of the Coral Sea had three distinct results. First, although US matériel losses were greater than those of the Japanese, it was an Allied tactical victory as naval air power and carrier warfare emerged as the key to future Allied success. The virtual loss of the two big carriers in the Coral Sea battle weakened the Japanese at Midway less than a month later. Here they lost four carriers and, effectively, the Pacific naval war. The 'breathing space' created for the Allies by the Coral Sea battle also meant the US Navy was able to deploy the *Hornet* and *Enterprise* to the central Pacific after their return from the raid on Japan.

Second, it was a strategic victory in that Japan was forced to fight a land campaign in New Guinea, which highlighted the poor support it was able to provide its troops so far from home. Plans for invading Fiji, Samoa and New Caledonia were shelved and the sea route to the north of Australia remained open to the Allies. And third, Allied success at Coral Sea was an overwhelming psychological victory. For the first time in six months, the Japanese had been stopped, and stopped where they least expected—at sea. The Americans saw Coral Sea as a psychological success as official historian Samuel Morison later recorded:

> There is no greater teacher of combat that can even remotely approach the value of combat itself; call Coral Sea what you will, it was an indispensable preliminary to the great victory of Midway. The morale value of the battle of all Allied nations, coming as it did immediately after the surrender of Corregidor, was immeasurable.

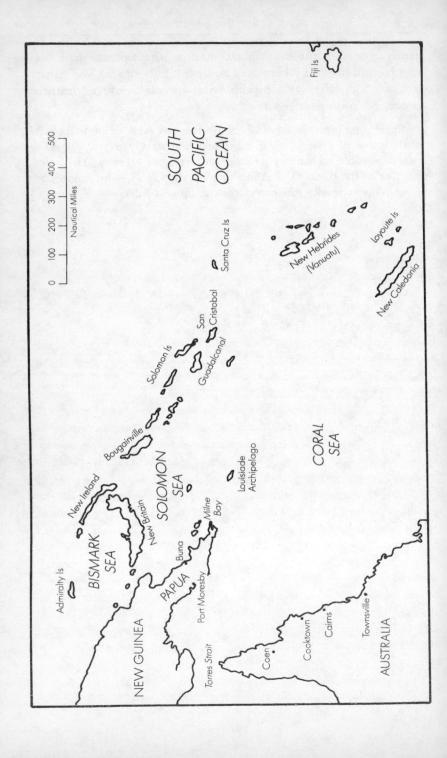

Bill Evans and Chris Coulthard-Clark

The battle*

4 May 1942

Under the protection of a dark night, Admiral Fletcher brought the carrier *Yorktown* to a position about 160 kilometres south-west of the island of Guadalcanal at 6.30 am on 4 May. At 7.01 am, he launched the first of three aerial attacks on Tulagi but much to Admiral Fletcher's disappointment, the Japanese supporting force had already departed and could not be located. However, the gung-ho US air crews sent back exaggerated damage reports while in reality, only four barges, two minesweepers, one converted minesweeper and one destroyer were sunk.

This surprise attack did result in the hasty evacuation of the Japanese landing force at Tulagi with one small garrison left behind when Vice-Admiral Inoue discovered that Vice-Admiral Takagi's two fleet carriers were too distant to provide assistance. However, the local Japanese commander's frantic appeals for support resulted in Rear Admiral Goto's light carrier, *Shoho*, and heavy cruisers racing toward Tulagi. He reached Guadalcanal late in the afternoon to discover that the US ships had disappeared south-east under the cover of a murky weather front. Meanwhile, at 8 am on 4 May, Rear Admiral Crace and his ships joined Admiral Fitch's TF11.

---

* First published under the title 'Four days to a hard-won victory', in *The Australian Special Edition*, 2–3 May 1992.

5 May 1942

The *Yorktown* group rejoined the *Lexington* group at 8.46 am on 5 May. The combined ships of Admiral Fletcher, Vice-Admiral Fitch and Admiral Crace cruised in clear weather throughout 5 May while refuelling from the fleet tanker *Neosho*. At the same time Japanese transports heading for Port Moresby had left Rabaul and were coming south. Admiral Goto's covering force was on the port side moving parallel to them to support the Port Moresby landing, while Admiral Takagi's strike force steamed down the eastern side of the Solomon Islands entering the Coral Sea late in the evening. Admiral Takagi's aim was to assault the rear of any Allied naval forces rushing to attack the Japanese transports. Rear-Admiral Marushige's support group was now south of Woodlark Island headed for Deboyne Island.

6 May 1942

At 7 am on 6 May, Admiral Fletcher merged the two carrier task forces and Admiral Crace's TF44 into TF17. Throughout the day, he was getting reports of Japanese naval forces including carriers south of the Solomon Islands. On 4 May a US plane based in Australia sighted *Shoho* and two heavy cruisers at 11.35 am in the region about 65 kilometres south of Bougainville. By the afternoon of 6 May, a reliable assessment of Admiral Fletcher's intelligence suggested that the Port Moresby invasion group would pass through the Jomard Passage between Misima and Tagula islands off the tail end of Papua on 7 or 8 May.

On the evening of 6 May, Admiral Takagi's strike force almost caught Admiral Fletcher's fleet while they were still refuelling. He was within 112 kilometres of TF17 when he shifted course to the north. Admiral Takagi's mysterious neglect to carry out long-range aerial searches from his carriers on 5 and 6 May prevented him from catching Admiral Fletcher's carriers unexpectedly.

7 May 1942

On 7 May, TF17 was just south of the Louisiade Archipelago, which forms an extension of the Papua tail. Just before 7 am, Admiral Fletcher ordered Admiral Crace to continue north-west with the heavy cruisers HMAS *Australia* and USS *Chicago*, the light cruiser HMAS *Hobart* and three US destroyers: the *Farragut*, *Perkins* and *Walke*. Admiral Fletcher's carriers turned north searching for the enemy carriers.

Admiral Crace's mission was to stop the Port Moresby invasion group from getting through the Jomard Passage no matter what happened to the US carriers. Admiral Fletcher anticipated that his carriers would be attacked this day but was willing to deprive the Anzac task force of carrier air support while simultaneously reducing his already feeble carrier anti-aircraft screen.

At this point, neither Admirals Fletcher nor Takagi was certain of the other's location in the Coral Sea. Admiral Fletcher possessed information that three Japanese carriers were supporting the Port Moresby thrust. His aerial reconnaissances were futile because of foul weather to the north-west where the two Japanese fleet carriers were. Japanese land-based aircraft actually sighted the US carriers but the vital message failed to reach Admiral Takagi.

The weather in the north-west was clear on the morning of 7 May and early that day US reconnaissance planes were searching in the north-west and sending in reports. A pilot reported at 8.15 am that he saw 'two carriers and four heavy cruisers' slightly north of Misima Island. In response at 10 am, Admiral Fletcher directed attack groups to be sent from both his carriers. These 93 planes were well out before the scout plane returned. Then it was found that the scout pilot really saw two cruisers and two destroyers. Nevertheless, Admiral Fletcher made the bold decision to let the attack continue, probably reasoning there had to be some profitable targets with the Port Moresby invasion group nearby. His gamble was rewarded at 10.22 am when a Japanese carrier and several other ships were sighted just kilometres from where the attack had been sent originally. About 11 am, the Americans made their first aerial attack on an enemy carrier. The *Shoho* was hit with thirteen bombs and seven torpedoes, and sank with most of her crew at about 11.50 am. When his planes returned to TF17, Fletcher assumed that now the Japanese knew his position, with their attack soon to come. He kept his planes ready until the *Shokaku* and *Zuikaku* could be found.

Also on 7 May, a Japanese seaplane from the base at Deboyne Island sighted Admiral Crace's group and shadowed, although keeping well out of gun range. It was not spotted until 11.30 am, when

Admiral Crace had to assume the Japanese had his location. When this scout reported back to Rabaul, it said Admiral Crace's group consisted of two battleships, a heavy cruiser and four destroyers. This error caused concern to Admiral Inoue after the loss of the *Shoho*. He immediately ordered Japanese Navy planes from Rabaul to attack Admiral Crace's ships. Just before 3 pm, the bombers from Rabaul were picked up by Crace's force on radar six minutes before they came into view. Bombs and torpedoes failed to make any direct hits in this attack and the second wave that followed at 3.13 pm. The Japanese were surprised at the skill and resistance put up by Admiral Crace's group, which cost them at least five aircraft. At 3.19 pm, three more aircraft appeared and dropped bombs, which also missed the ships. These were US Army B-17 bombers, which reported to Townsville that they had heavily damaged Japanese ships.

Meanwhile, initial Japanese misidentification of the *Neosho* as a carrier played havoc with their attack plans. Rear Admiral Chuichi Hara on the *Zuikaku* ordered a full attack up on the fleet oiler and her escort destroyer. The *Sims* took three bomb hits and went down with almost all her crew. The *Neosho* took seven hits but remained afloat until scuttled by the Americans on 11 May. As evening approached, the weather closed in and in a determined bid to find and strike the US carriers before nightfall, Admiral Takagi's air commander ordered a force of dive 27 dive-bombers and torpedo-bombers into the air at 4.15 pm. These were sent on a westerly course to look for their quarry near where Admiral Crace was attacked. However, natural factors intervened, with cloud cover from a cold front effectively shielding the US force, while the Japanese crews battled rain squalls and strong turbulence. Failing to find anything, and approaching the limits of their safe range, the Japanese planes jettisoned their bombs and headed for home.

As luck would have it, the course of the returning bombers actually brought them close to the force they had been seeking. And with the advantage conferred from having radar, the Americans scrambled fighters to intercept them. Nine Japanese planes were shot down in the resulting melee, fought out in conditions of half-light about 45 minutes after sunset. With fuel running low, the Japanese broke contact while the US pilots gathered to rejoin their carriers. In the course of recovering their aircraft in the falling darkness, personnel on *Yorktown* were dismayed to discover that several

Japanese crews—tired, confused and glad to have found what they thought was their own carrier—had joined the queue of circling planes, waiting their turn to land before discovering their mistake and making off. Ultimately, just six of the Japanese aircraft made it back to Admiral Takagi's carriers, which were 80 kilometres to 100 kilometres away from Admiral Fletcher at this time.

Knowing now of each other's presence within striking distance, both commanders weighed the idea of making a night surface attack. Instead, each decided to seek a decisive outcome the following morning, 8 May. During the night of 7 May, Admiral Fletcher moved to the south and west while Admiral Takagi went north.

8 May 1942

It was imperative for each to locate the enemy as soon as possible on the morning of 8 May. Searches were launched by both sides a little before dawn. Scouts of each side reported the other almost concurrently soon after 8 am. The decisive action of 8 May began on even terms. Each opponent had two carriers. There were 121 planes available to Admiral Fitch while Admiral Hara had 122 planes. The Americans had the advantage in dive-bombers but the Japanese had the advantage in torpedo planes and fighters. Moreover, the Japanese pilots had more combat experience. Japanese torpedoes were far superior to the defective US ones. In another respect, the Japanese obtained a great advantage. By his unnecessary move south during the previous night, Admiral Fletcher had lost the bad weather area in which he had been operating so now TF17 was exposed under clear skies. At the same time, the Japanese remained within the frontal area with the protection of clouds and rain squalls.

Both sides put scouts out at daybreak and, as chance again dictated, each found the other about 8.20 am and prepared to deliver knockout blows from the air. This battle on 8 May was a simultaneous exchange of aerial strikes by the opposing carrier forces, which was in fact the first great naval battle between ships that never actually sighted each other but fought one another solely from the air.

Both US carriers launched their attack groups between 9 am and 9.25 am. The *Yorktown* air group was launched first with 24 dive-bombers, nine torpedo planes and two fighters. About 10.30

am, the dive-bombers discovered the two Japanese carriers and their escorts in loose formation. But instead of splitting into two groups and attacking both carriers at once, the US dive-bomber pilots inexplicably hid in cloud cover until the torpedo planes arrived. This needless delay enabled the *Zuikaku* to disappear into a rain squall leaving only the *Shokaku* as a target. With the arrival of the torpedo planes, the dive-bombers began their belated attack with only moderate success. The slow US torpedoes were easily dodged but the dive-bombers were successful in planting two bombs on the *Shokaku*. The *Lexington* air group was launched about ten minutes after the *Yorktown* air group but its 22 dive-bombers failed to find the *Shokaku*. Only the eleven torpedo planes and the four scout bombers found the *Shokaku*. They added another hit to the two already inflicted on the *Shokaku*. These three hits prevented her from recovering her aircrafts. Admiral Takagi detached her and ordered her to proceed to Truk.

The Japanese had launched their air groups of 70 dive-bombers and torpedo planes with twenty fighters about the same time that the Americans launched their strike. US radar picked them up at 112 kilometres but only three US fighters intercepted them before they struck. When 32 kilometres away, untroubled by US fighters, the Japanese divided into three groups. There were two groups of torpedo planes and one group of dive-bombers. When the Japanese began their aerial attack, the two US carriers were together each in the centre of their circle of screening vessels. Their evasive tactics slowly separated them. Their screens were divided fairly equally but the disruption of the circle certainly assisted the Japanese. The Japanese first attacked the *Yorktown*, which easily avoided the torpedoes but took one bomb hit. This blow did not really hinder her fighting effectiveness. The *Lexington*, larger and less manoeuvrable, was caught in an 'anvil' attack on both bows simultaneously and received two torpedo hits on the port side. She also received two bomb hits about the same time, which caused further minor damage.

In the action that morning both the American carriers suffered multiple hits, the *Lexington* being the more badly damaged although its combat effectiveness had not been seriously impaired and, within an hour, it was able to resume flying operations. On the Japanese side, *Shokaku* was severely damaged, being forced to retire initially to Truk and eventually to Japan to undergo repairs. *Zuikaku*, although suffering no battle damage, was left with a much reduced number of its aircraft operational. The battle honours to this point seemed about even. But a failure of damage control procedures on *Lexington* now handed the Japanese a result they had been unable to achieve in combat. An internal explosion at 12.47 pm, caused by the ignition of vapours from ruptured fuel lines, started serious fires, which after several hours became uncontrollable. Soon after 5 pm, the order was given to abandon ship. After all living personnel were safely taken off, the grand old '*Lady Lex*' was sent to a watery grave by torpedoes fired from an accompanying destroyer. The *Yorktown* took aboard those planes of the *Lexington* still in the air.

Although Admiral Inoue was given reports claiming that both US carriers had been sunk, he was hesitant to continue the Port Moresby invasion group's progress in the face of overwhelming Allied air power in Australia. He felt he must postpone these landings at Port Moresby indefinitely and had made the decision later in the afternoon of 8 May. Combined Fleet headquarters that morning had given him permission to alter the date of the Port Moresby landings. He directed the invasion convoy and the Mo main force back to Rabaul. Admiral Yamamoto at Japanese Combined Fleet headquarters was angered at this cessation of activities on Admiral Inoue's part because a previous report from Admiral Inoue had claimed that the two US carriers had been sunk. Unaware of the low plane strength on the *Zuikaku* and the fuel situation, Admiral Yamamoto refused to let the US surface fleet escape without heavy losses. Late on 8 May he ordered Admiral Inoue to continue his pursuit to annihilate the enemy.

At 11.30 pm, Admiral Inoue ordered Admirals Takagi and Goto to recommence their strikes against the withdrawing Americans as quickly as possible on 9 May. Admiral Takagi changed course to search to the south and east. By now, Admiral Fletcher was well out of reach. Admiral Crace's task force was far to the west when the crucial struggle took place between the opposing carrier groups because of its course in the previous night. He continued his role on the blocking group of the Jomard Passage.

Throughout 8 May, Admiral Crace was not kept informed of events by Admiral Fletcher. After the air attacks of 7 May, Admiral Crace kept his ships at general quarters during daylight hours in the event of additional air attacks. He could only hear fragments of the

8 May battle from monitored radio communications. His force was consistently shadowed by aircraft and several sightings were made before noon.

On 9 May, Admiral Crace ordered HMAS *Australia* to transfer 300 tons of fuel to the destroyer *Farragut*, which was completed before noon. This enabled him to maintain his position and presence as the blocking group. With no word to the contrary, he assumed that Admiral Fletcher was still in the Coral Sea, which required him to stay in position. The reality was that Admiral Fletcher's TF17 was already proceeding south rapidly to leave the Coral Sea to the Japanese. Admiral Takagi's battle group was now the undisputed master of the Coral Sea and was hunting for the elusive Admiral Fletcher. It was fortunate for Admiral Crace and his four ships that he was more than 1100 kilometres to the west of Admiral Takagi.

At 7 pm on 9 May, Admiral Crace reached the conclusion that Admiral Fletcher's carriers urgently needed replacement aircraft, bombs and torpedoes while his destroyers were short of fuel. Orders and even information were still denied to Admiral Crace even though Admiral Fletcher had withdrawn from the Coral Sea. He had to assume Admiral Fletcher had departed, which meant he had to consider the same action. BBC Radio reports picked up by the task force confirmed what the rest of the world already knew—that the battle of the Coral Sea had been fought and won.

The battle of the Coral Sea opened the way for allied air raids on the Japanese headquarters at Rabaul in September, 1942. (*Arch Fraley Collection*)

The seven two-man crews who were to take part in the raids on Sydney Harbour and Diego Suarez in Madagascar. The midget submarine commanders are seated, with their navigators behind. Ban is front left, followed by Yamaki, Chuman, Akeida and Matsuo: all but Akeida were part of the attack on Sydney Harbour. (*Japan Midget Submarine Association*)

Captain F. E. Getting RAN. Despite mortal wounds, he continued directing rescue operations from the shattered bridge of his command, the *Canberra* during the battle of Savo Island, August 1942. (*Australian War Memorial AWM 106675*)

Before the war, it was thought impossible for Europeans to cross the mountains carrying a load, let alone fight along the track. (*Australian War Memorial AWM 54746*)

On the Kokoda Track near Oivi, troops from the 2/14th
Battalion slog through the mud. (*Australian War Memorial
AWM 13620*)

General MacArthur visits Aussies in the New Guinea jungle
near Port Moresby in October 1942. He is accompanied by
General Sir Thomas Blamey.

Papuan Raphael Oembani leads a wounded soldier to safety: one of the war's most famous pictures. (*Australian War Memorial AWM 14028*)

Right A Japanese light tank lies abandoned after the heavy fighting at Milne Bay. *Below* 'Bluey' Truscott: lost hero.

Allied infantry had to penetrate defences quickly to avoid hellish machine-gun fire during the battle of El Alamein, October 1942. (*Australian War Memorial AWM 10583*)

Montgomery: a guiding light and a point of focus, a master and a mascot. (*British Official Photograph No. BM 24498*)

William Dargie *Attack by 2/24th Battalion, El Alamein at night, October 25–26, 1942*, 1973, oil on canvas, 149.5 × 271.5 cm. (*Australian War Memorial AWM 27821*) *Below* Desert graves record the horrific toll of the battle of El Alamein. (*Australian War Memorial AWM 10583*)

Australians celebrate victory at El Alamein. (*Australian War Memorial AWM 13356*)

David Horner

The threat to Australia*

THE battle of the Coral Sea has been accepted in Australian folklore as the battle that saved the country from invasion. In the 1992 ABC television series, 'When the War Came to Australia', Australians recalled their experiences of the war. One commented: 'if they'd lost the Coral Sea battle the Japs would have come into Australia', while another said: 'the Coral Sea battle was a lot closer to an invasion of Australia than most people even now accept'. Shortly before the fiftieth anniversary of the battle, Sir Eric Neal, the Chairman of the Australia United States Coral Sea Commemorative Council, was quoted in the *Canberra Times* (1 April 1992) as saying that the battle saved Australia from invasion. Is this popular perception true?

The battle of the Coral Sea came at the end of five astonishing months in which victorious Japanese forces had carried all before them. Beginning on 8 December 1941 they had attacked Pearl Harbor and the Philippines from the air, had landed on the north coast of Malaya, had sunk the *Prince of Wales* and the *Repulse* in the South China Sea, had marched into Hong Kong, and had invaded the Philippines, driving the American–Filipino army back into the Bataan peninsula. On 15 February 1942 Singapore surrendered, and

---

* First published under the title 'Salvation folklore overlooks Japanese disarray on attack', in *The Australian Special Edition*, 2–3 May 1992.

Japanese forces pushed into the Netherlands East Indies. On 19 February, as cover for their landings on Timor, they bombed Darwin.

As early as 4 January Japanese planes bombed Rabaul in Australian New Guinea, and on 23 January their forces attacked and captured the town. The first air raids on Port Moresby began on 3 February, and on 8 March Japanese troops landed at Salamaua and Lae on the north coast of New Guinea.

Faced with this relentless onslaught, it was reasonable then for Australian political and military leaders to expect that the next step would be an attempted invasion of the mainland. On 27 February, for example, the Australian Chiefs of Staff advised the Government that after its success in the Netherlands East Indies, Japan was 'now at liberty to attempt an invasion of Australia should she so desire'. A possible Japanese line of approach was through Port Moresby, but the Chiefs knew that there was no prospect of reinforcing Port Moresby until the sea lanes were secure and additional aircraft were available.

On 5 March the Deputy Chief of the General Staff, General Rowell, advised the Government that the Japanese might mount an attack on Port Moresby in the middle of March, on Darwin in early April, on New Caledonia in the middle of April, and on the east coast of Australia in May. The US high command in Australia expected an attack on Darwin by three enemy divisions before the end of March, and on 25 March there was an invasion scare in Darwin when a Japanese fleet was detected in the Celebes; it went to the Bay of Bengal.

The Australian Government and the public were therefore fully justified in planning to repel an invasion, and by the middle of March an air of panic or desperation hung over some quarters of the Australian population. On 11 March Ek Dum wrote in the *Bulletin*: 'War has ceased merely to be on Australia's doorstep. It is on the mat reaching for the knocker.' The Sydney *Daily Mirror* discovered a 'reputed tremor of civilian morale through some sections in Australia', and Federal ministers were perturbed at what they considered to be a lowering of public morale.

Government concern was heightened by the lack of adequate defences. Three well-trained and experienced divisions (the 6th, 7th and 9th) of the Australian Imperial Force were in the Middle East or on ships returning from there, while units of the 8th Division had been captured at Singapore, Timor, Ambon and Rabaul. Remaining in Australia were some 270 000 militia troops, organised into ten divisions, who had been called up on the outbreak of war with Japan. They were under trained and lacked adequate equipment and weapons.

The air defences were in an even weaker state. On the outbreak of war with Japan the RAAF had a total of 306 planes, but most of these were obsolescent trainers such as Wirraways. It had only 53 Hudson medium bombers. By March many of these had been lost in action, while the US Air Force in Australia numbered only 39 bombers and 177 fighters.

Following its early successes the Japanese Navy was superior to the combined US, British, Australian and New Zealand navies. Off the east coast of Australia was Anzac Force, commanded by Rear Admiral Crace RN. It consisted of an Australian cruiser, a US cruiser, two New Zealand light cruisers and two US destroyers.

Although the threat of invasion remained, towards the end of March a number of events caused a revival of confidence. The first of these was the return to Australia of the 7th Division and one brigade of the 6th Division which, along with the headquarters of the 6th Division, was hurried north to help defend Darwin.

The second event was the reorganisation of the Australian Army and the appointment of General Sir Thomas Blamey as its Commander-in-Chief. His presence, along with other officers who returned to Australia with recent combat experience, helped raise the standard of the militia.

The third event was the arrival on 17 March of General Douglas MacArthur, to command the combined Australian, American and Dutch forces of the newly formed South-West Pacific Area. Already American forces had started to arrive in Australia, but MacArthur's presence underlined the fact that Australia would not be alone in the coming struggle. The threat of invasion had not passed, but the period of desperation was over.

In early April the US and Australian military chiefs concluded that there was a possibility of a Japanese attack on 'Australia's supply line and against Australia itself' in the very near future. They still recognised that the critical point was Port Moresby, but air and naval support for its reinforcement was not yet available. At this stage there was only one militia brigade around Port Moresby.

With the possibility of a Japanese attack Generals Blamey and MacArthur deployed most of their land forces along the east coast of Australia. The air forces concentrated their striking units in the Townsville–Cloncurry area, from which they could attack the Japanese base at Rabaul. It was too dangerous to base the air units at Port Moresby.

In deploying these forces MacArthur had the advantage that signals intelligence units were beginning to provide evidence that the Japanese would soon attempt an invasion of Port Moresby. According to Rear Admiral Layton, the head of US Naval intelligence based at Hawaii, as early as 3 April his staff had 'numerous indications' pointing to an 'impending offensive from Rabaul'. By 20 April his staff thought that the Japanese would attack Port Moresby on 3 May. On 24 April MacArthur issued a warning that a Japanese force of three aircraft carriers and five cruisers might strike the north-east coast of Australia between 28 April and 3 May. On 4 May General Milford, commanding the 5th Australian Division at Townsville, received this warning from his higher headquarters: 'An early attack on Port Moresby is probable and this may be followed by a landing on the north-east coast with a view to a progressive advance southwards covered by land-based aircraft'.

As the Battle of the Coral Sea approached, the Allied high command in Australia believed that the Japanese thrust towards Port Moresby posed a definite threat to the Australian mainland. This view was stated publicly by the Prime Minister, John Curtin, in Parliament on 29 April when he said that the Government 'regards an outright Japanese attack on Australia as a constant and undiminished danger. As part of this purpose. . . the Japanese may seek to isolate Australia by cutting the sea routes whereby essential supplies reach this country.' This last sentence was, in fact, a very clear statement of what the Japanese were actually trying to do, but was the Japanese thrust also part of an overall plan to invade Australia?

Japan's rapid successes in December 1941 and January 1942 caught their planners unprepared. For example, on 5 January, when it looked as if they would achieve all their targets by the middle of March, the chief of staff of the Japanese Combined Fleet wrote in his diary: 'Where shall we go from there? Shall we advance into Australia, attack Hawaii; or shall we prepare for the possibility of a Soviet sortie and knock them out. . . ?'

For the next two months Japanese Imperial General Headquarters debated this question. In the meantime, on 29 January the Commander-in-Chief of the Combined Fleet, Admiral Yamamoto Isoroku, was ordered to capture Lae and Salamaua and, at the proper time, Port Moresby. As related earlier, the first two localities were seized on 8 March.

The Japanese Navy General Staff were keen to mount an invasion of Australia, and in December they had calculated that they would need three divisions to secure footholds on the north-east and north-west coastlines. On 14 February, one day before the fall of Singapore, a Naval Ministry official told a conference of Navy and Army staff that they had 'a good chance to make a clean sweep of Australia's forward bases'. Again, on 27 February, after the successful strike against Darwin and the landings in the East Indies, the Navy General Staff insisted on an invasion of the north-east coast of Australia.

The Japanese Navy's plans were strongly resisted by the Army which estimated that it would need at least ten and perhaps twelve divisions to invade Australia. The Army did not believe that these divisions could be spared from China or Manchuria where they were located in case of war with the Soviet Union. If the Red Army collapsed before the German blitzkrieg, Japan might launch an invasion of Siberia. Even more crucial, a major assault on Australia would require 1.5 to 2 million tons of shipping, but most of this shipping was required to transport the newly gained raw materials back to Japan from South-East Asia. Instead, the Army wanted an offensive in Burma and India.

On the Navy's side there was no unanimity about the need to invade Australia. Admiral Yamamoto wanted to attack Midway Island, in the central Pacific, thus drawing the US Pacific Fleet into battle. Eventually a compromise was reached, and on 7 March the invasions of Australia and India were put aside. On 15 March it was agreed to capture Port Moresby and the southern Solomons, and 'to isolate Australia' by seizing Fiji, Samoa and New Caledonia. The Japanese planned to form a defensive ring around their Greater East Asia Co-prosperity Sphere, and if Australia could be isolated it would no longer be a base for a US counteroffensive.

Japanese plans in the New Guinea area were delayed for a time by a major Japanese naval raid into the Bay of Bengal in early April, and by Yamamoto's determination to continue preparations for his invasion of Midway Island. But by the end of April the Japanese forces at Rabaul were ready for the assault on Port Moresby.

The Battle of the Coral Sea caused the Japanese to call off their seaborne attack on Port Moresby, but the most serious aspect of the battle was that their losses meant that Yamamoto's forces were reduced for the Midway battle a month later. The absence of one fleet carrier was perhaps crucial to the outcome of that battle. In the New Guinea area the Japanese persisted with their strategy, landing troops on the north coast of Papua on 22 July to march on Port Moresby over the Kokoda Track. By that time the Allied forces in New Guinea had been built up to a point where they could just resist this new thrust.

Had the invasion fleet not been halted by the Coral Sea battle, Port Moresby would probably have been taken. From that base the Japanese air forces would have been able to attack northern Queensland. Certainly the war would have taken a different course. If all went well, perhaps the Naval General Staff might have persuaded Imperial General Headquarters to support a landing in Australia.

Undoubtedly, then, the Battle of the Coral Sea was crucial to the outcome of the war in the Pacific. But it is not true to say that it prevented a Japanese invasion of Australia because, as has been shown, such an invasion was not an agreed part of Japanese plans.

In recent years some historians have suggested that radio intercepts should have revealed to the Australian higher command that Australia was not under threat of invasion, and that the Government was not justified in raising that possibility. However, since the Japanese did not decide not to invade Australia until mid-March, the charge that the Government manufactured an invasion threat in February and March is false. It did not, however, take long for Japanese intentions to become apparent. As early as 11 April, Allied intelligence concluded that it was not practical for Japan to launch a major offensive against Australia at that time. Furthermore, MacArthur had access to American intercepts of Japanese diplomatic traffic known as 'Magic', and on 18 April these reported the discussions between the Japanese Foreign Minister and the German Ambassador to Tokyo, revealing that there was no plan to invade Australia. The same day the US Pacific Fleet intelligence staff concluded that there was no evidence that Japan intended to invade

Australia. On 23 April MacArthur told the Prime Minister's War Conference that 'a large scale attack on Australia was possible, but not probable. There might be predatory raids, but he did not think a major attack was likely.'

This view contrasted with Curtin's statement in Parliament on 29 April quoted earlier, when he said that a Japanese attack was a 'constant and unlimited danger'. Curtin continued to stress the threat of invasion for another year, partly to maintain Australia's war effort, and partly to gain additional men and aircraft from the United States. However, at the time of the Coral Sea battle it was a prudent approach on the part of both Curtin and MacArthur to plan on repelling a Japanese invasion. That the battle has gone into folklore as preventing an invasion of Australia is understandable, but as a statement of fact it is not true.

Gregory Pemberton

The political background to the battle's celebration*

'The people won't dare to throw away the value of the United States alliance when they recall the Coral Sea battle', enthused Allen Fairhall, the then Minister for Defence, to a fellow Cabinet colleague in the Liberal Government of Harold Holt in April 1966. With US and Australian involvement in the Vietnam war attracting mounting criticism, Fairhall had reason to worry about the consequences for Australia's relationship with the US. Twenty-four years after this relatively minor naval engagement in the Pacific War, Fairhall clearly appreciated the value in terms of present politics of the ritual celebration of a past event.

All such historic celebrations or commemorations are designed to serve present political purposes. Rarely are they spontaneous creations of the people *en masse*. Such celebrations are usually manufactured by a government or an interest group influencing the Government. Yet, to succeed, they have to touch a responsive chord in popular consciousness. If not, they will fail to capture popular sentiment, like Australia Day, for example, or they will lose their initial popular significance, as did Empire Day or Labour Day.

Anzac Day taps into a profound and genuine popular sentiment in Australia although both governments and groups such as the Returned and Services League have sought to channel the cultural

---

* First published under the title 'Military celebration owes much to politics', in *The Australian Special Edition*, 2–3 May 1992.

expression of that sentiment in a particular direction in terms of present politics. Because European Australia was constituted as part of an empire, much of its culture, including its celebratory rituals, was derived from the empire's centre—Britain. The NSW school magazine before World War I encouraged this process by printing on the top of one of its issues the semaphore message which Nelson made famous at the Battle of Trafalgar: 'England expects every man to do his duty'. The commemoration of the battle of Trafalgar still remains significant for the Royal Australian Navy, which for many years traced its cultural roots directly to the Royal Navy. The Royal Australian Air Force still holds as significant the Royal Air Force's victory in the Battle of Britain. The national commemoration of the Queen's birthday, which grew out of Empire Day, is another example.

Generally, 'Australian' events were often not seen to be worthy of such commemoration. Gallipoli was an ambiguous exception. Empire Day provides a good illustration of how such traditions are 'invented'. In 1905 the Conservative Government of George Reid agreed to proclaiming 24 May, the late Queen Victoria's birthday, as Empire Day following representations from the Australian branch of the British Empire League. It had been founded in 1901 in response to the Anti-War League's opposition to Australian involvement in the Boer War and was further disturbed by the decision of Edmund Barton's Government to prevent, under the Defence Act of 1903, the use of Australia's army in overseas (and therefore presumably imperial) wars. The rising Japanese threat then, as later, provided stimulus for the adoption of this celebration.

Many of the national celebrations sponsored by a state are to do with war. This is not a coincidence. The origins and the legitimacy of the modern nation-state are inextricably bound up with war. It was through war that a modern state usually carved out its new 'national' territory from the declining empires or from other weaker nation-states. Force was also often required to suppress those people within the new boundaries of the nation-state who would not accept its legitimacy to govern, such as was the case with the Aboriginal people in Australia. To preserve the myth of the united nation these usually are not celebrated. The Australian state certainly could not admit to the existence of this war because to do so would be to undermine the legitimacy of its claim to the land which became based on the doctrine of *terra nullius*—a legal fiction that Australia was uninhabited. Celebration of British victories (such as Trafalgar), partly through the medium of Empire Day substituted until Australia got the baptism of blood, which some but not all had sought, at Gallipoli. Thereafter, partly through the lobbying of returned servicemen's groups, Anzac Day became the nation's key celebratory occasion.

This new celebration of the battle of the Coral Sea, like Empire Day, did not arise spontaneously from the Australian people as a whole. Once again it was promoted by a small group of leading Australians—based around the Australian–American Association—who once again had to overcome some initial reluctance from the incumbent government before realising their objective with its successor.

Australian perception of the US Navy as a supplement if not a successor to the Royal Navy did not start with the Coral Sea battle. Fear of Japan had been growing in Australia since the 1890s. The Anglo-Japanese alliance of 1902 and the subsequent withdrawal of the Royal Navy from the China station three years later were signs that the pre-eminence of British power in the Far East was declining. Following this and Japan's victory over Russia in 1905, Prime Minister Alfred Deakin extended an invitation in late 1907 to President Theodore Roosevelt for the US Great White Fleet to visit Australian ports during its world voyage the following year. The fleet was greeted by enthusiastic crowds. Another US naval force which visited in 1925 was also warmly greeted. As the fear of Japan rose, Australians continued to look to the US to supplement British imperial power.

The Prime Minister Joseph Lyons proposed a Pacific pact embracing these two European civilisations at the imperial conference in London in 1937. This pro-US sentiment was given concrete form with the formation of the British American Co-operation Movement for World Peace on 15 July 1936 at the instigation of Sir Ernest White and with the support of prominent businessmen Sir Henry Braddon, W. S. Robinson and Sir Keith Murdoch. Significantly, it was formed in the Millions Club in Sydney, one of the organisations promoting Empire Day. Renamed the Australian–American Co-operation Movement in 1941 when it received a grant from the Australian Government to establish a permanent

Australian-based secretariat, it was eventually named the Australian–American Association. Formed partly to encourage anti-isolationist sentiment in the US and to improve economic relations after acrimonious trade disputes, this organisation did not represent an Australian break from the empire.

The promoters of closer Australian–US relations received a powerful boost on 7–8 May 1942, when a Japanese and a US fleet (including Australian cruisers) engaged each other solely with aircraft in the Coral Sea. The US lost the carrier *Lexington*, destroyer *Sims* and the tanker *Neosho*. The carrier *Yorktown* was badly damaged but repaired within 48 hours. The Japanese lost the small carrier *Shoho* plus many pilots and aircraft, while the fleet carrier *Shokaku* was so badly damaged it was not able to rejoin the fleet at the battle of Midway. Although it was the Japanese who held the field, continuing to seek out the US fleet, both sides claimed victory. The *New York Times* was particularly ebullient while the Australian press, relying on General MacArthur's press releases, also exaggerated Japanese losses. Later, more accurate reports were not published. Privately the Australian Advisory War Council considered the result 'rather disappointing' as the opportunity for a 'complete victory' had been missed.

After the war the Australian–American Association actively promoted the significance of the Coral Sea battle in conjunction with its attempts to encourage greater US commercial and investment interest in Australia. Unlike Gallipoli, the tone was to be celebratory, not solemn. In Melbourne in May 1946 the battle was commemorated for the first time with a charity ball and a luncheon address by the association's new president, Liberal Party president, Dick Casey. Sir Keith Murdoch's Melbourne *Herald* assisted the cause by publishing exaggerated claims of Japanese losses and their intentions to invade Australia. The following year the association told the Prime Minister, Ben Chifley, that 'it is desired to perpetuate the memory of this Australian–American victory, which as a matter of history is now known to have saved Australia from actual invasion'. This message gained prominence in the press and eventually became part of Australia's collective memory.

Chifley did not share Murdoch's enthusiasm. He declined to have Commonwealth buildings display US flags for the occasion and suggested Australia had sufficient commemoratory war days with

Remembrance Day and Anzac Day. By 1949 his Government was more amenable. It was an election year and the public was aware of acute differences between the US and Australia, which had culminated in Washington cutting off the flow of classified defence information to Australia in June 1948. Chifley now agreed to a request by Casey to invite a US naval unit to Australia for Coral Sea celebrations in 1950. Washington declined, however. After the two nations' relations improved with Menzies' victory in December 1949, Washington did agree to send the Commander-in-Chief of the Pacific Fleet, Admiral Arthur Radford, to the celebrations.

Ironically, the close US–Australian relations symbolised by Coral Sea Week and formalised by the ANZUS alliance initialled in April 1951 were now used by Washington to win the Australian people's acceptance of a 'soft' Japanese peace treaty. Asian communism was now seen as the greater threat. The signing of ANZUS in April 1952 did not obviate the importance of Coral Sea Week because the latter served as a public reminder of the alliance's value. Still, the Australian–American Association wanted a more tangible symbol. In 1948 they had decided on a public monument and Menzies launched the appeal in 1950. By March 1953 when construction started, £113 000 had been raised by the Government and public. An Australian federal election was pending in February 1954 when the young Queen Elizabeth toured Australia. While in Canberra, the Queen presented new colours to the corps of staff cadets at the Royal Military College, Duntroon, and unveiled the national memorial to the US.

Murdoch had said he wanted 'something soaring, something standing apart in lonely grandeur'. The final result was an obelisk 77 metres high surmounted by an eagle with a globe held in its talons and wings uplifted in a victory sign. Its plaque reads: 'In grateful remembrance of the vital help given by the United States of America during the war in the Pacific'. It was located at the base of Russell Hill, Canberra, at the exact centre of the proposed Defence department complex, soon to be relocated from Melbourne. The memorial faced Parliament House. The symbolism was obvious. The traditional imperial underpinning of Australian liberty was being reinforced by this virile symbol.

This reassurance was needed at the time. Japan was no longer a threat but 'Asia' still was. European colonialism was about to be delivered a death blow by the Vietnamese victory over the French garrison at Dien Bien Phu. Soon after, the 1956 Suez crisis would turn Britain and France back towards a greater focus on Europe, culminating in the formation of the European Economic Community a year later. Seeing its traditional 'protection' dissipating, the Menzies Government turned towards even closer military links with the US, announcing in April 1957 that Australia's armed forces would be standardised with those of the US. Following this decision, the biggest US fleet since the war visited Australia for Coral Sea Week. US naval supremacy was now seen as central to Australian security.

The battle of the Coral Sea was a significant moment in Australia but its importance has been exaggerated at the expense of independent achievements in the New Guinea campaigns. As Australia seeks to engage Asia constructively rather than be sheltered from it by Western naval power, Coral Sea Week may retain some value only if it can be used to influence Washington to a more sympathetic view towards Australia's economic complaints.

7

The attack on Sydney Harbour

David Jenkins

The Japanese midget submarine attack*

THE evening of Sunday, 31 May 1942 was dark and overcast in Sydney. Outside the Heads, the official Royal Australian Navy history notes, the wind was south by west, of moderate force, the sea rough with a fair swell running. Within about fifteen minutes of sunset, at 4.54 pm, the coast was dark. The moon was full and rose at 6.13 pm but until the middle watch (midnight to 4 am) its light was obscured by heavy cloud. Outer South Head and Inner South Head lights were burning but the main leads (harbour entrance alignment lights) were out. There were, however, patches of brightness within the harbour, and floodlights were on at the graving dock site at Garden Island where work was in progress. The harbour was open to traffic, which was proceeding normally. Ferries were running and ships departing and arriving.

On board the Japanese submarine I-22, cruising at reduced speed well below the surface off Sydney, Sub-Lieutenant Keiu Matsuo and his navigator, Petty Officer First-Class Masao Tsuzuku, were making final preparations for their mission. Together with other members of I-22's crew, they worshipped before a candle-lit Shinto shrine. Then, covers were removed from a photograph of their nine colleagues who had died in the midget submarine attack in Hawaii,

---

* First published under the title 'War Gods and Steel Coffins', in the *Weekend Australian*, 23–24 May 1992.

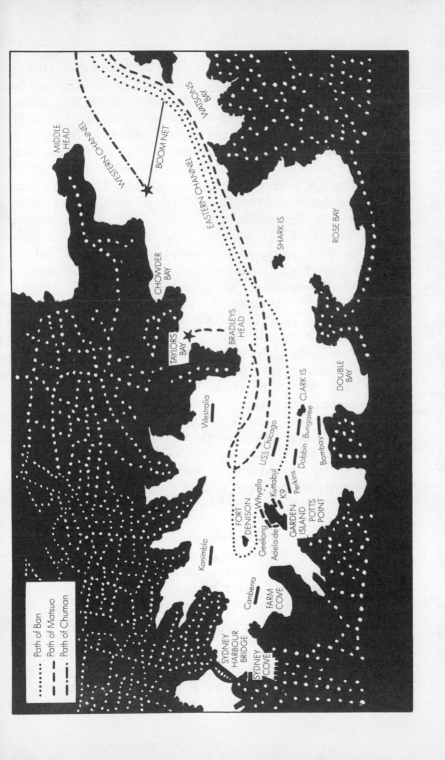

by then officially honoured as the Nine War-Gods of Pearl Harbor. A citation presented by Admiral Yamamoto to the First Special Attack Flotilla was also unveiled. A farewell meal was then taken.

Towards the end of the meal Matsuo asked Sub-Lieutenant Muneaki Fujisawa, I-22's assistant torpedo officer, to cut his hair. Fujisawa readily agreed. During the haircut, which left him so closely cropped he was almost bald, Matsuo said, almost to himself: 'I wonder what my mother is thinking at this moment?' Fujisawa said later he was convinced Matsuo had resolved to die. There can be little doubt that this was indeed the case. The young submarine officer's letter to his parents four days earlier and his poignant farewell to his fiancée made it abundantly clear that he did not expect to return from his mission. Tsuzuku, who was to accompany Matsuo, was also convinced he would not return from the attack. 'When you receive this letter', he wrote to his brother, 'you will know that I was killed in the Australia area on 31 May. I have nothing to regret.'

In an emotional farewell, Captain Ageta told Matsuo and his navigator to make every effort to return to I-22, which would be waiting for them after the attack. The sentiment, though doubtless well-intentioned, was part of the *tatemae*, an affirmation of a sanitised public position which served to disguise the uncomfortable reality that the two young men were almost certain to die. Six months earlier, Matsuo and Ageta had maintained a hopeless vigil off Pearl Harbour in this very submarine, waiting for Naoji Iwasa and his crewman to return from their mission there. Ageta had little reason to believe that this time it would be different. Now, Matsuo thanked Ageta and bade him farewell.

At about 9 pm, as darkness closed in on a heaving grey sea, I-22 moved forward at a depth of eighteen metres, making two or three knots, just enough to maintain steerage. Dressed in their work clothes and wearing soft leather flying helmets, Matsuo and Tsuzuku hauled themselves up through the trunk connecting the mother craft to the midget submarine. Once inside the smaller vessel, they dragged up the steel hatch cover, sealing themselves in. A control wheel on the inside of the hatch operated three securing lugs through a system of bell crank levers.

Tsuzuku, who steered the craft and who was responsible for the valves and ballast that controlled diving, squeezed on to a tiny padded seat tucked into the port side of the vessel. Matsuo, who determined the course, speed and depth at which the craft would travel, took up his customary standing position directly behind the periscope. A final check of the gauges and control confirmed that all was in readiness for the mission.

At 5.21 pm Sydney time, after the telephone line had been cut and the remaining clamp removed, Matsuo gave the order that would take his craft away from I-22. With the electric motors still dead, Tsuzuku released a carefully measured jet of compressed air into the main tanks, increasing buoyancy. Almost imperceptibly, the midget eased herself off the steel racks abaft I-22's conning tower and floated upwards. Only when he was clear of the parent vessel would Matsuo give the order to start the motor. The Japanese Navy had not had any real trouble with the electric motors in the midgets. This one came to life immediately, making only a soft hum inside the craft. With her clutch engaged and her large bronze propellers churning, the midget drew away at four knots.

At this depth, Matsuo was travelling blind, too deep to use his periscope. But he began nursing his midget towards the surface, ready to make the first of four navigational fixes. The time was 5.25 pm in Sydney, 1.25 pm in Tokyo. (Misleadingly, the official RAN history used Tokyo time, drawing on data recovered from Matsuo's vessel and failing to make the time conversion.) As he levelled out, the top of his conning tower less than a metre below the surface, Matsuo flicked the switch that would raise the periscope. There was a whine of electric motor as the glistening steel cable drew the periscope up from its well. Folding down the handles, Matsuo took his first glimpse of the approaches to the distant harbour. It was a glimpse, through choppy seas, of a cold and dark night, punctuated by the reassuring sweep of light from the Macquarie lighthouse at Outer South Head. The craft was in position Outer South Head Light 260 degrees 7.2 miles.

On board I-27, Lieutenant Kenshi Chuman had written a letter to his parents—to be delivered if he died—assuring them he would succeed in his mission. He also gave 500 yen to a crew member of the mother submarine to be passed on to the relatives of his navigator, Petty Officer First-Class Takeshi Omori, should he die in the attack. Both men left behind letters and mementos which made it clear they regarded the mission as suicidal. So, too, did

Sub-Lieutenant Katsuhisa Ban, whose writings give expression to their prewar indoctrination. 'Nations that fear death', Ban wrote, 'will surely be destroyed. It is necessary for the youth of Japan to take notice of this. "Sure-to-die" is the spirit that will bring about the final victory.'

At 5.28 pm, seven minutes after Matsuo's midget had been launched, Chuman's craft lifted off the cradle on the afterdeck of I-27, which was six miles east-south-east of Sydney Harbour. At 5.40 pm, Ban and his navigator, Petty Officer Mamoru Ashibe, were released from I-24, which was seven miles north-east of South Head. Under the carefully prepared attack plans, Chuman's midget was to enter the harbour first, at 6.33 pm, which was twenty minutes after moonrise. The vessels commanded by Matsuo and Ban were to follow at twenty-minute intervals. Chuman was closer to shore than his colleagues but he would have to work his way against the strong current.

For a while, the mother submarines monitored the progress of their charges on their hydrophones, picking up the distinctive beat of the electric motors, then, as the sounds faded, they set a course south for Port Hacking, where they would take up their positions for the retrieval. Chuman, travelling five or six metres below the surface, entered the harbour first, as planned. He passed undetected over the two working indicator loops at the harbour mouth, then swung his craft hard to port, which put him on course for the main anchorages. It had taken longer than expected to navigate the heavy seas and strong southerly current and he was now well over an hour behind schedule. Ban, who was to have entered the harbour forty minutes after Chuman, was running more than two hours behind time.

A large, well-lit Manly ferry was making for the eastern gate in the boom and Chuman apparently decided to follow in its wake. At 8.01 pm, the signature of an inward crossing was recorded as he passed over the second inner loop. To a trained eye the signature would have indicated that a submerged vessel had entered the harbour at a speed of 3–6.5 knots. The naval rating at Inner South Head had a commanding view of the inner loop area and it was the practice for the man on duty to give the loop station visual confirmation of any inward or outward crossing recorded on the stylograph. If no sightings could be made, he had a direct telephone link to the Garden Island Operations Room where a general alarm could be sounded. On this occasion, owing to ferry and other traffic, the significance of the loop reading was not recognised.

Chuman, undetected during his crossing of the two separate sets of indicator loops, seems to have fallen behind the ferry heading for the eastern gate in the boom net. Then, for reasons that are unclear, he seems to have set a course for the western gate. Here, his luck ran out. Chuman's craft, the indicator chart shows, was exactly two minutes behind the ferry as he crossed the inner loop. And though the ferry had probably drawn away from him in the 800 metres between the inner loop and the western entrance to the boom, the path towards the gate should have been fairly clear. Somehow, the midget submarine veered away, missing the opening.

Instead of passing effortlessly through the open gate, it ploughed into the steel mesh of the anti-torpedo boom, hundreds of metres off course. Chuman, realising his mistake, attempted to force his way through, but there was not much he could do. The midgets were not able to reverse. All he could do was drive forward at full speed, hoping the serrated steel teeth above his bow guard would tear an opening through the net. His efforts were in vain. The midget from I-27 was soon hopelessly entangled. It was 8.05 pm. The quiet young man who had trained for more than a year for this mission had come to grief at the first barrier guarding the enemy harbour.

At 8.15 pm, James Cargill, a Maritime Services Board watchman, sighted a suspicious object caught in the net near the west gate. A crusty 52-year-old Scot who had seen service in the merchant navy, Cargill was stationed on the pile-driving punts alongside the Western Channel near Pile Light. The water inside the harbour was calm and the moonlight strong. 'I was talking to another workman at 8.15 pm', Cargill recalled after the war, 'when I looked over to Pile Light and thought I saw a launch against it and just inside the channel. I knew it shouldn't be there without lights so I rowed over to see what was going on.' The object was about 45 metres from the western pylon. As Cargill approached, he saw a 'steel construction' protruding one or two metres above the waterline. At first, the object 'looked like a couple of oxy-acetylene bottles'. On closer inspection he decided he was looking at either a mine or a submarine.

Deeply concerned, the watchman rowed back to report his findings to Sub-Lieutenant H.C. Eyers, the captain of *Yarroma*, one of the two channel patrol boats on duty near the boom gates. It was 8.45 pm. Eyers had been a shipping clerk in Melbourne before the war and now found himself, aged 21, in command of a converted pleasure craft. He was sceptical about the report made by the watchman and slow to react. After turning a searchlight on the object, which was 250 metres away, he announced that it looked like naval wreckage. Cargill disputed the suggestion. 'It's not', he said. 'It's moving backwards and forwards. You'd better hurry up or we'li have no bloody Navy left.'

Increasingly concerned, Cargill invited Eyers to take his skiff and investigate for himself. The naval officer declined. He also declined to approach the object in *Yarroma*, explaining that he was afraid that the object might be a magnetic mine. His failure to do anything, Rear Admiral G.C. Muirhead-Gould wrote later in his official report on the incident, was 'deplorable and inexplicable'.

At 9.52 pm, more than an hour after Cargill had made his first report, Eyers reported a 'suspicious object in net'. He was ordered to close and give a full description. Eyers was still reluctant to approach the object but he did agree that a sailor from *Yarroma* should accompany Cargill back to it to seek more information. Cargill and the stoker from *Yarroma* set out in Cargill's skiff at about 10 pm. Before long, they had chilling confirmation of Cargill's fears. 'When we pulled alongside', Cargill said, 'I got my pocket torch out. The "thing" was an oar's length away. I could see it was a submarine just below the surface. By the time we had got there the submarine had stopped struggling to get free of the net.' At 10.10 pm, while the two men were carrying out their investigation, Eyers reported that the object was 'metal with serrated edge on top, moving with the swell'. Ten minutes later, the sailor with Cargill confirmed that the object was indeed a submarine.

In the meantime, *Lolita*, another converted pleasure cruiser, had joined *Yarroma* and been ordered by Eyers to investigate. *Lolita*'s commander, Warrant Officer Herbert Anderson, was an experienced master mariner. But he had not been long in the navy and was now faced with a dilemma that might well confound an experienced naval officer. Anderson brought his craft to within six metres of Chuman's midget submarine, and examined it with an Aldis lamp.

Like Cargill, he had no difficulty in recognising a 'baby submarine'. The bow of the intruder was about one metre out of the water, the periscope plainly visible and the stern entirely submerged. The periscope was rotating and the beam of the Aldis lamp reflected in the periscope mirror.

The correct procedure in these circumstances, according to Lieutenant Commander L.E.C. Hinchcliffe, the staff officer for the channel patrol boats and the Naval Auxiliary Patrol boats, was to retire and open fire with the .303 Vickers machine-gun. Instead, Anderson backed his vessel up to the midget and dropped three depth charges. 'He may have felt the bullets wouldn't penetrate the hull', Hinchcliffe said, 'but at least he could have tried. We had been informed, wrongly as it turned out, that Japanese midget submarines were quite vulnerable to attack'. The depth charges had been set to explode at seventeen metres. But the water was too shallow and none of them detonated. In the meantime, *Yarroma* had reported that the object was a submarine and requested permission to open fire.

Chuman and Omori, their craft hopelessly ensnared in the boom net, decided *jibaku* (self-destruction) was the only honourable way to end their mission. At 10.35 pm, before either of the two small harbour patrol boats could take any further action, the Japanese submariners, fired a demolition charge which ripped open the quarter-inch steel plating of the forward section of their craft killing them. The explosion, which was accompanied by a large orange flash, was so great that it lifted the eighteen-ton *Lolita* on a surge of water and hurled debris from the submarine more than ten metres into the air.

Meanwhile, at 9.48 pm, another inward crossing was recorded on the inner indicator loop as Ban's midget moved in to attack. Once again, the passage of the intruder went unnoticed. Ban, proceeding up-harbour in the wake of a Manly ferry appears to have had no trouble with the anti-torpedo nets, where Chuman's midget, struggling to break free, had already attracted the attention of the defence forces. Ban's midget appears to have glided through the eastern gate in the boom at about 10 pm as Cargill was setting off in his skiff for a second look at the object in the net.

At 10.27 pm, a few minutes before the midget from I-27 blew herself up, and again at 10.36 pm, the general alarm was given by

Muirhead-Gould, who had been having dinner at Tresco with the commander of *Chicago*, Captain H.D. Bode, and some of his officers. The 10.27 pm warning instructed all ships in Sydney Harbour to take anti-submarine precautions and the port was closed to outward shipping.

Ban had done well to get this far but his progress was being impeded by the sort of depth-keeping difficulties that had hampered several of the midgets at Pearl Harbor. Instead of sliding obediently along at periscope depth, Ban's midget kept bobbing to the surface, the curved black plating of her conning tower plainly visible in the moonlight. (He was spotted by the watch on *Chicago*.) The 5-inch gun crew opened fire but could not lower the gun enough to score a hit because Ban's vessel was too close. A quad mount (machine-gun with four barrels) also opened up, with a similar result.

Soon afterwards, sailors on the corvettes *Geelong* and *Whyalla*, which were refitting alongside the oil wharf at the north-western tip of Garden Island, sighted the conning tower to their north. The midget was proceeding west at about eight knots and was about 200 metres away. The cutting wire from the conning tower to the bow made its progress quite conspicuous. The captain of *Geelong* ordered his gunnery officer to open fire but the latter held back for fear of hitting a passing Manly ferry, which was travelling east. When the ferry had cleared the area, *Geelong* opened fire, pouring about a hundred 20-mm rounds at the target, some of them tracer, and churning the water to white foam. The two corvettes swept the area with searchlights for half an hour.

In the control room immediately under the exposed conning tower, Ban and Ashibe were working feverishly to get their vessel under water. Machine-gun bullets were ricocheting off the steel plating and they knew that one round from a heavier gun would be enough to rip their vessel apart. Their immediate task was to adjust their trim. This was done by redistributing the lead ballast pieces, each of which weighed five kilograms. Eventually the pair's efforts proved successful. With her vents open to flood the negative tank and her ducktail stern planes hard a-dive, the midget disappeared beneath the surface. Ban let her go deep and stole away.

After lying low for some time, Ban eased his vessel up to periscope depth. He was now close to Fort Denison. He had travelled further up the harbour than intended and now called for full starboard rudder. With her propellers churning and her upper and lower rudders hard a-starboard, the midget came effortlessly around. Having passed alongside *Chicago* and confirmed she was the richest prize in the harbour, Ban made for Bradleys Head, on the north shore, close to Taronga Zoo. From there, he would be in an ideal position to fire his torpedoes at the US cruiser.

While shells had been falling around Ban, Matsuo and Tsuzuku were approaching the Heads in the midget from I-22. They, too, had taken longer than expected to reach the harbour. And they, too, were having trouble holding their vessel down. At 10.52 pm, HMAS *Lauriana*, an unarmed naval auxiliary patrol boat on duty in the loop area with HMAS *Yandra* (990 tons), sighted a flurry on water ahead. The object seemed to be on the same course, heading towards the Eastern Channel. Turning their searchlight on the area, the crew of *Lauriana* saw Matsuo's conning tower only 20–75 metres away.

The owner-commander of *Lauriana*, Sydney biscuit baron Harold Arnott, turned to starboard and came back but the submarine had disappeared. *Lauriana* flashed an L signal (submarine or other suspicious vessel sighted) to the port war station but this went unanswered. In an official report later, the flotilla skipper H.L. Winkworth complained about this. He also noted with regret that 'had we had our promised depth charges, we could have certainly sent the sub to the bottom, or rammed him had we been given an alert earlier in the evening'.

Two minutes later, *Yandra* locked on to the submarine. 'Sighted conning tower ahead distant approximately 400 yards and steering same course (265 deg) at about 5–6 knots,' it reported. As *Yandra* increased speed to 8.5 knots, the submarine altered course to port to proceed down the East Channel. The craft 'appeared to be on a steady course of approximately 186 deg at same speed, hull slightly awash, no periscope visible, trimmed slightly by the stern, stem which appeared to have a large towing eye on top, sloped sharply away to waterline'. At 10.58 pm, *Yandra* tried to ram the intruder. A slight impact was felt on the bridge. Five minutes later the submarine was seen to break surface 600 metres away. Roaring in at full speed, *Yandra* dropped a full pattern of six depth charges set to 30 metres. The sea heaved as each depth charge exploded, the detonations shaking houses and breaking windows.

When there was no further sign of the submarine, it was assumed, wrongly, that *Yandra*'s attack had been successful. What seems to have happened is that Matsuo decided to take refuge on the harbour bottom, perhaps because his craft was damaged, perhaps because he was waiting for the tumult to subside. As they waited, Matsuo and Tsuzuku would have heard clearly the thrash of propellers as the hunting patrol boats passed directly over them. With their passive sonar, they would have heard the sounds of all manner of other vessels moving about as the harbour responded to each new alarm.

Although two submarines were simultaneously under attack in different parts of the harbour, the ferries continued to run. This was on the orders of Muirhead-Gould who felt that 'the more boats that were moving around at high speed the better the chance of keeping the submarines down till daylight'. Ships continued to show lights, the official RAN history records, and it was not until 11.14 pm that the instruction 'All ships to be darkened' was issued.

Deciding to make a first-hand inspection, Muirhead-Gould and his chief staff officer boarded the admiral's barge and set off down the harbour towards the boom net. At midnight, his vessel came alongside *Lolita*, which was still patrolling the boom net. Steven Carruthers, author of *Australia Under Siege*, has given a vivid picture of the admiral's demeanour at the time, based on interviews with *Lolita*'s captain, Anderson, and her coxswain, Able Seaman James Nelson. Muirhead-Gould had evidently been drinking at Tresco. His manner was at once fatuous and frivolous. 'What are you fellows playing at?' he asked Anderson and his crew. 'What's all this nonsense about a submarine?' Muirhead-Gould, Nelson said, seemed rather sceptical and treated the whole matter in a light-hearted and facetious manner. He asked Anderson why he had thought there was a submarine caught in the net. Anderson replied that Nelson and another crew member, Able Seaman Crowe, knew what submarines looked like.

In response to further questioning, Nelson said he had sighted submarines while serving in the Mediterranean. Crowe had served in submarines in World War I. Seemingly unimpressed, Muirhead-Gould continued in a bantering tone. 'Did you see the Japanese captain in the submarine?' he asked. 'Did he have a black beard?' Nelson said he and Anderson were taken aback by the admiral's manner. But the jocular, casually dismissive tone continued. 'If you see another submarine', said the admiral, as he prepared to leave, 'see if the captain has a beard as I would be most anxious to know'.

Although Muirhead-Gould had ordered all ships darkened at 11.14 pm, it was another 71 minutes before he gave the order to extinguish the floodlights on the huge Garden Island graving dock. This delay was a mistake. The floodlights appear to have been a boon to Ban, who, after surviving the pounding from *Chicago* and *Geelong*, was manoeuvring into a torpedo-firing position near Bradley's Head. His target was the US cruiser, which was silhouetted against the graving dock floodlights. He was, however, still having trouble keeping his vessel down.

At 12.29 am, Ban was in position to attack. *Chicago*, still riding at anchor, was a sitting duck. One well-placed torpedo would tear a hole in the warship's side below the waterline, sending her to the bottom. A spread of two would make her destruction a certainty. Blown from the tube by the burst of low-pressure air and with its clover-leaf propellers churning the water into a spiral of white foam, the torpedo began its run towards the target. At first the 'fish' seemed sluggish and unwilling, sinking to a depth of six metres and running well below full speed. But as the oxygen-driven motor reached full revolutions, the torpedo rose slowly to the correct running depth of 2.4 metres. It also gained speed. By the end of the run it would be racing through the water at 45 knots, or more than 80 kilometres per hour. According to Ban's calculations, it would slam into the bulging underbelly of the US cruiser in exactly 40 seconds. Ban, however, had not time to watch what happened next. Once the torpedo had been blown free, his craft lost all longitude stability, its bow rearing to the surface. It would be two or three minutes before it could be brought down again.

The torpedo, meanwhile, had veered off course. It passed well in front of *Chicago* and continued harmlessly under the 20-year-old Dutch submarine K9 and on beneath *Kuttabul* (147 tons), the former harbour ferry secured alongside Garden Island. It exploded against the retaining wall on the eastern side of Garden Island, lifting *Kuttabul* high out of the water and killing 21 naval ratings, most of whom were sleeping below. The K9 was also badly damaged.

Muirhead-Gould had spent thirty minutes on *Lolita* grilling the crew about their report of a submarine. He was about to reboard his barge when the harbour was rocked by a tremendous explosion.

'What the hell was that?' he asked. 'If you proceed up harbour, sir', Anderson replied, 'you might find your Japanese captain with a black beard'.

When his midget had regained her stability Ban tried again, using the torpedo that remained in the lower tube. Once again his shot went wide, this time missing *Chicago* by four metres. The second torpedo ran aground on rocks near the gun wharf on the eastern side of Garden Island and failed to explode. Once again, Ban had to wait several minutes before he could bring his submarine under control.

Having fired both torpedoes, Ban had only one remaining weapon, his 8-mm Taisho service pistol—and that was hardly much use. But the craft also carried two 350-kg demolition charges. In theory, it would have been possible for Ban to carry out the sort of *tai-atari* (body-crashing) attack that Kazuo Sakamaki had envisaged at Pearl Harbor, ramming *Chicago* and blowing his own vessel up in the not unreasonable hope that this would also take the enemy cruiser to the bottom.

The fate of Ban's midget has never been established. If, as seems likely, Ban had left the harbour by 2 am, he may have had a chance to keep the rendezvous with the mother submarines—without having to make radio contact. Even if his batteries were exhausted, there was a strong possibility he would be carried towards the submarines by the offshore current. In these circumstances it may not have been necessary to make radio contact. Given all this, it is difficult to resist the conclusion that Ban knew he could make the rendezvous but chose not to. If his batteries were not flat, he may have headed out to sea, travelling east and keeping clear of the large submarines to the south. Some of Ban's former colleagues believe this is what happened. Ban, they say, would have headed out to sea, scuttling his vessel once the batteries were exhausted and going down with it.

Meanwhile Matsuo was preparing to make his attack. At 2.56 am, lookouts on *Chicago*, which was making for the open sea after a night of alarms in Sydney Harbour, sighted a submarine periscope almost alongside the warship as it passed South Head. *Chicago*, which may even have struck the midget a glancing blow, sent a 'submarine entering harbour' signal at 3 am. A minute later, an inward crossing was registered on the No 12 indicator loop. This, the offical RAN

182

history presumes, was Matsuo's midget making a belated entry after recovering from the attack by *Yandra* four hours earlier. It was nearly ten hours since Matsuo and Isuzuku had pulled away from I-22. They were still outside the anti-submarine boom and they were still having depth-control problems.

Sydney Harbour's so-called 'Hollywood Fleet' of converted pleasure cruisers had the job of patrolling the channel and reporting any untoward developments. But it was six hours before Muirhead-Gould ordered two of the four stand-by boats in Farm Cove to proceed down harbour. It was another 45 minutes before that order was passed on. Only at 3.10 am were *Steady Hour* (Lieutenant Athol Townley) and *Sea Mist* (Lieutenant Reginald Andrew) ordered to patrol between Bradleys Head and the boom.

For Townley, the acting flotilla leader, this was a welcome call to arms and he rapidly made preparations to cast off. For Andrew, the order aroused a deep sense of misgiving. He had assumed command of *Sea Mist* only eleven hours earlier and was not at all sure what was expected of him. And, having allowed five of his nine-man crew to go ashore for the night, he had only three others with him—a coxswain, a stoker and a signalman. As the two vessels set off, Townley instructed Andrew to set his depth charges to explode at fifteen metres. This was not—as some writers have suggested—a breach of naval regulations. But it would give the patrol boat little time to get clear in a depth charge attack and might put it at some risk.

At 3.50 am the British armed merchant cruiser *Kanimbla*, lying at a buoy in Neutral Bay, opened fire on what appeared to be a submarine. An hour later, the auxiliary minesweeper *Doomba* reported a submarine off Robertson Point. Then, at about 5 am, *Sea Mist*, patrolling the West Gate area with *Steady Hour* and *Yarroma*, observed a dark object off Taylors Bay. On approaching the object, the crews saw it was a midget submarine, its conning tower protruding about one metre above the water. 'It was a shattering experience', Andrew told Carruthers. 'It caught me very much off guard and I was far from ready to deal with the situation.'

That reaction was understandable. The reserve naval officer had joined *Sea Mist* only two days earlier on completion of six weeks' training at Flinders Naval Depot. Nevertheless, he put in a more than creditable performance. As the submarine started to dive,

Andrew fired a red Very light to warn shipping to remain clear. Then, coming in over the disturbed patch of water with his throttle wide open, he had his crew drop a depth charge over the stern. This gave *Sea Mist* only five seconds to get clear of the area, too little for safety. When, all too soon, the depth charges detonated, the 35-ton *Sea Mist* was thrown forward on a wall of water. The attack, however, had hit home. Returning to the scene, Andrew heard a splashing sound and saw Matsuo's craft rise helplessly to the surface, inverted and with its contra-rotating propellers revolving inside their steel tail cage. As the submarine sank, he dropped another depth charge. Once again, the sea heaved under the impact of 180 kilograms of TNT detonating under water. Once again *Sea Mist* was thrown forward by the force of the explosion.

Regaining control of the vessel, Andrew found that one of his two engines had stopped, reducing his maximum speed to five knots. It would be impossible for him to carry out further attacks and clear the area in time.

With *Sea Mist* disabled by the explosions, Andrew retired to watch from the sidelines as *Steady Hour* and *Yarooma* moved in for the kill. In the next three and a half hours, sixteen or seventeen depth-charge attacks were made on submarine contacts recorded by detection gear and visual sightings.

Matsuo's position was hopeless. His submarine lay crippled on the floor of Sydney Harbour, unable to fire its torpedoes and subject to repeated depth-charge attack. Escape was impossible, surrender unthinkable. Matsuo was armed with an 8-mm Taisho service pistol. Tsuzuku carried only a ceremonial sword. Now, some time in the early hours of Monday morning, Matsuo seems to have killed his navigator, then turned the gun on himself.

The attack on Sydney Harbour had been a big undertaking tying up six ocean-going submarines and four midgets. But it had accomplished little. One of the six large submarines had been lost on the way south, as had one of the midgets. Of the three midgets to reach Sydney, one had blown itself up in the boom net, one had apparently escaped to sea and had been so badly damaged that the commander and his petty officer had chosen to commit suicide. For those on the waiting parent submarines there was no way of knowing what, if any, damage had been inflicted. No midgets had returned bearing news and neither float plane was available for a post–attack reconnaissance of the harbour.

At 11.30 am on Tuesday, 9 June, the bodies of the four Japanese crewmen were cremated with full naval honours at Sydney's Eastern Suburbs Crematorium. Before the cremation, the coffins were draped with the Japanese ensign and three volleys were fired into the air by a RAN saluting party wearing navy blue greatcoats and white belts and gaiters. A trumpeter sounded the Last Post. The service was attended by Muirhead–Gould, the Swiss Consul-General and members of the press.

Muirhead–Gould came in for considerable criticism over his action in according the Japanese submariners military honours at their cremation. But in a later radio broadcast he defended his actions:

> I have been criticised for having accorded these men military honours we hope may be accorded to our own comrades who have died in enemy lands. But I ask you—should we not accord full honours to such brave men as these? It must take courage of the very highest order to go out in a thing like that steel coffin. I hope I shall not be a coward when my time comes, but I confess that I wonder whether I should have the courage to take one of those things across Sydney Harbour in peacetime. Theirs was a courage which is not the property or the tradition or the heritage of any one nation: it is the courage shared by the brave men of our own countries as well as the enemy, and however horrible war and its results may be, it is a courage which is recognised and universally admired. These men were patriots of the highest order. How many of us are really prepared to make one thousandth of the sacrifice that these men made?

8

Guadalcanal

Michael O'Connor

A forgotten Pacific battle*

FOR seven months, from August 1942 to early February 1943, an immense battle of attrition was fought on and around Guadalcanal, one of the Solomon islands. The struggle for control of that blood-soaked coastal plain and its airfield became the central focus of the Pacific War. Yet few know much about Guadalcanal: in part, this is due to a preoccupation at the time with the equally important New Guinea campaign to expel the Japanese from Papua. It was also due to the control of the PR machine in Australia by General MacArthur's headquarters. MacArthur had no part in the Guadalcanal campaign, which was controlled by Admiral Nimitz from Pearl Harbor. The popular view here was that Guadalcanal was an American show, of marginal interest to Australians. The reality was quite different.

The strategic moves which led to the campaign can be said to have begun two years earlier. On 22 June 1940 France surrendered to the Germans and set up a collaborationist government at Vichy under the aged Marshal Pétain. The virtually unknown Brigadier General Charles de Gaulle left France and set up a Free French government in exile in London. Throughout the succeeding months there ensued a bitter struggle between the two groups for control

---

* First published under the title 'Guadalcanal: a forgotten Pacific battle', in the *Weekend Australian*, 1–2 August 1992.

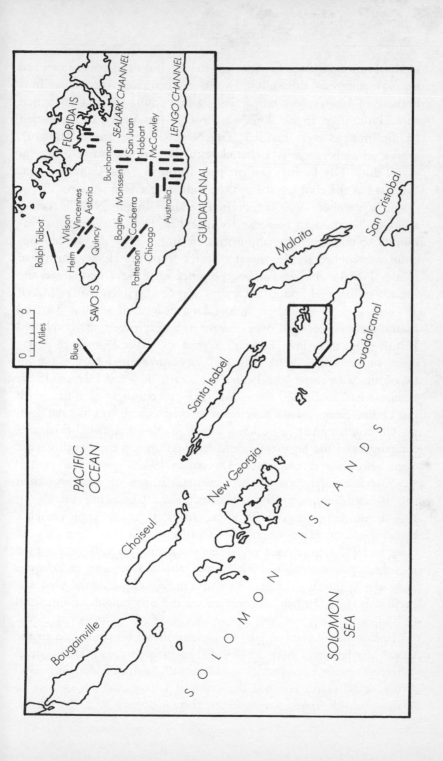

of the French empire. In Asia and the Pacific the Japanese evinced no little interest, although this was concentrated on Indo-China because of Japan's continuing war against China itself. The French administration in Indo-China was strongly pro-Vichy. In the distant Pacific loyalties were divided. The New Hebrides (now Vanuatu), whose administration was shared with the British, was Gaullist, as was Tahiti. The French civilian population in New Caledonia was Gaullist but the civil service and the military garrison was pro-Vichy.

In September 1940 the French resident in the New Hebrides went to Noumea in response to an appeal from the French community to take over the administration on behalf of de Gaulle. This coup was backed by the threat of force from the elderly Australian cruiser HMAS *Adelaide*, whose presence effectively neutralised the French military, although not a shot was fired. Given that in March 1941 the Vichy regime in Indo-China bowed to a blunt demand by the Japanese to hand over control in that territory, the combined British–Australian–Free French exercise in classical gunboat diplomacy in New Caledonia may well have prevented Noumea from becoming a Japanese base before the attack on Pearl Harbor. If the Japanese had succeeded then, Australia's increasingly vital link with the United States would have been severed. There would have been no US commitment to building a base in Australia, no Guadalcanal campaign and the Japanese would have controlled the South Pacific even before war broke out in December 1941.

Guadalcanal is one of the five main islands of what was then the British Solomon Islands Protectorate. Consisting mainly of rugged mountain ranges with a wet, tropical climate, it nevertheless boasts a coastal plain suitable for transformation into a military air base. In 1942 Guadalcanal was inhabited mainly by villagers engaged in subsistence agriculture. There was also a scattering of coconut plantations, mostly managed by Australians. The colonial Government was small, British and centred on the tiny neighbouring island of Tulagi.

In the only successful part of Operation MO—which led to the Coral Sea battle in May 1942—the Japanese invaded Tulagi on 3 May and set up a seaplane base. The small Australian Air Force and Army detachments left and the colonial Government withdrew to Malaita island where the resident commissioner, W.S. Marchant, controlled an intelligence network of his district officers, many of whom remained behind in Japanese-controlled territory.

After the Japanese were checked at Coral Sea, the Joint Chiefs of Staff in Washington issued a directive on 2 July for the expulsion of the Japanese from the New Guinea–New Britain–New Ireland areas. Part of this strategy was Operation Watchtower, the recapture of Tulagi and adjacent areas. That task was given to Nimitz, the Pacific area commander-in-chief, because he had the ships and the 1st Marine Division, the only troops in the Pacific trained and equipped for amphibious warfare. Watchtower was given added urgency when Marchant reported on 9 July, from Malaita, that 2000 Japanese labour troops had started building an airfield on the coastal plain on Guadalcanal.

From Australia, MacArthur objected to Watchtower. He wanted the resources for the New Guinea campaign, where troops, aircraft, ships and supplies of all kinds were in short supply. He understood that the Japanese wanted Port Moresby and was working to build up the defences there. On 26 June the first of two Australian brigades with American airfield construction troops had landed at Milne Bay to pre-empt what was expected to be a Japanese seaborne move against Moresby. Other Australian troops would soon begin the long trek across the Owen Stanley Ranges to occupy the north coast of Papua and build airfields there. On 22 July they would collide with the Japanese at an insignificant outpost named Kokoda, thus launching a bitter five-month struggle for the Australian territory.

In Washington, the Joint Chiefs rejected MacArthur's plea. Despite suggestions that the traditional army–navy rivalry plus an element hostile to MacArthur himself were instrumental in the decision, the Joint Chiefs pointed out quite properly that a key element in the strategy was to protect the vital US–Australia sea link against any Japanese naval and air thrust based in the Solomons. Fortunately for Australia, the bitter struggle of the next six months would prove MacArthur wrong and the Washington strategists right.

The planned landings at Tulagi and Guadalcanal were entrusted to the 1st Marine Division. Unlike the British who had closed their amphibious warfare school in 1939, the Marines had spent two decades studying the lessons of an earlier amphibious operation at Gallipoli. They had developed specialised equipment and tactical doctrine which would soon be put to the test. The Americans scraped together just about every ship available in the Pacific, including the Australian cruisers *Australia, Canberra* and *Hobart*. At 9 am on 7 August, after rehearsals in Fiji, 16 000 Marines went ashore on Guadalcanal and at Tulagi.

The Japanese response was immediate. Within an hour they launched air strikes from Rabaul against the invasion fleet. These raids were to become an almost daily affair for the next six months. Later the same day a force of seven cruisers and a destroyer under Vice-Admiral Mikawa sailed from Rabaul to Guadalcanal. A transport loaded with troops also sailed but this would be sunk en route by a US submarine. Unfortunately for the Japanese pilots, their course took them directly over Bougainville where Australian coastwatchers spotted and reported them, giving the US carrier pilots ample time to gain height before the Japanese arrived.

Jack Read, a district officer at Sohano on the northern tip of Bougainville, and Paul Mason, a planter at Buin in the south, had remained on the Japanese-held island since January 1942 and would stay there for eighteen months, evading increasingly intensive Japanese patrols before their evacuation in mid–1943. Together with others further south they would be commissioned into the RAN or other Australian forces and their radios would provide such timely and accurate intelligence for months that Admiral Halsey was to declare that 'the coastwatchers saved Guadalcanal and Guadalcanal saved the Pacific'. Astonishingly, Read's performance was never recognised by the Australian Government, although the Americans would decorate him with their highest bravery award available to a foreigner, the Distinguished Service Cross.

The Marines quickly captured Guadalcanal and Tulagi, although on Guadalcanal the Japanese garrison was able to withdraw in good order into the mountains. The Marines established a perimeter and concentrated on developing the airfield and getting their supplies ashore.

Meanwhile, Mikawa's cruiser force hastened down 'The Slot' towards Guadalcanal where the Allied cruisers under Rear Admiral Victor Crutchley, the commander of the Australian squadron on HMAS *Australia*, had the job of screening the beachhead against several possible lines of approach. Although Mikawa's force had been reported, Crutchley did not get word in time. In a shattering night action known as the Battle of Savo Island in the early hours of 9

August, Mikawa sank four Allied heavy cruisers, including HMAS *Canberra*. In fact, it was an unequal contest between a Japanese force superbly trained in night fighting and equipped with the best torpedoes in the world against a divided and inferior Allied force which had not worked or trained together to any significant extent. This relative inferiority would persist almost until the end of the campaign.

By day, only the Japanese aircraft would challenge the Marines and the US Navy around Guadalcanal but the Japanese strength would be whittled away because of the early warnings provided by the coastwatchers. The Marines completed the airfield, now named Henderson Field, and land-based fighters as well as those from the carriers were to cripple Japan's reserve of naval aircrews. By night it was a different story. Both sides used the night to pour in reinforcements and supplies for the bitter struggle on land. The waters around Guadalcanal were a battlefield in their own right as the Americans strove to overcome a lack of night-fighting experience with their new radars. The so-called 'Tokyo Express' of fast transports and converted destroyers would make the run down The Slot bringing troops and supplies for their beleaguered garrison. Supporting cruisers and destroyers would seek out the US patrols or bombard the Marine positions. So great were the shipping losses in the strait between Guadalcanal and Savo Island that it has been known as Ironbottom Sound since that time.

After the Battle of Savo Island, four massive naval battles would be fought around Guadalcanal. Both sides actively sought these engagements in an attempt to cripple the other's power. Tactically, the Japanese won a number of victories which left the Marines virtually unsupported. At one time the Americans did not have a single undamaged aircraft carrier in the Pacific.

On land, repeated battles of attrition depleted the Japanese force, which was hard to reinforce. By January 1943 General Headquarters in Tokyo had decided enough was enough; it ordered the evacuation of Guadalcanal within a month. Despite heavy losses the Tokyo Express took off 11 700 men and on 9 February the Americans declared Guadalcanal and the supply line to Australia secure.

Guadalcanal was vitally important to Australia. History makes clear the reality that the Guadalcanal campaign derived from the need to keep open the sea lines of communication (SLOCs) between the US and Australia. If they had been cut, this country would have been isolated from its source of modern aircraft and other sophisticated military hardware; the US Joint Chiefs of Staff would have been left with little alternative but to abandon MacArthur and the Australian and American forces to subsist on whatever a primitive Australian manufacturing industry could provide.

The Japanese understood the significance of Guadalcanal, too. When faced with the choice of continuing the struggle for Guadalcanal or for Papua, they abandoned their forces in Papua so as to focus on Guadalcanal. They had lost the struggle in Papua partly because the growing Australian and American air forces were able to cut the Japanese SLOCs. That was not true of Guadalcanal, where the Japanese managed to run supplies in on an almost daily basis and even evacuate their ground forces at the end. As always in modern warfare, the logistics factor was the vital element. The Japanese lost 14 800 troops, killed or missing in action on land. Another 9000 died of wounds or disease and 1000 were captured.

At sea, the Americans lost two fleet carriers, eight cruisers and fourteen destroyers. The Japanese Navy lost two battleships, one light carrier, four cruisers, eleven destroyers and six submarines. But by early 1943 the American defence build-up was in full swing while the Japanese were unable to replace their losses in ships, aircraft and specially trained aircrews. Damaged Japanese ships were likely to be out of action for long periods contrasting with the experience of the carrier USS *Enterprise*: badly damaged at the Battle of East Solomons on 23 August, she returned to Pearl Harbor for repairs which were completed in time to return to the Guadalcanal area early in October; damaged again at the Battle of Santa Cruz on 26 October, she was repaired at Noumea in time for the naval Battle of Guadalcanal on 14 November. The American industrial machine was building ships in a matter of weeks. By the end of 1942 the 33 000-ton Essex-class aircraft carriers were being delivered in eighteen months from keel-laying. Similar production performances were experienced for all types of war material, while large numbers of well-trained aircrews were coming out of pilot schools. By contrast, the Japanese were rushing ill-trained crews into action to replace their heavy losses.

Above all, Guadalcanal is important for the lesson that an Allied strategy is a single entity, not dependent upon any one member for success or failure in any one battle. Australia was an important, if small, member of the Allied forces in the Pacific theatre, but its war was not merely to defend Australia against the invasion that the Japanese had eschewed in early 1942. Australia's effort was to contribute what it could to the defeat of fascism, Nazism and militarism. Any lesser view would have been unworthy of the Australian people.

Denis and Peggy Warner with Commander Sadao Seno

The sinking of HMAS *Canberra**

The sea below was blue and the cumulonimbus cloud that was to gather so densely and soar so high toward evening was no more than a wisp in the sky. For the crew of the RAAF Hudson reconnaissance bomber approaching the halfway mark in a long patrol, there had been nothing to report. Then they saw eight ships ahead.

The biggest, with its raked funnels, led four others, all evenly spaced in line astern. Some distance away, visible through a slight haze, were three smaller vessels heading south-east at a leisurely pace, their wakes like small white ribbons on the calm surface of the sea. For the crew of the Hudson, unaware they were about to experience their first contact with the enemy, it seemed a tranquil scene.

It was 10.27 am on 8 August 1942, 60 kilometres north of the coastal village of Kieta on the island of Bougainville. The Hudson's signal lamp blinked the letter of the day. The answer should have been the corresponding letter. Instead, it came in brilliant flashes of gunfire from the larger ships. 'My God, they're Japs', shouted Sergeant Bill Stutt, the 24-year-old pilot. But Stutt and his men— navigator Sergeant Wilbur Coutis, radio operator Sergeant Eric

---

* First published as 'Scapegoat: the truth behind an Australian tragedy', in *The Australian Magazine*, 1–2 August 1992.

Geddes and gunner Sergeant John Bell—were under instructions to break radio silence only in an emergency. While Stutt and his crew considered the implications, he spotted two float planes. They seemed to be the naval seaplane version of the Zero, with a maximum speed of 430 kph—much faster than the Hudson—and thus they presented danger.

Stutt identified the ships as three cruisers, three destroyers and either two gunboats or two seaplane tenders. What he was looking at, in fact, were the heavy cruisers *Chokai*, *Aoba*, *Kako*, *Kinugasa* and *Furutaka*, the light cruisers *Tenryu* and *Yubari*, and the destroyer *Ynagi*.

Geddes, who had topped his class at the RAAF's radio school, hastily abandoned the signal lamp when the aircraft appeared and turned to his radio. It was time to break radio silence. Home base at Milne Bay could not hear him. But others did, including the Japanese and the Allied naval task forces off Guadalcanal, in the Pacific, where US Marines had landed the previous day. Stutt still vividly recalls Geddes repeating the signal over the radio and the urgency with which they raced back to Milne Bay when they thought the radio had failed. 'I would have jumped out of the plane and run if I could have got there faster', he says.

Aboard the *Chokai*, Vice-Admiral Gunichi Mikawa's flagship, there was consternation when the signal was intercepted. Surprise, the key to the success of the lightning night raid Mikawa planned against the Allies at Guadalcanal, had been lost. To continue might be suicidal. For more than two hours, Mikawa weighed the chances, then, although expecting an air attack from US carriers he knew to be in the area, he decided to head towards Savo Island.

As it turned out, Geddes's radio signal hardly caused a ripple among the Allied ships. Despite repeated warnings from Pearl Harbor code-breakers and traffic analysts of a Japanese naval build-up in the Rabaul area, and confirmation by B-17 and submarine signals, the captain of only one US cruiser and a handful of junior officers thought Geddes's signal might herald a surface attack at night.

Meanwhile, Vice-Admiral Richmond Kelly Turner, US Navy, the amphibious force commander, an intelligent, dominating and arrogant officer, received the report in the afternoon. He checked the night-time disposition order prepared by Rear Admiral Victor Crutchley, VC, Royal Navy, the screening force commander of the

Australian squadron. Turner read it thoroughly but made no changes.

Crutchley, a tall man with a flaming red beard known to Australian sailors as 'Old Goat's Whiskers', had newly arrived in the Pacific. He had not even met his subordinate American captains. He discussed Stutt's report during the day with his senior staff, who were sceptical about the RAAF and its intelligence-gathering capabilities. Crutchley later asked Turner what he believed the Japanese intentions were. Turner said he thought the force was headed for Rekata Bay, on the north tip of the island of Santa Isabel, about 190 kilometres away.

As for Vice-Admiral Frank Jack Fletcher, in command of the aircraft carrier force operating south of Guadalcanal, instead of sending his planes to meet Mikawa's force, he pleaded shortage of fuel and loss of aircraft, exaggerating both in his request to withdraw. He turned south and headed for safer waters. The decision meant that the transports would have to depart also (with much of the vitally needed equipment, ammunition and food still aboard ship), leaving the Marines in Guadalcanal to fend for themselves.

So was the scene set on the Allied side. At dusk, the forces took up their night dispositions with two destroyers, USS *Blue* and *Ralph Talbot*, acting as radar pickets north and west of Savo Island, which was to give its name to the battle. The two Australian heavy cruisers, HMAS *Canberra* and HMAS *Australia*, with the USS *Chicago*, patrolled the strait between Savo Island and Guadalcanal (with destroyers USS *Bagley* and *Patterson*). The US cruisers *Vincennes*, *Quincy* and *Astoria* worked a box to the north-east, between Savo and Florida Island (with destroyers *Helm* and *Wilson*). Some hours before the battle, Crutchley in the *Australia* left the line for a conference with Turner in the transport area. He did not inform the *Vincennes* group of his departure.

In the *Canberra*, not one senior officer was on the bridge. The fore control crew was closed up, but the torpedo tubes were maintained. All guns were empty. Captain Frank Getting had retired to his cabin. The commanders of the other Allied cruisers, Captain Riefkohl in the *Vincennes*, Captain Moore in the *Quincy*, Captain Greenman in the *Astoria*, and Captain Bode in the *Chicago*, equally exhausted after the strenuous activities of the previous two days of landings and air attacks, had already retired.

At 12.43 am on 9 August, Mikawa was heading for the south strait (between Guadalcanal and Savo Island) when a lookout spotted the picket destroyer *Blue*. Mikawa changed course 20 degrees to port and ordered that the fleet would attack through the north strait (between Savo and the Florida Islands). Seven minutes later, a lookout sighted the *Ralph Talbot* and, to avoid it, Mikawa again ordered a change of course. With every gun trained on the *Blue*, Mikawa had to decide whether to attack. The *Blue* decided it for him. A lookout on the *Chokai*'s bridge shouted: 'The enemy ship has reversed course'. The southern channel was open. Unlike the night-vision trained Japanese lookouts, the guardians of the gate saw nothing, their radar proving as ineffective as their eyes. The Japanese slipped between the two American destroyers and disappeared into the dark morning.

At 1.37 am, Mikawa saw the *Canberra* and the *Chicago* in column, 12.5 kilometres away. A minute later, he sighted another cruiser. This was the *Vincennes*, leading the northern group and heading towards the *Chokai*. He was now targeting both forces. At 1.40 am, as the Japanese ships skirted the tip of Savo Island, parachute flares dropped by the Japanese cruisers' planes silhouetted the Allied ships, lighting up the transports and the entire area like a stage backdrop.

Sub-Lieutenant M.J. Gregory, officer of the watch on the *Canberra*, was conscious of the fact that he had to call Lieutenant Commander J.S. Mesley, the navigator, at 1.45 am. He had his eyes on his watch when, at 1.42 am, he saw a flash and what appeared to be an explosion to starboard. Lieutenant Commander E.J. Wight also saw an explosion and immediately reported down the voice-tube to Getting in his sea cabin. Mesley, summoned by Gregory, jumped from his bunk and put on his boots. Gunnery Officer Lieutenant Commander D.M. Hole and torpedo officer Lieutenant Commander John Plunkett-Cole, both sleeping in the admiral's sea cabin, also rallied to Gregory's call. It was just after 1.43 am.

Temporary Surgeon Lieutenant J.E. Newton, sleeping at his medical party station on B turret, was awakened by a flash and saw three torpedo racks, one of which was on the port side and which he thought would hit the ship. Somehow, all three missed. He also saw one of the attacking ships when it was briefly lit up. 'I formed the impression that it had two funnels, for'd thick and after thin. I placed it as a large destroyer or small cruiser. The distance was about 1500 yards [1.35 kilometres]'.

It was a cruiser, but it was not small. The ship with the odd-shaped forestack and slimmer afterstack was the *Chokai*, which launched torpedoes at the *Canberra* and *Chicago* at 1.38 am. As the *Canberra* swung to port helm, one of them passed down the starboard side. Getting ordered 'hard to starboard full ahead' and then 'tell *Chicago* three cruisers'. Armament was immediately trained on the targets. Mesley shouted, 'Torpedo tracks approaching the port bow, sir'. Through the dark, low cloud and heavy rain he saw at least two tracks heading across the *Canberra*'s course. They, too, missed the manoeuvring *Canberra*. Hole ordered 'open fire' and Plunkett-Cole crossed to the port torpedo control position to fire the tube there.

But before the *Canberra* could fully man its guns or train its main battery, the first shell hit from port. Mesley saw flashes from both ends of one of the enemy ships and was temporarily blinded by an explosion on the port side abaft, just below the compass platform. Plunkett-Cole was knocked to the deck and momentarily blinded as a shell hit the plot room just behind him. He was about to press the torpedo triggers when the ship received a second hit on the port quarter. The torpedoes did not fire. Nobody on the compass platform had had time to recover from the first salvo before this one came in. Shells hit both boiler rooms and steam to all units failed. All power for pumps, fire-fighting and armament had gone.

When Mesley could see again, several people were lying on the deck of the compass platform. One was the captain, his head within a metre of the compass to which Mesley himself was clinging. Hole was dead, as were several others. There were bodies everywhere and men screaming. The Walrus plane was on fire, the catwalk was shattered and guard rails twisted. The 100 mm gun deck was a shambles. Fires were burning in the airmen's workshop and out of control.

Getting was conscious but in great pain and growing weaker. His right leg had been shattered from the knee down, practically shot away. He had arm and head injuries, including shrapnel in the face. He refused attention, ordering that others wounded should receive it, and asked what signals were being made and how things were going. Chief Engineer McMahon came to the platform and bent over the captain. 'Sir, I'm afraid things are bad', he said. 'We've been hit in the engine room.' 'Do your best, Mac', Getting whispered.

Survivors dived to the magazine doors to free men trapped as smoke, steam and fumes poured out of the boiler rooms. Only one escaped. Men with terrible wounds lay for hours on the forecastle in the pouring rain sheltering under any available blankets, coats and hammocks. Parties called to dump ammunition overboard struggled over the bloodied buckled decks and burning debris. Fires burnt out of control throughout the ship. Boats, rafts and anything that would float were lowered over the side and secured, and orders given to flood any remaining unflooded magazines.

Under attack for nearly three minutes, and without firing a shot, the *Canberra* was out of the fight. Between 1.44 am and 1.47 am it had received about 28 large-calibre shells, all square amidships. The ship slowed then came to a standstill. The *Canberra* was about twelve kilometres from Savo Island, and like its captain, only just alive.

The Japanese fired seventeen torpedoes at the southern group of ships. Only two scored hits, on the *Chicago*, causing damage and casualties. The *Chicago* became lost in the confusion and, like the *Bagley*, took no further part in the battle. The southern group was finished off as a fighting force in under six minutes, mainly by gunfire. The *Patterson* managed to engage the Japanese fire and, although suffering damage and casualties, was able to assist in later rescue efforts. Meanwhile, the Japanese had torpedoes to spare.

Now the *Chokai* used lights to pick up targets in the northern group and to inform its other ships of its location. The lights pinpointed ship after ship, controlling the performance of the other cruisers like a conductor of a symphony orchestra. Riefkohl, in the *Vincennes*, believing the southern group was using lights, sent a message requesting they be turned off. 'We are friendly', he signalled. The *Quincy*, centre ship in the line, was alerted by the lights, and was in the process of assuming 'Condition 1' (action stations). In the *Astoria*, lookouts saw the enemy ships before the attack but its captain ordered cease fire when firing began. 'I think we are firing on our own ships', he called. 'Let's not act too hasty.'

When the torpedoes came, the fates of the *Vincennes*, *Quincy* and *Astoria* were inevitable. At 1.55 am, the *Vincennes* was hit by two or three torpedoes fired by the *Chokai*. The first enemy shells on the bridge killed many men in the pilot house. Shells exploded in the hangar, where planes burst into flames. No water was available. The ship could not remain afloat and orders were given to abandon ship. Riefkohl literally walked into the sea ten minutes after the abandon order but was rescued later. The *Vincennes* turned turtle and went down at about 2.50 am.

The *Quincy* was practically shredded during the fight. In return, it inflicted the heaviest damage on the Japanese (scoring several hits on the *Chokai*, one of which exploded dangerously close to Mikawa and his staff). At 2.04 am, at least two torpedoes struck the *Quincy*. By then, the bridge was a shambles of dead bodies, including the captain's. There was no general order to abandon. As the *Quincy* turned over, hundreds of men crawled, ran and slid down the sides. It capsized to port, its mast like a huge burning cross. The bow went under, the stern rose and it slid from view.

In the *Astoria*, by 3 am, more than 400 men, including wounded and dead, were on the forecastle, while on the fantail men worked slowly toward the well deck. Separated by a wall of fire, neither group knew of the other's existence. After many hours of rescue attempts, the *Astoria* also sank.

By the time Mikawa departed, almost unscathed, hundreds of American and Australian men were in the dark, oil-covered, shark-infested water. Rescue efforts continued for six or seven hours (one group floated on rafts for several weeks). The *Canberra*, with a heavy list, lay motionless with fires blazing amidships. When rescue ships appeared, able-bodied men refused to leave until all the wounded were taken aboard. Getting died on board a rescue ship during the passage from Tulagi to Noumea, a few days after his 43rd birthday. He was one of 84 Australian seamen dead or missing from the *Canberra*.

The sun was rising on 9 August when an American ship was sent to sink the burning cruiser. It fired an incredible 263 rounds of 120-mm shells and four torpedoes, one of which exploded under the *Canberra*. Two others passed beneath without exploding. The *Canberra* refused to go down. Nine minutes later, a second ship completed the job, firing one torpedo into the cruiser's starboard side, under the mangled bridge. Just on 8 am the *Canberra* went down.

In 37 minutes' fighting, more than 1000 Australian and American sailors had been killed or forced into the sea to drown. Another 700 were wounded. Four valuable Allied cruisers had been lost.

The disaster off Savo Island stunned the US Navy. It was the worst blue water defeat in US history. 'The blackest day', Admiral Ernest J. King, Chief of Naval Operations and Commander-in-Chief of the US Fleet, called it. His immediate response was to accord the news of the lost American ships such a high security classification that even senior Army and Air Force officers with important claims for 'a need to know' were kept in the dark. Australia announced the loss of the *Canberra* after a couple of weeks. Two months passed before the US Navy released news of the American losses.

Soon after the battle, the US Navy began a series of inquiries. Vice-Admiral L. Ghormley conducted the first and presented a critical report on 17 October 1942. This was followed by a more detailed inquiry under the direction of Rear Admiral R.S. Edwards, Admiral King's chief of staff. Both indicated errors in the disposition of the Allied force but produced no real scapegoats. These were found, or more correctly invented, by Admiral Arthur J. Hepburn, a former commander-in-chief of the US Fleet, who was charged with conducting an 'informal inquiry'.

Hepburn interrogated the principal officers involved, including Crutchley and senior surviving officers from the sunken American cruisers. It was then that, despite evidence to the contrary from Turner and other senior officers, Hepburn found that Sergeant Stutt and his Hudson crew had not broken radio silence. He maintained that their reports, and those of other Hudsons on reconnaissance on 8 August, were not received by the task force until after dark—too late to take action against Mikawa's forces. This thereby cleared Vice-Admiral Turner and Rear Admiral Crutchley of any dereliction of duty.

Hepburn was not the author of his report, though. That task fell to Commander Donald J. Ramsey, his aide, who wrote later: 'The most vitally interesting part of the report is what I did not put into it'. He did not exaggerate.

The public did not get access to the report until 1971. By then, many of the major players were dead, though not Stutt and his crew. But the report was made available in the late 1940s to Rear Admiral Samuel Eliot Morison, the celebrated US naval historian.

His account of the battle reflected Hepburn's, but with major embellishments of his own. Of Stutt, he wrote:

> Instead of breaking radio silence, as he had orders to do in an urgent case, or returning to base, which he could have done in two hours, [he] spent most of the afternoon completing his search mission, came down at Milne Bay, had his tea, and then reported the contact . . . Thus, the faulty and long-delayed report of one pilot completely misled both American commands as to Japanese intentions.

Thereafter, all the popular American historians barked at Stutt's footsteps. According to one account, 'The pilot was an inexperienced and not very intelligent Australian who winged his way blithely on to complete his reconnaissance leg without breaking radio silence and sending the crucial information from his plane. He then landed and nonchalantly drank his tea before reporting.' Another 'historian' even professed to know the brand of tea Stutt drank—Lipton's.

The crew of the Hudsons seethed with anger when they read this. But it took A.J. Sweeting, then acting general editor of the Australian war history published by the Australian War Memorial, to stir them, or more accurately, Nancy Milne, wife of Flight-Lieutenant Lloyd Milne, into action. Milne, leader of the Hudson group, claims he shadowed the Japanese force off the Bougainville coast, after Stutt's sighting. For years, Nancy Milne burrowed into files in search of the facts, meeting obstruction along the way.

In 1984, she turned to us for help. Did we have anyone in Japan who could search the Japanese records for her? We did. A month or two later, Commander Sadao Seno, co-author of *Disaster In The Pacific: New Light On The Battle of Savo Island*, produced an authenticated extract from the *Chokai*'s action report which established Stutt had broken radio silence.

After Nancy Milne's death, her family passed her research to us and we continued our investigations in the Public Record Office in London and the Navy Yard archives in Washington, DC, where the office files of Hepburn and Morison are housed. Hepburn's interviews with the surviving captains of the US ships left no doubt that they had received Stutt's signal about the time it was dispatched. 'The report was made to me some time after an air attack we had that morning', Greenman of the *Astoria* told Hepburn. 'The report was made either in the morning or some time before the afternoon action.'

Riefkohl of the *Vincennes* insisted he got the signal in the morning: 'Everybody knew the attack was coming in the morning'. Alone among the senior officers, Riefkohl warned his ship's company, yet, because of the Hepburn report, saw his career ruined. Hepburn's interrogation was so tough the unfortunate Captain Bode of the *Chicago* blew out his brains two weeks later, in April 1943. Yet Vice-Admiral Turner, who also told Morison he received Stutt's signal during the day, escaped without criticism. Morison, too, elected not to accept the facts and to shift responsibility for the task forces' inaction to Stutt's alleged failure to break radio silence. But Morison went further, making his findings public during the 1950s.

For years, the Hudson crews have lived with these outrageous charges. Today, they have been cleared. The Naval Institute Press in the US will publish our book on the affair, thus putting the imprimatur of the US Navy on the efforts to establish the innocence of Stutt and the Hudson crews.

All the crew members survive—Geddes in Sydney, Bell in Perth and Courtis in Melbourne. Stutt, 74, who lives in the Melbourne suburb of Kew, turned to his passion for horses after the war. He was Chairman of the Moonee Valley Racing Club and the Bill Stutt Stakes is one of the races in Melbourne's spring carnival.

For Stutt's crew a great weight has been lifted from their shoulders. 'It didn't hit us until the sixties', says Courtis. 'We just couldn't believe it. I always believed we acted responsibly and intelligently.' 'I was very bitter', adds Geddes. 'I just couldn't believe that all those knowledgeable people would write such things about us without even trying to find the facts. It's great to know that someone has taken up the cudgels and come up with the truth.'

Stutt, who was awarded his commission soon after the fateful flight, has always been more phlegmatic than his crew. Like Courtis he was later awarded the Distinguished Flying Cross. With Bell and Geddes he also joined an American squadron, flying B-24s. 'I don't think any of these things would have happened if anyone had believed that I was responsible for the disaster at Savo Island', he says. 'My crew was far more steamed up than I.' Morison's fabrication about the tea still irritates him. Ironically, he doesn't drink tea. 'I wouldn't have had more than a half a dozen cups in all my life', he says. Even with this small detail Morison helped to trap himself in his own web, although half a century has passed since the battle was fought and the cover-up began.

9

The Kokoda Track

David Horner

The strategic setting*

AUGUST 1942 was a crucial month in the defence of Australia in the Second World War. Of the five major battles that saved Australia in 1942, three were fought in August. Following the Japanese surprise attacks on Pearl Harbor, the Philippines and Malaya on 7–8 December 1941, it took barely two months before Australia was faced with a real threat to its own security. On 23 January 1942 Japanese troops overwhelmed the small garrison at Rabaul in Australian New Guinea. On 15 February Singapore fell, and four days later, to cover their landings on Timor, Japanese planes bombed Darwin.

Australia's political and military leaders were fully justified in believing that the country was under a real threat of invasion. But, unknown to the Australians at this time, Japanese Army and Navy leaders were deep in argument about whether or not to invade Australia. Meanwhile, on 8 March Japanese forces landed at Lae and Salamaua on the north coast of New Guinea. On 15 March the Japanese leaders finally put aside plans to invade Australia; instead they decided to capture Port Moresby and the southern Solomons, and then 'to isolate Australia' by seizing Fiji, Samoa and New Caledonia.

The security of Australia would therefore depend on the battle

---

* First published under the title 'Battle owed little to strategy', in *The Weekend Australian*, 29–30 August 1992.

for Port Moresby, for if it were captured the Japanese could strike at will at the north coast of Queensland. Furthermore, if the Japanese extended their air and naval bases to Fiji they could interdict the lines of communication between Australia and the United States, making it extremely difficult to build up Australia as the main base for a counteroffensive against the Japanese East Asia Co-Prosperity Sphere. Perhaps, if the Japanese had succeeded in these plans, they might have later changed their minds and landed in northern Queensland. That the Japanese high command never agreed to invade Australia does not detract from the crucial importance of the battles for Port Moresby in 1942. The struggle for Port Moresby determined the fate of Australia, and was decided in five major battles.

Delayed by operations in the Indian Ocean, the Japanese were not able to mount a major invasion force against Port Moresby until early May and then, in the first major battle, the Battle of the Coral Sea, they were beaten back by planes from two US carriers, plus land-based planes from Townsville. Japanese plans to take Port Moresby were further delayed by the second major battle, the Battle of Midway, fought between US and Japanese carrier fleets in the central Pacific Ocean in early June. The Japanese lost four carriers and the Americans one, and thus the Japanese were forced to postpone their plans to seize New Caledonia, Fiji and Samoa. Instead it was now even more urgent to capture Port Moresby. But with the loss of the carriers, an amphibious operation was no longer possible, and General Hyakutake in Rabaul was ordered to plan an overland drive over the Owen Stanley Ranges to Port Moresby. The scaling down of the Japanese offensive plans indicated that strategically the tide of battle was beginning to turn, but the Japanese were still capable of mounting a deadly offensive. The stage was set for three major battles in August—Kokoda, Milne Bay and Guadal-canal.

The American success at Midway had a remarkable effect on both the US Joint Chiefs of Staff in Washington, and on General Douglas MacArthur in Melbourne, commanding the South-West Pacific Area. MacArthur wanted to seize the opportunity to mount a major assault against the Japanese base at Rabaul. But the US Navy was not willing to allow MacArthur to take full control of the offensive. Eventually, after weeks of bickering, it was agreed that the offensive would be shared. US Naval forces under Admiral Ghormley would seize and occupy Santa Cruz and Tulagi Islands in the southern Solomon Islands. Then MacArthur's forces would capture the remainder of the Solomons and the north coast of New Guinea.

In preparation for these operations, MacArthur ordered the construction of an airfield at Milne Bay at the south-east tip of New Guinea, and moved his headquarters forward to Brisbane. Meanwhile, Admiral Ghormley was preparing for his Solomons operations. At the time of the Coral Sea battle the Japanese had landed a small force on Tulagi Island, but in June the Americans received reports that the Japanese were building an airstrip on the larger Guadalcanal Island which was nearby. Ghormley was ordered to seize it, using the 1st US Marine Division. Once the Marines had landed on Guadalcanal, MacArthur planned to occupy the Buna area on the north coast of Papua, where airstrips would be prepared to support his advance towards Rabaul.

Unfortunately for MacArthur's grandiose plans, the Japanese moved first. Indeed, from the beginning the Papuan campaign was shaped by inaccurate strategic assessments by MacArthur's headquarters. Following the Battle of the Coral Sea, the Australian garrison at Port Moresby was increased from one to two militia brigades, and a little later another militia brigade was sent to Milne Bay to protect the airfield being built there. But with his eye on his coming offensive MacArthur disregarded intelligence reports that indicated that the Japanese were about to strike again at Port Moresby. For example, in May MacArthur's code-breakers deciphered a Japanese message that their next operation would be over the Owen Stanley Ranges. This message, which one senior code-breaker called 'one of the three most important to be decoded in the war', formed the basis for a General Headquarters Intelligence Summary on 23 May 1942, but was disregarded by MacArthur's intelligence staff.

Certainly, MacArthur and his Land Force commander, General Sir Thomas Blamey, reacted to the news that the Japanese were likely to land a small force at Buna. They ordered the Commander of New Guinea Force at Port Moresby, General Morris, to send troops across the Kokoda Track to secure the Buna area. But Morris did not have sufficient forces to conduct a proper defence of Papua.

The 39th militia Battalion from Port Moresby had just begun to move towards Buna when the Japanese landed there on the night of 21 July. But even then MacArthur refused to take the Japanese threat seriously, believing that once the US Marines landed at Guadalcanal on 7 August the Japanese might withdraw from the Buna area. Blamey was not as confident as MacArthur and, after the 39th Battalion was driven out of Kokoda on 29 July by superior forces, it became obvious that reinforcements would have to be sent to New Guinea.

It was agreed that Lieutenant-General Sydney Rowell and the headquarters of the 1st Australian Corps, plus the 21st Brigade of the 7th AIF Division would go to Port Moresby. The 18th Brigade of the 7th Division would join the 7th militia Brigade at Milne Bay and would form a small division, known as Milne Force, under Major-General Cyril Clowes.

But the dispatch of these reinforcements, which would not arrive in New Guinea until mid–August, did not mean that MacArthur or Blamey were taking the Japanese threat as seriously as they should have. As MacArthur told the US Army Chief of Staff, General George Marshall, on 2 August, he planned to 'secure the crest of the Owen Stanley Range . . . and to provide an airfield at Milne Bay to secure the southern end of the Owen Stanley bastion'. After that he could advance with amphibious forces along the north coast of Papua.

It is true that the Japanese were thrown off balance by the landing of the US Marines at Guadalcanal on 7 August. On 28 July Major-General Horii, the commander of the Japanese South Seas Detachment in Rabaul, had been ordered to attack Port Moresby over the range. This assault was now postponed until later in August when it was to be coordinated with a landing at Milne Bay.

Nor were the Japanese content to be pushed off their new airstrip at Guadalcanal. On the night of 8–9 August their cruisers struck at the Allied naval forces protecting the US landing. In the disastrous battle of Savo Island, the Australian cruiser *Canberra*, and three US cruisers were sunk. Following up this victory, the Japanese landed 1000 men on Guadalcanal to drive the Americans off. On 21 August the Japanese lost heavily in an attack on the perimeter of Henderson airfield. While the Americans held the airstrip they could control the surrounding seas by day. But at night the Japanese dominated, bringing in reinforcements for another effort to seize the vital airstrip.

As General Harmon, the Commander of the US Army, Pacific, reported to General Marshall in Washington, 'We have seized a strategic position. Can the Marines hold it? There is considerable room for doubt!'

In Papua, General MacArthur's Australian forces were about to face a similar challenge. The Japanese offensive began on 26 August with two simultaneous attacks—one against Isurava on the Kokoda Track, and the other a landing by Japanese Marines at Milne Bay. It took some days before the troops at Isurava and the commanders at Port Moresby realised that the Japanese there had been reinforced for an offensive, and thus for a number of days the action at Milne Bay attracted the greatest attention. There General Clowes was fighting a difficult battle. Hampered by constant rain, endless mud and poor communications, and threatened with a landing to his rear, he was wary of committing his forces to an immediate counter-attack.

The Milne Bay landing, followed soon after by news of a Japanese victory at Isurava, caused intense anxiety at MacArthur's headquarters in the AMP building in Brisbane. On 28 August he warned Marshall in Washington that the situation might become critical unless he was provided with naval support. Two days later he sent a long message to Marshall in which he started to lay the blame for any possible defeat on the Australian troops: 'This is the first test of Australian troops under my command . . . With good troops under first class leadership I would view the situation with confidence unless reinforcements are landed but . . . I am not yet convinced of the efficiency of the Australian troops'. He continued that the failure to review the strategic situation would have a 'disastrous outcome'. Without additional naval forces, he predicted 'the development within a reasonable period of time of a situation similar to those which produced the disasters that have successively overwhelmed our forces in the Pacific since the beginning of the war'.

The root of the trouble was that MacArthur's strategy was at fault. He had based the defence of Port Moresby on the belief that a garrison at Milne Bay and a picket on the crest of the Owen Stanleys, in addition to air and naval forces, would be sufficient, while he prepared for his spectacular offensive bounds. But now his strategy was looking dangerously unrealistic. The Japanese had decimated the US Navy in the Solomons and were challenging the security of Milne Bay and the Owen Stanley Range.

Despite MacArthur's misgivings, by 6 September Clowes had defeated the Japanese at Milne Bay, but by this time it was obvious that there was an even greater threat on the Kokoda Track, where the Australian troops were conducting a desperate withdrawal. On 6 September MacArthur again asked Marshall for more naval forces. 'If New Guinea goes the result will be disastrous. This is urgent.' And again he shifted the blame, adding that 'the Australians have proven themselves unable to match the enemy in jungle fighting. Aggressive leadership is lacking.'

Eventually the Japanese failed on the Kokoda Track, and there were three reasons for this. First, the track was much more difficult than they had expected and they had made insufficient provision for supplies. Second, their advance was seriously delayed by the hard fighting of the Australians, which bought time for reinforcements to arrive and caused the Japanese to exhaust their supplies. And third, the Guadalcanal campaign caused the Japanese high command in Rabaul to divert resources to that area, and eventually to order a halt to the Owen Stanley advance.

The American determination to hold Guadalcanal was therefore doubly important to the successful defence of Australia. On the one hand, if the Japanese had regained the Guadalcanal airstrip they could have dominated the southern Solomons and would have made it extremely difficult for the US Navy to operate in that area. They could have attacked New Caledonia and perhaps even Fiji, in pursuit of their strategy of isolating Australia. On the other hand, the battle of attrition on Guadalcanal drew Japanese resources away from Papua and made the Australians' task there easier.

By the end of September the Allies were beginning to gain the upper hand at both Guadalcanal and on the Kokoda Track, but in each area there were to be many more months of fighting before the Japanese were finally defeated. By the time the Japanese had been driven into the sea at Sanananda on the north coast of Papua on 22 January 1943 they had suffered over 13 000 killed. The Australians lost over 2000 killed and the Americans more than 600. The Guadalcanal campaign finished on 8 February 1943; there the Japanese lost perhaps 24 000 killed, while US fatal casualties numbered some 1600.

Without doubt the Allied successes on the Kokoda Track, at Milne Bay and on Guadalcanal ensured the security of Australia. In the first two battles the Australians played the major role, while the work of the Australian coastwatchers in saving Guadalcanal was crucial. Had Milne Bay been taken by the Japanese the Allied position would have been threatened. If Port Moresby had been taken by General Horii's troops advancing over the Kokoda Track, the whole strategic situation would have been transformed. In that sense, Kokoda was the most important battle fought by Australians in the Second World War. But contrary to later claims by General MacArthur, it was a battle fought in reaction to a Japanese offensive. It owes nothing to strategic prescience among the high command in Australia.

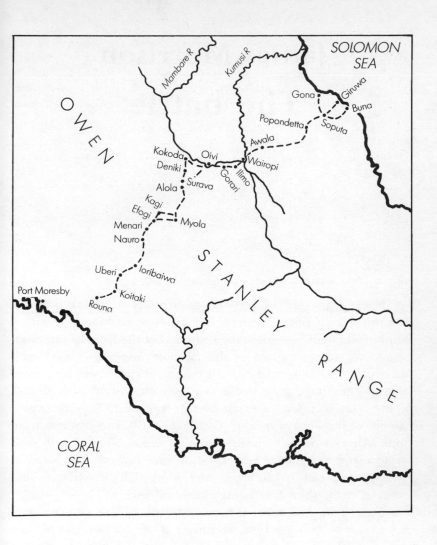

James Morrison

The battle*

ABOUT 4 pm on 23 July 1942, about thirty Australian troops—
armed with rifles, revolvers and a Lewis machine-gun with a
drum of ammunition—made the first stand of the Kokoda campaign
against the advance guard of the Japanese invaders—armed with
heavy machine-guns, mortars and a mountain gun. It was an uneven
contest. The Australians were the raw militiamen of the 11th platoon
of the 39th Battalion, with an average age of 18.5 years, plus a
handful of the Papuan Infantry Battalion (PIB). The Japanese were
from Major-General Tomitaro Horii's Nankai Shitai (South Seas
Detachment) veterans of China, Guam and Rabaul. The stand at
Awaia, north-east of Kokoda, was short. The Australians and
Papuans, outnumbered and outgunned, fell back to Gorari, leaving
a section (about nine men) as forward patrol at Wairopi. Two days
earlier about 7000 Japanese, including 2700 combat troops, had
landed at Basabua, about one kilometre east of Gona Mission, on
the north coast of New Guinea.

Only two weeks before the Japanese landed, B Company of the
39th, under the command of Captain Sam Templeton, had left Ilolo
to cross the Owen Stanley Range to secure Kokoda and provide a

* First published under the title 'Outnumbered Aussie battlers
  marched from defeat to victory', in *The Australian Special Edition*,
  29–30 August 1992.

protective force for American engineers building an airstrip at Dobodura. Captain Templeton, more than fifty years old and a submariner in World War I, led his men in a rearguard action against overwhelming numbers from Gorari to Oivi. Captain Templeton was killed at Oivi as he went back alone to guide reinforcements from Kokoda. The junction of the Kagi and Myola tracks is named after him.

The commanding officer of the 39th, Lieutenant-Colonel W. T. Owen, a survivor of the Japanese massacre of the Australian garrison at Rabaul in that January, ordered his troops to fall back through Kokoda to Deniki. But on 28 July the Australians reoccupied Kokoda. About 2.30 am on 29 July the Japanese attack began on Kokoda with mortar and heavy machine-gun fire. The Australians had nothing to throw back at the Japanese; their mortars and heavy Vickers machine-guns had been left behind in Port Moresby. The Australians were also outnumbered—about 100 troops facing an estimated 400. The attack proper began at 2.30 am, with an assault on the Australian northern perimeter. Colonel Owen exposed himself to enemy fire as he fought with his men. About 3 am Colonel Owen was mortally wounded as he threw a grenade from the forward trench. The Japanese soon penetrated the Australian flanks and, in the confusion, the Diggers withdrew in the mist through the rubber plantation south of Kokoda, down the track towards Deniki. The Australians had lost seven, including their commanding officer, but a captured Japanese document estimating they had faced 1200 enemy at Kokoda gives some indication of the quality of the Australian defence.

Within eight days of the landing of his advance party General Horii had achieved the first of his objectives: the capture of Kokoda. His advance party set about consolidating the beachhead at Buna and Gona for the landing of the main force, which at its height was to number 10 000 combat troops.

By 2 August the 39th Battalion had consolidated at Deniki under the temporary command of Major Alan Cameron. Major Cameron had 480 men, which combined with the remnants of the PIB, was now called Maroubra Force. Major Cameron had at his disposal 31 122 rounds of Thompson machine-gun .45 calibre, 64 561 rounds of small arms .303 and 1021 grenades—barely sufficient for immediate use and a reserve. Before their departure from Port Moresby, the remaining companies of the 39th had been equipped with Thompson submachine-guns. The weapon had been issued only the day before the troops left and they had to learn how to use them as they marched over the Owen Stanleys. But the .45 calibre Thompson was an ideal weapon for the close contact of jungle fighting.

On 8 August Major Cameron ordered an attack on Kokoda, the efficacy of which divides historians. Raymond Paull in *Retreat from Kokoda* wrote that it allowed Cameron to blood his untried troops and upset General Horii's build-up of force. But Peter Brune in *Those Ragged Bloody Heroes* argued it was unwise and broke two of the most elementary military rules: concentration and economy of force. Major Cameron sent out one company to cut the Japanese line of communications east of Kokoda, a second was to follow and then move north-west to recapture Kokoda and a third was sent straight down the track. Captain Cyril Dean leading the attack down the track was killed in the first contact with a strong Japanese patrol moving down from Kokoda and his assault was called off. Captain Bidstrup's company succeeded in cutting the Japanese line of communications for a few hours but was forced to withdraw in the face of overwhelming opposition.

Captain Noel Symington's C Company retook Kokoda from a handful of Japanese about 1.30 pm on 8 August. The Australians captured a map clearly marking the intended Japanese advance over the Owen Stanleys to Port Moresby and a history of the Japanese campaign in Malaya. Captain Symington then deployed his 100-odd men on the plateau overlooking the airfield. Late the following morning about 200 Japanese, smeared with mud and wearing jungle greens, launched their attack through densely wooded cover and were beaten off. At 5.30 pm with 300 men and supporting mortar fire, later at 10.30 pm and 3 am on 10 August, the Japanese renewed their attacks but were beaten back each time.

After two days of fighting, the Australians were practically out of ammunition, augmenting their .303 supply from Lewis gun drums left behind in the first battle of Kokoda. Unable to be reinforced and with no supplies of food and ammunition dropped to them by air, they faced annihilation if they remained and Kokoda was abandoned. While the Japanese had suffered significant casualties in the second battle for Kokoda, Brune argues Major Cameron now

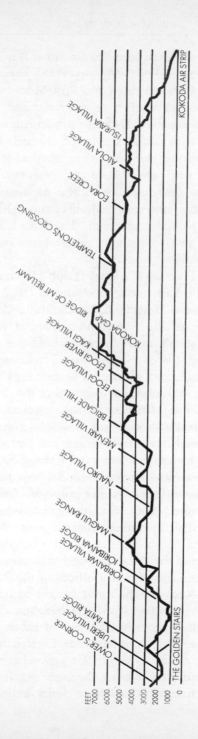

KOKODA AIR STRIP

ISURAVA VILAGE

AIOLA VILAGE

EORA CREEK

TEMPLETONS CROSSING

RIDGE OF MT BELLAMY

KOKODA GAP

KAGI VILLAGE

EFOGI RIVER

EFOGI VILLAGE

BRIGADE HILL

MENARI VILAGE

NAURO VILLAGE

MAGULI RANGE

IORIBAIWA RIDGE

IORIBAIWA VILLAGE

IMITA RIDGE

UBERI VILLAGE

OWER'S CORNER

THE GOLDEN STAIRS

FEET
7000
6000
5000
4000
3000
2000
1000
0

did not have a sufficient force to make a stand at Deniki, a far better defensive position than Kokoda. Moreover, the Japanese knew just how weak the force between them and Port Moresby was, because of the failure of Major Cameron to reinforce and hold Kokoda. The Japanese had the initiative. During early 13 August the Japanese attacked Deniki, and the battle see-sawed through the afternoon. On the following morning the Japanese committed fresh troops and when their assault eased, about 8.30 am, Major Cameron broke contact and withdrew his troops to Isurava. At Isurava they dug in using steel helmets, bayonets and bully beef tins. This was the end of first stage of the Kokoda campaign. The 39th had lost 41 men but were no longer raw militiamen, rather battle-hardened jungle troops.

On 16 August Lieutenant-Colonel Ralph Honner DSO MC, a veteran of the Middle East, took command of the 39th at Isurava. On the same day General Horii landed at the Buna–Gona beachhead with the main force of the *Shitai* and arrived at Kokoda on 24 August. Colonel Honner's orders were to hold the enemy on the northern side of the Owen Stanleys until relieved by the 21st Brigade. The Japanese attacked Isurava at first light on 26 August with three battalions, as the leading elements of the 2/14th Battalion approached Alola. Strong Japanese patrols attacked the Australian perimeter and launched a mortar and mountain gun bombardment on Isurava. 'We would have been wiped out that evening or the next morning if we had stayed there and I was going to stay there because reinforcement was promised—and I was just hoping like hell it was coming because if it hadn't come we would have been done', Colonel Honner said. 'I couldn't implement a plan of withdrawal in face of an incoming reinforcement. We had to stay. They had to get to us.'

The first elements of the 2/14th arrived at Isurava that afternoon. The following day the commanding officer of the 2/14th Lieutenant-Colonel Arthur Key, marched into Isurava to relieve the 39th. Colonel Honner told Colonel Key one battalion could not hold Isurava and declined to be relieved. One of those reinforcements was the then Captain Phil Rhoden, later Lieutenant-Colonel and commanding officer of the 2/14th. 'We saw what was left of the 39th. We heard what they'd been through and I was personally surprised to see that men who looked so down and out could come back for more', Colonel Rhoden said. 'They were volunteering to stop with us and we were gratified because we needed every person. Anyone that could hold a rifle or a gun was needed. It was amazing how the two sides of the Australian Army (AIF and militia) came together without let or hindrance. It was encouraging. It was a morale booster.'

On the afternoon of 29 August, the fourth day of the battle of Isurava, the Japanese broke through the Australian perimeter and the wounded Corporal Lindsay Bear DCM MM and Private Allan Avery and Private Bruce Kingsbury insisted in joining a counterattack to repel the enemy. When Corporal Bear was so badly wounded he could no longer continue to fight, he handed over his Bren gun to Private Kingsbury. Private Kingsbury, firing the Bren gun from his hip, cleared a path 100 metres through the Japanese, inflicting an extremely high number of casualties. He was then killed by a single sniper's bullet. Private Kingsbury's action restored the position and denied the Japanese their breakthrough. He was posthumously awarded the VC, arguably the first to be awarded on Australian soil. 'I reckon he almost gave his life away. There was nothing scared about it. He just went straight into them as if bullets didn't mean anything', Private Avery said.

Captain Toshiya Akizawa of the 144th Regiment provided the Japanese perspective on the battle of Isurava. 'I remember that all my junior officers, my NCOs and most of my men lost their lives', he said. 'Accordingly, all we could think of doing was leaving the place we were in and attacking up the hill and we were being told by the officer from behind: "Attack! Attack!". 'So there is no courage. Just without thinking we attacked and attacked.'

On 30 August General Horii, frustrated at the delay to his advance, threw his huge reserve into the attack. At 3 pm the Australians began their fiercely fought withdrawal from Isurava to Eora Creek. The Australians had held Isurava for four days. They strained General Horii's supply lines and held up his advance to Port Moresby. This was the culminating point of the campaign; the advantage passed from the Japanese to the Australians, although it was not to be apparent for some time. From 31 August to 15 September the Australians, against vastly superior numbers, fought a decisive military game of cat and mouse along the track. Company by company, platoon by platoon, section by section, they defended until their comrades passed through their lines, broke off contact sometimes only 20 or 30 metres from the enemy and repeated the procedure again and again down the track. On 5 September, the commander of the 21st Brigade, Brigadier Arnold Potts, dug in with 1000 troops on a ridge, rising south of Efogi. The area was to be the scene of some of the bloodiest fighting of the campaign and was later called Brigade, or Butcher's Hill.

At 4.30 am on 8 September General Horii, reinforced by 1500 fresh troops and outnumbering the Australians by more than six to one, launched a three-pronged attack on the Australians' front, rear and flank. The forward position repelled eight attacks that morning but Brigadier Potts's headquarters was cut off. Despite a number of counterattacks, Brigadier Potts was unable to dislodge the Japanese and in fading light the Australians withdrew. Although Brigadier Potts had suffered heavy casualties, he had succeeded in delaying the Japanese advance by a further three crucial days.

By 11 September the Australians had withdrawn to Ioribaiwa. The commander of the 25th Brigade, Brigadier Ken Eather, planned to launch a twin-flanking movement against the Japanese. But two things went wrong: the 2/31st Battalion became disoriented and was briefly lost in its left flank thrust and the 3rd Battalion on the right flank was routed by a strong Japanese patrol, which was able to occupy the high ground between the 3rd and the 2/31st. If Brigadier Eather continued to hold Ioribaiwa he would have lost the freedom of movement vital to his planned offensive. He therefore decided on 16 September to withdraw to Imita Ridge, a natural defensive position. It enabled Brigadier Eather to strike out against the Japanese with strong patrols and to deploy artillery for the first time in the campaign.

On 25 September the Japanese high command, wanting to concentrate its forces on Guadalcanal and frightened that General Horii would be cut off by an Allied landing at the Buna–Gona beachhead, ordered a fighting withdrawal along the Owen Stanleys. The Japanese concentrated their defence on the track at Templeton's Crossing and Eora Creek. They offered no resistance at Kokoda, for fear of being outflanked and annihilated by an Australian push through Abuari–Missima–Oivi. On 2 November Kokoda was retaken.

Christopher Dawson

Brigadier Eather at Imita*

AMONG the survivors of the Owen Stanley campaign is the commander who turned back the Japanese rush towards Port Moresby at Imita Ridge on the Kokoda Track. Major-General Ken Eather was brigadier in command of the fresh 25th Brigade which arrived at Ioribaiwa on 14 September after a few days marching from Port Moresby. Major-General Eather, an energetic 41, had led battalions before the outbreak of World War II and took the 2/1st Battalion, City of Sydney Regiment to North Africa with the 6th Division.

Until their arrival, the outnumbered Australian forces had been relentlessly driven back, despite brave resistance. The Japanese South Seas Detached Force, a divisional-sized unit built largely around the experienced 144th Regiment under Major-General Tomitaro Horii, landed at Gona on the Solomon Sea coast of New Guinea on 21 July with the aim of taking Port Moresby. Pitted against the Japanese initially, were untried Australian militra units. As the Japanese pushed further south over what had been considered the impenetrable Owen Stanley Range, the Australians were reinforced by the 7th Division's 21st Brigade from Western Australian, South Australia and Victoria. By September, all those fighting on the Kokoda Track were at the limits of their endurance.

---

* First published as 'Imita end of road for the Japanese', in
  The Australian Special Edition, 29–30 August 1992.

Major-General Eather's task was to halt what appeared to be the enemy's inexorable advance. The 21st Brigade had been instructed to hold a defensive position north of Ioribaiwa, but the Japanese kept up their advance around the flanks. It was then that Major-General Eather made his fateful signal to his divisional commander, Major-General A. S. 'Tubby' Allen: 'Enemy feeling whole front and flanks. Do not consider can hold him here. Request permission to withdraw to Imita Ridge, if necessary.' In a later telephone call to Major-General Allen, Eather was told of the importance of remaining on the offensive and retaining Ioribaiwa. But the final decision was left to him. It was not so much the mauling that two of his battalions had received at the hands of the Japanese but the terrain that led to this decision. 'Imita was a much more decisively defensive position', he said recently in Sydney. 'In order to go forward, we first had to go back.'

The *Official War History* said Major General Eather decided to move back because if he continued to hold the Ioribaiwa position he would have committed all his force to defensive tasks and would have lost freedom to adopt the offensive. 'Ioribaiwa was a hopeless bloody thing while Imita Ridge, which was just behind it, was a much more pronounced feature. There wasn't much between them. Just a few yards', Major-General Eather said. In one of the latest books on Kokoda, *Those Ragged Bloody Heroes*, author Peter Brune described the withdrawal, completed on 17 September, as 'a sound military decision'. The Japanese had the momentum and initiative. But they had also been fighting an unrelenting struggle for two months across the most rugged terrain and were stretching their supply lines. The withdrawal to Imita Ridge allowed Major-General Eather to create a reserve and to push forward to engage Japanese patrols. 'I did not allow them [the Japanese] to probe', he said. 'It was always my policy to obtain and retain control of no-man's land.'

From a political point of view, Major-General Eather's withdrawal had momentous consequences: it lead to interference by the commander of the South-West Pacific Area, General Douglas Mac-Arthur, the journey to Port Moresby by the Australian Commander-in-Chief, General Sir Thomas Blamey, and the removal from command of Lieutenant-General Rowell, Major-General Allen and the gallant Brigadier Arnold Potts. For the Japanese, it was the breaking point. Major-General Horii had gone a long way quickly but had extracted the last ounce of energy from his troops. 'They were now so hungry, so physically weary, that Horii doubted their ability to even hold their position', the military analyst, Colonel E.G. Keogh, wrote. 'The position was now reversed. The Australians had a relatively short line of communication while Horii was at the end of a long and difficult one with scarcely a crumb to eat in the forward area.'

Major-General Eather, who commanded the 11th Division at the end of the war, is the only surviving Allied general. In 1945 he was commander of the Australian contingent at the Victory Parade, London. He was on parade again at the Anzac Day march in Sydney in April. [Major-General Eather died in May 1993.]

David Horner

The command crisis*

T HE Kokoda campaign placed both the high command in Australia and the senior military commanders in New Guinea under intense strain. As it looked as though the Allies would soon be faced with another disaster—one that would directly threaten Australia— senior commanders felt that their own positions were under threat. As a result, within a space of five weeks three senior commanders, Generals Rowell and Allen and Brigadier Potts, were relieved of their commands.

But they were not the real culprits. Responsibility for the command crisis must be spread widely, but in the main it rests on three individuals: the Prime Minister, John Curtin, the Commander-in-Chief South-West Pacific Area, General Douglas MacArthur, and the Commander-in-Chief of the Australian Army, General Sir Thomas Blamey.

The full weight of the command crisis fell on Lieutenant-General Sydney Rowell. A 47-year-old Duntroon graduate, Rowell had served at Gallipoli in the First World War and in 1940–41 had been chief of staff to Blamey in the Middle East. There he had performed outstanding work during the Greek campaign but had fallen out with Blamey over the latter's performance during the campaign. He had returned to Australia to become Deputy Chief of the General

---

*   First published under the title 'Commanders' errors almost led to ruin', in the *Weekend Australian Special Edition*, 29–30 August 1992.

Staff, and then in April 1942 had been given command of the 1st Australian Corps. Despite this excellent record, he had had very little command experience.

Following the Japanese landing at Buna on 22 July 1942, and their seizure of Kokoda at the end of the month, the Australian higher command belatedly decided to reinforce New Guinea. As a result, on 11 August 1942 Rowell and his headquarters staff arrived in Port Moresby to take command of the campaign. It was a difficult assignment.

Rowell immediately sent the 21st Brigade, commanded by Brigadier Arnold Potts, along the Kokoda Track to reinforce the 39th Battalion at Isurava, but a few days later Potts reported that there were insufficient supplies on the track and that his advance would have to be delayed. Perhaps there had been bungling in the supply arrangements, but Rowell's predecessor, Major-General Basil Morris, had been given few resources to prepare the defences of New Guinea. The situation became worse when, on 17 August, all five transport planes at Port Moresby were destroyed in a Japanese air attack. The Allied shortage of transport ships and naval and air units limited the number of troops that could be supported in New Guinea.

Faced with these problems, Rowell also had to deal with a lamentable lack of understanding of the conditions in New Guinea by MacArthur's General Headquarters (GHQ) in Brisbane. For example, on 13 August GHQ suggested that the 'pass' through the Owen Stanley Ranges could be blocked by demolitions. Rowell replied that since parts of the track already had to be negotiated on hands and knees, explosives, which would have to be man handled up the track, could hardly block it.

The lack of understanding at GHQ was revealed further after the Japanese landed at Milne Bay on the night of 25–26 August. MacArthur started to send peremptory messages to Port Moresby ordering the Australians to rapidly destroy the Japanese. Confident of the ability of General Clowes to conduct the battle at Milne Bay, Rowell refused to pass on these messages.

The pressure on Rowell is revealed in a letter to Major-General George Vasey, Blamey's chief of staff in Brisbane, on 28 August: 'I'm personally very bitter over the criticism from a distance and I think it damned unfair to pillory any commander without any knowledge of the conditions'. Two day later he added: 'I know how you are faced [*sic*]. I do hope that there is a show-down between Blamey and MacArthur. Taking it by and large, we do know something about war after three small campaigns.' The latter comment referred to the campaigns in Libya, Greece and Syria the previous year.

Rowell's letter highlighted the main problem. Not only was the American-staffed GHQ inexperienced, but there was an unhappy relationship between MacArthur and Blamey. Less than five months earlier the Australian Prime Minister, John Curtin, had given MacArthur complete control over the Australian forces. MacArthur had become the chief military adviser to the Australian Government and Blamey, the Commander-in-Chief of the Australian Army, had to threaten to resign before he too was given access to his own Prime Minister. Blamey had been appointed Commander Land Forces under MacArthur, but MacArthur had no intention of allowing Blamey to act as his deputy. It later became obvious that MacArthur planned to direct his operations from GHQ, through Task Force commanders in the field, such as Rowell, the commander of New Guinea Force.

Blamey quickly saw that his own position was under threat from MacArthur. But MacArthur too believed that his position was in danger. The deteriorating strategic situation in New Guinea related directly to his own faulty plans. He had to find someone to blame and settled on the Australian soldiers and commanders. After his failure in the Philippines MacArthur knew that knives were out for him in Washington; the fall of Port Moresby would not be just another military disaster, it would be the end of his military career.

In Port Moresby Rowell believed that it was Blamey's role to shield him from these pressures. But he did not appreciate that since Curtin supported MacArthur, Blamey's own position was in jeopardy. An accomplished and ruthless political general like Blamey would fight for his own survival not just for himself, but also because he believed that, for the sake of Australia, he was the best man to resist MacArthur.

Rowell had problems enough in New Guinea. Despite Clowes's victory at Milne Bay, the Japanese had secured a bloody victory at Isurava and were continuing a relentless advance against the hard-fighting Australians on the Kokoda Track. Brigadier Potts with 21st

Brigade had taken command of the fighting but on 8 September, after a fortnight of non-stop fighting, Rowell relieved him of command and replaced him with Brigadier Porter.

The recall of the brave, solid, inspiring Potts underlines a serious fault in command, for neither Rowell nor the commander of the 7th Division, Major-General Arthur Allen, had been able personally to inspect the conditions in the mountains. No man could have done more than Rowell in the busy fortnight between the time he took command and the Japanese attacks on 26 August. However, to inspect Potts's brigade forward at Isurava would have meant an exhausting week's journey by foot. Later Rowell reinstated Potts as commander of the 21st Brigade, once it had returned to the Port Moresby area.

Rowell was now faced with his most critical and trying test. On 8 September the Japanese had attacked and isolated the headquarters of the 21st Brigade, which was fighting desperately to regroup south of Efogi, about 70 kilometres from Moresby. The 25th Brigade had not yet arrived in New Guinea and the 21st Brigade now had a strength of less than half a battalion.

Despite the tremendous strain Rowell remained calm and planned for victory. His chief medical officer wrote that he was 'amazed at his equanimity and unruffled demeanour'. On 14 September Brigadier Ken Eather's 25th Brigade, which had just arrived in New Guinea, reached Ioribaiwa Ridge to take over from the 21st Brigade. The next day the Japanese breached Eather's line, and Eather decided to withdraw to Imita Ridge, about 60 kilometres from Port Moresby. Eather was ordered that there was to be no further withdrawal. But, short of supplies and exhausted, the Japanese could advance no further. Imperceptibly at first, the initiative was returning to the Australians.

This was not the perception in Brisbane. There MacArthur received a report from his Air Commander, Major-General George Kenney, that Rowell had become defeatist and that Moresby would be lost 'if something did not happen'. Kenney had not even met Rowell when he had visited Port Moresby, but MacArthur was already deeply worried about events there. On the evening of 17 September he telephoned Curtin and advised him that Blamey should go to New Guinea to take command personally 'not only to energise the situation, but to save himself' and 'to meet his responsibility to the Australian public'.

Inexperienced in military affairs, Curtin agreed to MacArthur's request, no doubt encouraged by a reported comment of one of his senior Ministers, John Beasley: 'Moresby is going to fall. Send Blamey up there and let him fall with it!' After a background briefing by the Prime Minister, the General Manager of the Melbourne *Herald* wrote about Blamey: 'They are not satisfied with him . . . His every move is watched. He was sent to New Guinea . . . to give him one final chance.'

Uncomfortable with this order, Blamey dallied and did not arrive in Port Moresby until 23 September. By this time the Japanese offensive on the Kokoda Track had stopped, and on 2 October the Australians, reinforced by the 16th Brigade, began their counter-offensive.

But this was too late for Rowell. He had seen Blamey's arrival as evidence that Blamey had no confidence in his ability to command the campaign. Furthermore, if Blamey were to take command, it was not clear what role was left for Rowell. Given their antipathy from the Greek campaign it was inevitable that they would clash, and on 29 September Blamey relieved Rowell of his command. Lieutenant-General Edmund Herring was brought north from Australia to take command of New Guinea Force.

Despite Blamey's later claims, Rowell did not fail as a commander in New Guinea. But he did fail to establish a working relationship with a man whom he disliked intensely. The underlying reason, however, was MacArthur's overreaction after the Japanese had exposed his faulty strategy. Supported by Curtin, MacArthur had forced Blamey to act against his better judgment.

Blamey's inability to stand up to MacArthur continued as the campaign unfolded. Throughout October the 7th Australian Division, commanded by General Allen, fought its way back along the Kokoda Track. Again the troops were short of food and ammunition as supplies had to be brought forward by native carriers. And the Japanese resisted stubbornly from dug-in positions. Unlike Rowell, Allen was a militia officer, but in two world wars he had commanded a platoon, a company, a battalion and a brigade in action. He was highly respected by his men.

In Brisbane, MacArthur again showed a lack of understanding

of conditions on the Kokoda Track. When in mid–October Japanese naval guns and bombers attacked Henderson Field on Guadalcanal and Admiral Ghormley, who was commanding the US Forces around Guadalcanal, was relieved of his command, MacArthur again faced the threat of his own removal. On 17 October MacArthur signalled Blamey in Port Moresby: 'Press General Allen's advance. His extremely light casualties indicate no serious effort yet made to displace enemy.'

When Blamey passed a similar message to Allen, the latter drafted his reply: 'If you think you can do any better come up here and bloody try'. In his actual reply Allen said that he 'was singularly hurt' by MacArthur's signal. He was also hurt by news that on 23 October Herring had relieved Potts of command of the 21st Brigade, which was resting and retraining near Port Moresby. Herring did not know Potts, had no knowledge of his performance on the Kokoda Track, but wanted to install an excellent brigadier who had served under him in Darwin.

Unwilling to risk his own position and in an effort to placate MacArthur, on 27 October Blamey signalled Allen that he was to be replaced by Major-General George Vasey. Few division commanders in history have been replaced without having been visited by either their army commander or corps commander, or indeed by anyone above the rank of lieutenant-colonel.

Personally, Blamey had survived a difficult period, but not without cost to his prestige in the Army. His standing was not helped when he addressed the 21st Brigade, which had fought so gallantly on the Kokoda Track, and reportedly told them they had run like rabbits. As the medical officer of the 2/16th Battalion recalled: 'The entire parade, officers and men, were almost molten with rage and indignation'.

The bitterness has lingered. In a television documentary produced by the Australian Army in 1992 Lieutenant-Colonel Ralph Honner, who commanded the 39th Battalion on the track, recalled being sent to meet Blamey when he had visited Port Moresby on 12 September 1942. It seemed to Honner that the fact that the 21st Brigade was at that time 'fighting for their lives' was 'of no importance to him. He didn't know who I was. I had been his commander of the Australian forces opposing the Japs. He didn't know. He didn't care.'

Against the suffering and heroism on the Kokoda Track the arguments between generals and politicians might seem of little consequence. But the opposite is the case. It was errors by men like MacArthur and Blamey which led to the near disaster in New Guinea. As usual, it was the men in the front line who paid the heaviest price. But as the fate of Rowell, Allen and Potts, shows, they were not the only ones to suffer.

10
Milne Bay

David Horner

The battle[*]

COMPARED with the fighting on the Kokoda Track and at Guadalcanal, the battle for Milne Bay was of only minor proportions. In the Papuan campaign, which began on 22 July 1942 and ended on 22 January 1943, more then 2000 Australians, 600 Americans and about 13 000 Japanese were killed. In the Guadalcanal campaign, which began with the US landing on 7 August and lasted six months, 1600 Americans and 24 000 Japanese were killed. By contrast, the battle at Milne Bay lasted from 26 August to 7 September 1942 and resulted in the deaths of less than 200 Australians and Americans. About 2800 Japanese landed in the area and, of these, perhaps 750 were killed.

These statistics, however, do not provide a true picture of the importance of the battle for Milne Bay, and the fact that it was fought at all relates to the strategic importance of this otherwise remote area. Situated at the south-east tip of New Guinea, it provided a secure anchorage for Allied or Japanese ships. More importantly, in May 1942 General MacArthur, the Commander-in-Chief of the South-West Pacific Area, had ordered the construction there of airstrips from which Allied planes would be able to attack

---

[*] First published under the title 'Masterstroke a turning point for Allied morale', in the *Weekend Australian Special Edition*, 29–30 August 1992.

234

Rabaul and operate along the north coast of Papua and into the Solomon Sea.

Conversely, for the Japanese to approach Port Moresby along the south coast of Papua they would have to seize the vital Milne Bay airstrips. Believing that there were about twenty or thirty aircraft based at Milne Bay, and that the airfields were protected by only two or three companies of infantry, the Japanese decided to land about 2000 Marines, in an offensive to be coordinated with an attack on Port Moresby over the Kokoda Track.

But they grossly underestimated the number of Allied troops that had been deployed by MacArthur. In July Brigadier John Field had arrived with the 7th Australian Infantry Brigade (militia), and then in mid-August this force had been reinforced by the 18th Brigade (AIF), under Brigadier George Wootten, which had fought at Tobruk in 1941. When Major-General Cyril Clowes, a graduate of the Royal Military College, Duntroon, who had served in the Middle East, assumed command on 22 August, Milne Force numbered 8824 (Australian Army 7459, US Army 1365). Of these only about 4500 were infantry; the remainder were engineers (mainly American) building the airstrips, and anti-aircraft units to protect them from air attack. In addition, two RAAF Kittyhawk fighter squadrons, Nos 75 and 76, commanded by Squadron Leaders Les Jackson and Peter Turnbull, were based at Milne Bay.

In preparing the defences of Milne Bay, General Clowes and Brigadier Field faced substantial difficulties. There were few roads or bridges and Field's militiamen had to spend much time on labouring tasks, rather than training for operations. It rained constantly, turning the area into a sea of mud, and communications between units were poor. The soldiers even had to draw their own maps of the area. Troops were unused to the tropics and Milne Bay was one of the worst malaria areas. Brigadier Wootten's AIF brigade was more experienced, but arrived only a short time before the Japanese attack.

In deploying his forces Clowes was faced with a number of problems. Milne Bay is situated between two peninsulas and is roughly rectangular in shape, running about forty kilometres from east to west and ten kilometres wide at the open, eastern end. On the north and south coasts the jungle-covered mountains come down almost to the coast, but at the western end there is a swamp

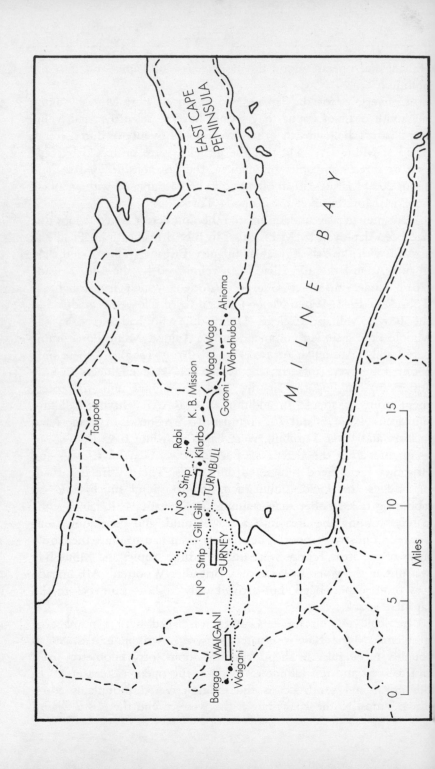

plain where the airfields were being built near the Gili Gili coconut plantation.

In many ways it was like defending an island. There was, and still is, no road to Port Moresby. Not only could the Japanese sail at will into Milne Bay, but they could land troops either to the north or south of the peninsulas and approach the airstrips overland. The Allies could only resupply Milne Force by sea, and Allied vessels were exposed to Japanese naval and air attacks.

Clowes assessed that the Japanese would probably land on the north coast of the bay and advance along it towards the airstrips at the western end. He therefore gave Brigadier Field's 7th Brigade the task of defending the head of the bay, near Airstrip No. 3, while he kept Wootten's 18th Brigade in reserve further inland near Airstrip No. 1 (later named Gurnery Field). Thus he gave the more static task to the less experienced militiamen, keeping the Middle East veterans for the mobile counterattack role.

Since Allied intelligence had intercepted Japanese radio messages, Clowes was warned, in general terms, that his force was soon to be attacked. But he could do little to interfere when the Japanese landed on the north coast of the bay near Wahuhuba on the night of 25–26 August. He had no naval forces, coastal guns or searchlights, and the Japanese forces could land where they wished.

During the night and the next two days the 61st militia Battalion fought a determined delaying action as it was driven back along the north coast towards Airstrip No. 3. The defence was assisted by strafing by the Kittyhawk squadrons. Australian aircraft also destroyed several Japanese barges which otherwise might have been used to move men and supplies along the coast.

Uncertain as to whether the Japanese were going to land more troops at his rear, Clowes kept most of his forces in reserve, but he assigned the 2/10th AIF Battalion to Field to relieve the 61st Battalion. Believing that the Japanese numbered some 5000 men, the commanding officer of the 2/10th Battalion moved east along the coast to meet the invaders.

During the night of 27 August the Japanese attacked the Australians in a vicious battle around KB Mission. The Japanese had two small tanks which roared into the forward Australian positions. As the tanks sprayed machine-gun fire and tried to crush any wounded who could not move out of the way, the Australians had no means of retaliation. Their 'sticky' anti-tank grenades failed either to stick or explode.

By the morning of 28 August the 2/10th Battalion had lost 43 killed and 26 wounded. As the official history puts it:

> The 2/10th Battalion, a proud and experienced battalion of volunteers, had been thrust back in their first fight with the Japanese—and by forces which, as it was learnt later, were not overwhelmingly superior but which were made of brave and determined men whose plan of attack, centring on the use of their two tanks, worked well.

To assess the situation, during the morning a patrol from the 2/10th Battalion returned to the battle-site and came across Private Abraham, who had a leg riddled with bullets and had been left behind in the dark. Five times he had rolled aside to avoid a charging Japanese tank. The patrol found that Abraham was still holding off four Japanese. They had originally numbered ten. He had killed six. The Australian patrol killed the other four and carried Abraham out.

By this time General MacArthur in Brisbane was becoming concerned about the apparent Japanese success. On 28 August he sent a message to General Rowell in Port Moresby that Clowes was to 'clear the north shore of Milne Bay without delay'. Confident of Clowes's handling of the battle Rowell did not send on the order. With torrential rain, poor communications and few roads, Clowes could not move quickly. And he still faced the threat of a landing at his rear. On the afternoon of 29 August aircraft reported a cruiser and nine Japanese destroyers heading towards Milne Bay, and about midnight they shelled positions in the Gili Gili area, although it was comparatively light and caused no casualties.

Clowes gathered his forces to defend Airstrip No. 3, where he could make full use of his defensive firepower. The airstrip was defended by the 25th and 61st militia Battalions and US engineers, and they were supported by field, anti-tank and anti-aircraft artillery. Meanwhile patrols were sent forward to locate the enemy.

At 3 am on 31 August the Japanese mounted the expected attack on Airstrip No. 3. Three times they formed up and attacked but were cut down by artillery and machine-gun fire. Just before dawn three bugle calls were heard and comparative silence followed, except for the groans and cries of the wounded.

The diary of a Japanese Marine in the *3rd Kure Naval Landing Force* gives an attacker's view:

A red signal went up and fell to the right of where we were. Heavy machine-gun volleys started and trench mortars and grenade throwers went into action. There didn't seem to be any place where we could put ourselves but nevertheless we advanced. We were like rats in a bag and men were falling all around. I thought we were going to be wiped out and then we were told to withdraw for the time being and we retreated.

Soon after 9 am the 2/12th AIF Battalion moved through the forward militia defensive positions and began the counteroffensive, encountering determined Japanese rearguards. The advance was coordinated by Brigadier Wootten and the headquarters of the 18th Brigade, while the rear was protected by the 9th militia Battalion. That night about 300 Japanese suddenly appeared from the jungle valleys on the left of the advancing Australians and attacked elements of the 2/12th Battalion. In a savage two-hour battle the Australians claimed that they killed 90 of their attackers.

Next day Wootten resumed the advance, bringing the 2/9th AIF Battalion forward by boat to take over from the 2/12th Battalion. By 4 September the Japanese had been driven back about ten kilometres but were still fighting stubbornly. About midday most companies of the 2/9th Battalion were in action. When one of the forward sections was held up by fire from three enemy machine-guns, the section commander, Corporal French, moved forward and with grenades and a Thompson submachine-gun cleared all three Japanese positions. He was killed as he cleared the final Japanese position and was posthumously awarded the Victoria Cross.

On 5 September Clowes received word from Brisbane that the Japanese would land more troops during the night, and during the night his forward troops could hear the sound of boats moving between ship and shore. Next day the Australians reached the main Japanese base area, but met little opposition.

About 10 pm that night Japanese ships once more sailed up the bay. At the head of the bay the British merchant vessel *Anshun* was unloading urgently needed ammunition and stores while nearby were the colours and lights of the hospital ship *Manunda*. A Japanese cruiser turned its searchlights onto both Allied ships, sunk the

Anshun, but did not fire on the hospital ship. The Japanese also shelled various Australian shore positions. The Japanese ships returned the following night, again illuminated the *Manunda*, and shelled the Airstrip No. 1 area.

During the night of 6 September the last Japanese forces were evacuated. The troops remaining ashore were left to make their way overland towards Buna. Most were tracked down and killed by Australian patrols.

The Japanese Navy's respect for the Rules of War in not firing at the *Manunda* was not matched by their Marine counterparts ashore. As the Australians regained the territory held temporarily by the Japanese they found instances of atrocities committed against captured or wounded Australians and also against the local natives. These atrocities were later investigated and confirmed by the Australian judge, Sir William Webb. It was a sobering experience for both the militiamen and the Middle East veterans. But then, after the Japanese failed in their attack on Airstrip No. 3, they apparently had also shot their own wounded comrades.

The battle of Milne Bay was significant for a number of reasons. Field Marshal Sir William Slim commented in his book *Defeat into Victory* that his Fourteenth Army in Burma took heart from the 'first undoubted defeat' of the Japanese on land. There is an element of truth in this claim, although the Japanese garrison on Tulagi near Guadalcanal had been defeated by the US Marines earlier in August, so it was not strictly the first defeat on land. But as General Rowell has pointed out, Milne Bay was the first time that 'the Japanese had been defeated at a time and on the ground of their own choosing'. For the first time in nine months since their invasion of Malaya, a Japanese invading force had been thrown back into the sea.

With fighting in the balance at Guadalcanal and on the Kokoda Track, the Japanese defeat instilled much needed confidence in Allied commanders and their forces. The battle had shown that the Japanese were not infallible. They had made a strategic error, while the Allied decision to build a base at Milne bay had proven to be a masterstroke.

Following the outstanding performance of the 39th militia Battalion on the Kokoda Track, the militia battalions at Milne Bay had performed well, considering their inexperience and lack of training. As Brigadier Field, the only member of his brigade to have served in the Middle East, commented, 'for untried troops . . . they had done splendidly'.

At Milne Bay, as well as on the Kokoda Track, two views of Australian politics and two sides of the Australian Army came together in defence of Australia. For the first time the hardened men of the AIF, who had volunteered to serve in the imperial cause overseas, fought beside young conscripts, whose service was restricted to Australian territory. For the first time an Australian division was commanded in action by a graduate of the Royal Military College, Duntroon.

The battle was also the first action by American Army units in New Guinea. Fourteen Americans, mainly from the 43rd Engineer Regiment, were killed. The Australians lost 167 killed and 205 wounded, most from the 18th Brigade.

For the first time in the Pacific the RAAF was able directly to support Australian infantry. General Rowell thought that the action of Nos 75 and 76 Squadrons on the first day 'was probably the decisive factor'. Beaufighters from No. 30 Squadron also operated from Milne Bay.

Airstrip No. 3 was later renamed Turnbull Field in honour of Squadron Leader Peter Turnbull, the commanding officer of No. 76 Squadron, who was killed in action while strafing the Japanese on 27 August. The airstrip is no longer in use, but the kunai-covered strip through the jungle and oil palms is still clearly visible. There, beside a memorial to Peter Turnbull is another memorial and a plaque with these words:

> In memory of the officers, NCO's and men of the 7 & 18 Aust Inf Bdes who gave their lives in defending Turnbull Field. This marks the western most point in Milne Bay of the Jap advance Aug–Sep 42, also the southern most point of the Jap advance in the S.W. Pacific. 83 unknown Jap Marines lie buried here. Erected as a tribute by Australian forces serving in this area. June 1944.

Gregory Pemberton

The role of the Air Force*

O N the Anjou peninsula in an obscure part of the Kimberleys in Western Australia, where the white-beached mainland reaches its closest point to the island of Timor, there is a primitive dust-swept airstrip of World War II vintage carved out of the dense scrub and red bauxite soil, named Truscott Field in memory of the Australian fighter ace who led 76 Squadron in the courageous defence of Milne Bay against the Japanese in August–September of 1942. Truscott Field is only one of a series of such airstrips strung out along Australia's northern frontier for wartime air defence against the repeated Japanese air strikes against the Australian mainland. Most were named after dead Australian fighter aces and some after the American pilots who died in the defence of Darwin. The Australian names of these remote and now neglected airfields stand in stark contrast to the choice of British placenames for the RAAF's more permanent air bases—Richmond, Laverton, Edinburgh and Amberly.

Construction of Truscott Field commenced in March 1944 with hundreds of workers, including more than 60 Aborigines from the nearby Drysdale River (now Kalumburu) mission, using heavy earthmoving machinery to level a basic airstrip. Soon after, the

---

* First published under the title 'Aces who held Milne Bay fight obscurity of time', in *The Australain Special Edition*, 29–30 August 1992.

242

bombers of Australia's newly formed 79 Wing conducted from Truscott Field a succession of raids against Japanese positions in the islands to the north. From desperate defence in 1942, the Australian forces had by then gone on to the offensive as the Japanese forces were gradually rolled back. A neglected Truscott Field remains a more poignant memorial to Squadron Leader Keith William 'Bluey' Truscott's deeds in the defence of Australia than the sculptured bust of him sitting between spreading wings of bronze in the grounds of Melbourne's Royal Children's Hospital.

'Bluey' was a foundation member of the RAAF's 452 Squadron in the Battle of Britain. He became such a charismatic figure there that the Marquess of Donegal organised the 'Redhead's Spitfire Fund' to buy 'Bluey' his own Spitfire. He returned to Australia in March 1942 as a fighter ace credited with fourteen 'kills', a Distinguished Flying Cross and Bar. In July he went to Milne Bay in New Guinea with the RAAF's 75 and 76 Squadrons to await the expected Japanese attack. The former was led by Les Jackson, whose brother John, a veteran of the Western Desert, had previously led 75 in the defiant defence of Port Moresby. The 78 Squadron was under the command of the dashing Peter Turnbull and 'Bluey' commanded one flight along with his longtime mate from 452, 'Bardie' Wawn. 'Bluey' was dismayed to swap his sleek thoroughbred Spitfire for the more cumbersome American-built Kittyhawk. But he soon came to see their value in this very different theatre.

Gurney Field at Milne Bay (named after Australia's Squadron Leader Bob Gurney) was only a narrow steel mesh laid out on the perpetual bog among the (world's largest) coconut plantations at the head of the bay. The conditions were appalling but Milne Bay was critical in what the then Prime Minister, John Curtin, had called the 'Battle for Australia'. On 26 August the Japanese at Kokoda resumed their advance towards Port Moresby and simultaneously commenced their landing at Milne Bay. There waited the 18th Australian Infantry Brigade, which had never fought in the jungle, and the 7th Brigade, which had never fought anywhere. The only other support was from American engineers and anti-aircraft gunners.

Former diplomat and writer Ric Throssell was a young signaller in 11th Division Signals at Milne Bay. He and his mates soon appreciated the importance of the Kittyhawks without whose support Milne Bay could not have been held. They were excellent ground-attack aircraft and were even competitive with the Japanese Zeros in aerial combat. He remembers the American squadron of heavily armoured Bell Aerocobras were virtually useless, despite their fierce, pointy-nosed appearance, against the lightly armoured Zeros. On 'scramble', they headed out to the safety of the sea. The night of their arrival. Throssell and some of his mates sneaked out of camp up a hill to a deserted plantation homestead where they slept on the floor. Throssell still recalls vividly the strong scent of the frangipani in the tropical garden while fireflies danced among the coconut palms. The next day, 24 August, their tropical paradise was disturbed when a Japanese Zero strafed the homestead, signalling the beginning of the long-awaited Japanese attack. On returning to camp Throssell discovered their 'paradise' was marked on the map as Target Hill.

The Kittyhawks drove off the Zeros and next launched a successful raid against the troop barges and transport ships of the Japanese invasion fleet. The Kittyhawks returned, rearmed, refuelled and repeated the raid in the fast-dwindling daylight. 'Right', yelled Turnbull, 'rearm and refuel—they'll be here tonight'. He was right. Around midnight, the shelling began. Major-General Clowes, the Australian commander, issued his order: 'No retreat or surrender, whatever the size of the attacking force'.

At 1.30 am, 26 August, with a dense fog making visibility zero, the Japanese Marines landed at KB Mission on the bay's north-eastern shore and engaged the Australian ground forces which were holding the front-line of defence of the airstrips where the pilots were sitting in their aircraft waiting to be able to see. It was mutual support; the troops needed the air support to survive and the air force needed the troops to defend the strips. Suddenly, the fog lifted and the Kittyhawks roared into life. Again and again they strafed the Japanese force. Eight American Flying Fortresses joined the fray, then five B-25s, and finally a few RAAF Hudsons all made bombing raids. But it was the Kittyhawks who went in, time after time, their pilots tired, filthy and even stricken by malaria. The American engineers worked ceaselessly to scrape away the mud oozing up through the mesh of the strips, threatening to ground the aircraft. Having survived a Japanese strafe while the Kittyhawks were caught rearming, Turnbull went up again to destroy a threatening enemy tank. He came in too low, possibly was struck by ground fire, and crashed straight into the ground. Throssell happened to be in divisional headquarters repairing a line to the air operations tent when the message of 'Red Leader Down' arrived and he recalls the great consternation this caused. But the war went on and Truscott stepped in to take over from Turnbull. The squadron could not have had a more able replacement.

On the night of August 27, the Japanese seized KB Mission. The road to the airstrips was now open. Nobody slept that night. By dawn, the Japanese held one end of Airstrip No. 3 while the Australians held the other. The Japanese were only two miles from the Kittyhawks at Gurney Field. 'Bluey' refused to withdraw. His name was a legend and his presence inspired the troops. At dawn he, Jackson and the Hudsons were in the air again. They knew this was the decisive day. In appalling visibility they strafed the edge of the plantations and held back the Japanese from overrunning Airstrip No. 3. As the rain and cloud swept across the bay they again attacked the Japanese barges, supported by B-26s from Moresby. When the order came to withdraw the aircraft to the safety of Moresby, 'Bluey' and 'Bardie' Wawn alone stayed back and watched as, despite the tanks, flamethrowers and constant naval bombardment, the infantry denied the possession of the vital airstrips to the Japanese. Later that day, the Kittyhawks returned and 'Bluey' led them against the Japanese with Jackson having ditched on his way back. When night came, 'Bluey' again refused orders to withdraw all aircraft to Moresby.

Over the next 36 hours the battle hung in the balance. The Kittyhawks strafed until the rifling in their gun barrels was smooth. About 150 000 rounds of .50 calibre had been fired. On the night of 30 August the Japanese massed for their last desperate assault. Clowes now threw in his reserves. That night and into the early morning the infantry held the Japanese back and then in torrential rain and bitter hand-to-hand combat they forced them back through the swamp and sodden bush. By 5 September it was clear the Australians had won. Soon after, 'Bluey' received on behalf of 76 Squadron a letter of commendation from the US Major-General George Kenney, Commanding General of Allied Air Forces in the South-West Pacific.

Following the Milne Bay victory, 'Bluey' and 76 squadron were withdrawn to Darwin for the relatively quiet tasks of escorting convoys and intercepting air raids. On 28 March 1943, 'Bluey' and his colleague went out to escort a Catalina home. The air was still and the sea so glassy it was difficult to judge one's height above it. 'Bluey' was never at his best at low levels. As they approached the Bay of Rest, they suddenly realised they were too low. 'Bluey's' airscrew bit into the sea, then flipped the Kittyhawk on its back in an eruption of foam and flames. At 26, 'Bluey' was gone forever and Australia had lost a hero. His virtually unmarked body was recovered and buried in the War Cemetery near Perth and his first Spitfire stands in the War Memorial in Canberra.

The great Marlene Dietrich once sang 'Where have all the flowers gone?' The 82nd birthday of Australia's greatest flying ace, Clive Caldwell, passed recently without public notice. Keith Miller recently complained publicly that a horse race at Randwick named after the Australian pilot Bill Newton, who was beheaded by the Japanese, had its name changed to that of its new corporate sponsor. 'Bluey' Truscott's name is also in danger of being lost once the World War II generation has passed away. Australia's rich history will be a little poorer for the loss of his memory.

11

The battle of El Alamein

Gavin Long

The battle*

A s the moment for the opening of one of the great battles of
history drew near, flights of British bombers surged across the
night sky, but the sounds soon faded. Then exactly at 9.40 pm the
whole wide arc of the battlefield was rimmed with flickering yellow
light as 900 medium and field guns opened up against the enemy
gun lines. Seconds elapsed before the first detonations reached the
troops waiting on their start lines. They could have believed they
were watching a silent display of summer lightning, until the thunder
burst upon their eardrums in a swiftly mounting crescendo. For
fifteen minutes this counter-battery bombardment continued, then
stopped as suddenly as it had started.

There followed five minutes of eerie silence while the men of
the Eighth Army awaited the signal to advance. At 10 pm it came.
Two parallel searchlight beams reaching high into the moonlit vault
of the sky swung inwards and crossed. Instantly the guns belched
fire again with a barrage of unbelievable intensity. The floor of the
desert shook, vehicles shuddered without pause, men's bodies and
their very voices quivered under the mighty shock waves. This time
the barrage crept forward ahead of the infantry to assist them on to
their objectives.

---

*   Frist published under the title, 'Heroism that conquered the enemy
    yard by yard', in *The Weekend Australian, Special Edition*, 24–25
    October 1992.

The first to cross the Australian start lines were the 2/24th Battalion of Brigadier D. A. Whitehead's 26th Brigade on the right and the 2/17th and 2/15th Battalions of Brigadier W. J. V. Windeyer's 20th Brigade on the left. Almost immediately they ran into machine-gun and mortar fire as they threaded their way through mines and booby traps. At the enemy wire the men were held up for a few minutes until the barrage lifted and moved on ahead of them through the enemy minefields. Where the barrage had failed to smash down the wire, engineers blew gaps through it with bangalore torpedoes, and the infantry passed through and started methodically mopping up the enemy posts. In the smoke and dust raised by the bombardment, visibility was limited to a few yards, but lines of tracer shells fired from the rear as guides helped to keep the attackers on their correct line of advance. Shortly after midnight the three battalions had reached their objective and dug in. They had achieved a considerable success at a total cost of 24 dead and 140 wounded or unaccounted for. Indeed, along the whole of the 30th Corps' front the first objectives had been taken in about two hours without great opposition. The second phase of this opening night's attack was to prove more difficult. The assaulting divisions were soon to discover that the first line of defence, which on the British maps had been shown as bristling with obstacles and weapons of every kind, was in fact comparatively lightly held as an outer line to cover the main line of defence sited in the rear at considerable depth.

As the battalions assigned the task of achieving the second—and final—phase of the night's attack were moving up to pass through the foremost battalions, the artillery continued pounding the advanced enemy positions. An hour was allowed for the second wave of attackers to move into position. In the 9th Division's sector only one battalion in each brigade was employed in the final phase—the 2/28th Battalion on the right and the 2/13th on the left.

In the face of stiff opposition the 2/48th (Lieutenant-Colonel H. H. Hammer) fought its way to its objective, which it reached at 3.45 am. During this advance, Sergeant W. H. Kibby attacked an enemy post which was holding up the advance, killing three with his Tommy gun and accepting the surrender of twelve others.

Having penetrated 3.5 kilometres into enemy territory from the

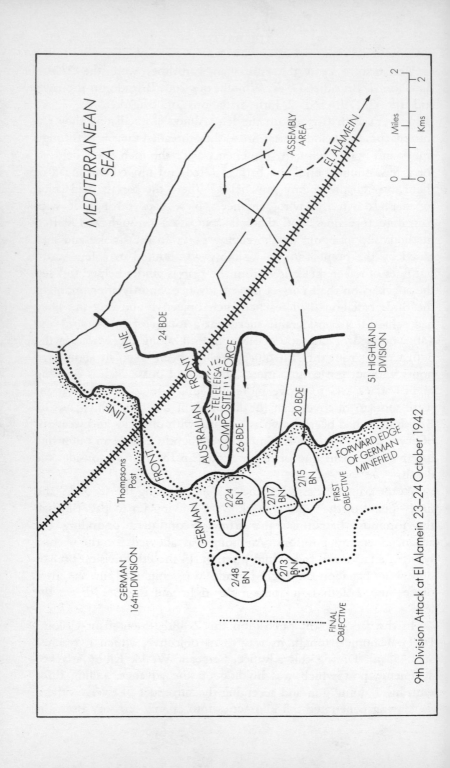

9th Division Attack at El Alamein 23–24 October 1942

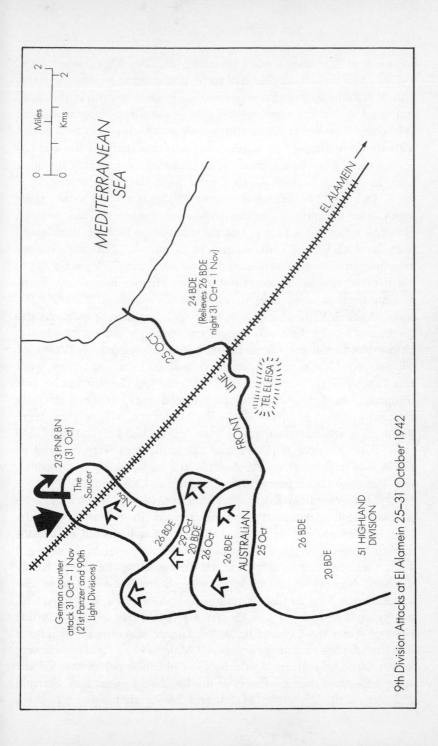

MEDITERRANEAN
SEA

2/3 PNR BN
(31 Oct)

The
Saucer

German counter
attack 31 Oct – 1 Nov
(21st Panzer and 90th
Light Divisions)

1 NOV

26 BDE

29 Oct
20 BDE

26 Oct

26 BDE

AUSTRALIAN

25 Oct

FRONT LINE

TEL EL EISA

24 BDE
(Relieves 26 BDE
night 31 Oct – 1 Nov)

25 OCT

EL ALAMEIN

26 BDE

20 BDE

51 HIGHLAND
DIVISION

0   Miles   2

0   Kms   2

9th Division Attacks at El Alamein 25–31 October 1942

brigade start line the 2/48th Battalion, like the 2/24th in its rear, had an open right flank that had to be protected as well as the front. Both battalions stationed companies facing north to protect this flank and lined up on the right with a composite force, commanded by Lieutenant-Colonel E. Macarthur-Onslow, which was in turn linked with the 24th Brigade to extend the northern flank to the coast.

On the left of the advance the 2/13th Battalion, having no open flank to protect, had to advance on a front three times as wide as the 2/48th's—2200 metres as against 730 metres—and to the same depth. The strength of the enemy defences made the task beyond the capacity of the infantry, but the attack was to have been made with the 40th Royal Tank Regiment in support. The main enemy minefield in that area was expected to be about 230 metres deep, but it proved to be almost 1460 metres. Despite herculean efforts, the engineers were unable to clear lanes through in time for the tanks so the 2/13th attacked on time without their support. As the companies fought their way deeper into enemy territory, opposition stiffened and soon they were taking very heavy casualties. Wounded officers and NCOs continued leading their men until they were killed or severely wounded and put out of the battle. In one company, the few survivors were forced back under their only remaining leader to the intermediate objective, where they were absorbed in another company. Dawn approached before the 2/13th could reach its final objective and the companies were ordered to dig in where they were. At daylight the tanks finally got through and destroyed some posts threatening the 2/13th's positions.

On the Australian front soon after sunrise on 24 October, the German 15th Armoured Division moved in to stage the first counterattack on the bridgehead. Three Australian field regiments, the 7th Medium Regiment and some British Sherman tanks engaged them. German lorry infantry entered the battle but the enemy finally fell back, leaving several tanks burning. Some Shermans were also knocked out. The 2/13th Battalion, still short of its final objective, was practically without officers. At 4 pm that day its commanding officer, Lieutenant-Colonel R. W. N. Turner, was mortally wounded and his adjutant seriously wounded. Major G. E. Colvin was sent forward to take command and he then obtained permission for the other left-out-of-battle officers of the battalion to join him. Starting at 2 am on the 25th, the 2/13th and 2/17th Battalions, supported by the 40th Royal Tank Regiment, completed the 20th Brigade's task by fighting their way forward to the final objective and digging in.

The task now given to the Australians was the tentative portion of the original El Alamein battle plan of cutting off and capturing the enemy between the 30th Corps's northern flank and the sea. To open the attack the 26th Brigade, already facing north as well as west, was to drive 1.2 kilometres northwards into the enemy salient to capture Trig 29, the highest ground in the area, and the slope that ran north-east from the Trig down to a feature called the Fig Orchard. Across part of the ground to be captured ran a switch defence line leading through the Fig Orchard to Thompson's Post, the scene of bitter fighting in the days to come. The attack on Trig 29 was to be carried out by the 2/48th, that on the Fig Orchard by the 2/24th.

The attack opened at midnight with an artillery barrage. Pressing forward through heavy defensive fire two companies of the 2/48th stopped as planned 200 metres short of Trig 29 while carriers with another company aboard charged through to the dusty smoke-shrouded objectives, where the infantry leaped among the enemy and overcame them with bayonets, grenades and small-arms fire. Advancing with the left-hand company, Private P. E. Gratwick, a 40-year-old West Australian prospector, charged an enemy post with a rifle and bayonet in one hand and a grenade in the other. Throwing one grenade into the pot, then another, he jumped in among the surviving defenders with his bayonet and killed them all, including a complete mortar crew. He then charged a second post but was killed by machine-gun fire as he reached it. He was posthumously awarded the Victoria Cross.

The 2/24th Battalion had the difficult task of advancing 2.7 kilometres along a line of enemy posts, one of the advanced companies moving down the left of the enemy wire and the other to the right of it. They captured the Fig Orchard post after heavy fighting, with severe losses on both sides; one company, overshooting its objective, reached the perimeter of Thompson's Post before the fourteen survivors of the 63 who had started were withdrawn to the Fig Orchard position. Lieutenant-Colonel C. G. Weir, commanding the 2/24th, found the forward companies surrounded by German dead, but at 4 am decided the battalion as too depleted to hold such an extended front and withdrew.

During the previous night of violent action the 20th Brigade, which had taken over the 26th Brigade's front, was attacked by tanks and infantry. Against the 2/13th Battalion the Germans followed up by dark the daylight attack that had failed earlier, but they were again routed, this time losing three tanks and tow-tracked troop carriers when they were within 55 metres of the Australians. Artillery and infantry-weapon fire broke up the attack. On the 2/17th Battalion's front, twelve enemy tanks appeared at dawn on a ridge to the north-west where they remained all day harassing the Australians.

The day of 27 October was also marked by very fierce fighting. A pre-dawn attack on the 2/13th Battalion by infantry assisted by fifteen tanks was dispersed by a concentrated artillery bombardment with an infantry fire curtain in front of it. A second attack was also dispersed. But it was on the Australian's new northern front that Rommel threw the main weight of his armour, artillery and infantry that day. While forming up for the attack near the Sidi Rahman mosque on the coast road in the afternoon, the enemy concentration was pounded by British bombers, but an attack by an enemy infantry battalion supported by a heavy German artillery barrage was launched against the 2/48th Battalion on Trig 29. The artillery supporting the 2/48th put down a wall of fire and the battalion joined in with mortars, machine-guns and rifles.

The enemy was driven back with very heavy losses. The German left wing came up against the 2/24th with tanks and infantry, but there too the attackers were dispersed with heavy losses. An attack on the 2/17th was also beaten off. Rommel later wrote of the attacks on the Trig 29 positions: 'Attacks were launched by elements of the 15th Armoured Littorio Division and a Bersaglieri Battalion, supported by all the local artillery and anti-aircraft. The British resisted desperately. Rivers of blood were poured out over miserable strips of land.'

On 28 October the British stood on the defensive during the day while regrouping, but at 10 pm the 9th Australian Division again struck northwards on the right flank towards the coast road. Brigadier Windeyer's 20th Brigade opened the attack with the 2/13th Battalion driving along the switch line through the Fig

Orchard to the outskirts of Thompson's Post—the area from which the 2/24th had been withdrawn on the morning of 26 October—and the 2/15th Battalion taking over from the 2/48th and striking north from Trig 29.

The 2/13th was an exhausted and depleted unit, with its rifle companies down to 35 of all ranks. It had been attacking and beating off counterattacks for five sleepless nights and had been on the march throughout the preceding night. Forced to advance on a narrow front because of its reduced numbers, the battalion inevitably left unsubdued enemy posts on the left flank, which caused casualties among the Australians after they had advanced to their objective—across ground strewn with anti-personnel mines. A patrol of ten men led by Lieutenant S. C. F. North was hit by a mortar bomb that killed or seriously wounded all except Lieutenant North, who returned and organised another patrol which brought back the casualties while a patrol under Corporal R.V. McKellar moved through a minefield and attacked with grenades two machine-gun crews who were covering the troublesome mortar crew. This patrol then rushed the mortar crew, overcame them and returned with the weapons.

As the 2/15th was forming up for its attack on the left it was heavily shelled and its commanding officer, Lieutenant-Colonel C. K. M. Magno and his adjutant were wounded, Magno mortally. Advancing through heavy machine-gun and mortar fire the battalion secured its objectives. In the attack the counted Italian dead numbered 89 and 130 German and Italian prisoners were taken.

At dawn on 29 October the 2/13th Battalion was heavily shelled in its isolated position. Three shells penetrated dugouts of battalion headquarters, wounding Major Colvin, killing his adjutant and wounding his anti-tank officer. But is was on the 2/15th and 2/17th that the enemy's main efforts were directed that day. Fourteen enemy tanks stood on a hill near Trig 29 and poured heavy fire into the Australian positions all day. But repeated attacks on the Australians by tanks and infantry were repelled by artillery and infantry fire that inflicted severe losses on the enemy.

These operations caused Rommel to concentrate even more forces in the north, and in the next four days the Australian sector became the focal area of the battle. The 9th Division was called on to maintain the relentless pressure on the enemy 'to eat the guts out of them', as Montgomery had expressed it, and open the way for the British armoured break-out farther to the south. In London Churchill was becoming highly critical of Montgomery's apparent inactivity.

The Australian commander, Lieutenant-General Sir Leslie Morshead, attacked again on the night of 30 October, employing four battalions under the command of Brigadier Whitehead, with the intention of cutting the coastal road, sending two battalions eastwards along it to break through the enemy front line from the rear, and then having another battalion turn north and drive to the coast, thus penning in the enemy between it and the 24th Brigade, which was still holding the coastal sector.

The 2/32nd Battalion (Lieutenant-Colonel J. W. Balfe) opened the attack, covered by a heavy barrage, at 10 pm and reached the railway (the intermediate objective) in good time, capturing 175 prisoners, mostly Germans, in the course of its advance. The battalion then moved on to the road in the face of stronger opposition but left two companies south of the railway to guard the left flank while engineers made a gap through the 3.6 metre-high railway embankment to enable supply vehicles to pass through.

The 2/3rd Pioneer Battalion (Lieutenant-Colonel A. V. Gallasch), the 2/48th and the 2/24th moved off at intervals and fought their way to positions near the 2/32nd, where they dug in shortly after midnight while preparing to move forward to complete their respective tasks. The area in which the battalions had gathered was a wide depression that the troops quickly named the Saucer. In the two days to follow the Saucer was to become the focal point in the bloody struggle between the two armies. The enemy had begun closing in by midnight and casualties were mounting among the Australians as the Pioneers toiled to complete the gap in the railway embankment.

At 1 am the 2/48th and 2/24th Battalions left their start lines. They were charged with the desperate task of fighting their way eastwards down the road and railway for two kilometres through the rear of the recently reinforced enemy positions. They advanced into a receding British barrage laid down by guns massed farther east. After a week of almost continuous fighting the combined strength of these two battalions had been reduced from a total of 1300 officers and men to a meagre 450 between them. Now they became involved in some of the most bitter fighting of the battle. They stormed through machine-gun, mortar and 88-mm gunfire to subdue post after post, all of them stoutly defended. Companies were reduced to a few men without officers, but they were rallied by NCOs to join with other groups to continue the fight. On the left of the attack, the 2/48th reached its final objective, where Sergeant Kibby, whose gallantry in this and earlier fighting could not have been surpassed, was killed attacking the last enemy post blocking the advance.

On the right the 2/24th found its final objective, Thompson's Post, strongly held, contrary to intelligence reports. The depleted battalion, now deprived of artillery support, was unable to press on with the attack. Independently, the two battalions had to retire to the Saucer as the last day of October dawned. Captain E. P. Harty led back the 54 survivors of the 2/24th and Lieutenant-Colonel Hammer, himself wounded, brought back the 41 men of the 2/48th still on their feet. Territorially their mission had failed but the division had captured 544 prisoners and a formidable array of weapons.

The 2/3rd Pioneer Battalion in its drive to the coast before dawn on the 31st was halted one kilometre from its objective. Later in the day its positions were overrun by enemy tanks and the survivors had to retire to the Saucer.

At dawn, the newcomers to the Saucer, who had taken up improvised positions in the darkness, found numerous enemy positions sited all round them at distances of between 700 metres and one kilometre. The enemy opened up with small arms, mortars, 88-mm guns firing air-burst shells and a variety of field guns. At 10 am, British intelligence intercepted a message from Rommel ordering his 21st Armoured and 90th Light Divisions to attack down the road and railway and capture the Australian position. At midday the attack began through clouds of dust and smoke raised by the shelling, aerial bombing and movement of tanks. Enemy assaults were maintained throughout the afternoon and well into the night, but every attack crumbled in the face of the spirited defence of the 9th Division. That evening, after about a half-hour of continuous fire, an enemy shell scored a direct hit on the 24th Brigade's tactical headquarters, mortally wounding Brigadier Godfrey and killing three other officers.

Late that night all the divisional line communications were cut by British tanks moving through the area, but the battle continued to rage. It died down at 2.30 am on 2 November. An intense British barrage had started farther south signalling the beginning of Operation Supercharge. The long awaited break-out was under way. The 9th Division had completed its vital 'crumbling' mandate of drawing upon itself as much of the enemy's fighting strength as possible and destroying what it could.

David Horner

The importance of
Australia's role*

THE battle of El Alamein was the Australian Army's last engagement in the Middle East in the Second World War. Since
arriving in early 1940 Australian units had fought with distinction
in the first Libyan Campaign, in Greece, Crete, Syria and Tobruk.
Sometimes the Australians formed the majority of the forces
involved; their role was usually crucial, and in all cases substantial.

At El Alamein, however, the 9th Australian Division had a
different role. The British commander, Lieutenant-General Montgomery, had four armoured and seven infantry divisions, more than
220 000 men, over 900 tanks and 900 field and medium guns. For
the first time in a major battle the Australians provided only a
fraction of the force employed.

Montgomery's original plan did not envisage that the Australians
would play a greater role than any of his other infantry divisions.
On the night of 23 October four infantry divisions, the 9th
Australian, the 51st Highland, the 2nd New Zealand and the 1st
South African, would attack side by side in order from the north
to south across a twelve-kilometre front in the northern sector of
the Alamein line. These four divisions, forming the 30th Corps
under Lieutenant-General Oliver Leese, were to force their way
through the German minefield, clearing corridors for the advance

---

* First published under the title 'Final engagement proved one of the
best', in *The Australian Special Edition*, 24–25 October 1992.

of two armoured divisions in the 10th Corps. After that, the British tanks would hold off the German tanks while the British infantry destroyed the Axis infantry in what Montgomery called 'crumbling operations' or the 'dog-fight'.

On the first day of the attack the infantry, including the Australians, achieved about 80 per cent of their objectives, but the German defences were stronger than expected and the armoured thrust did not begin until the night of 24 October. Then Montgomery's plan began to unravel. The tanks came up against strong German resistance, and the idea of superimposing the tanks of one corps on the infantry of another led to problems of command and control.

Fighting continued through 25 October, but it became clear that the crumbling operations would be costly. Already the Highlanders, New Zealanders and South Africans had taken considerable casualties. The 20th and 26th Australian Brigades had also suffered casualties, although slightly less than the others, but their exposed position offered the possibility of changing the direction of the attack. In their initial assault the Australians' line of attack had been some six kilometres from the coast, and they had left a large pocket of enemy defences around Thompson's Post to the north of their positions. The Australians also had more reinforcements than the New Zealanders and South Africans, and they were a well-trained and highly experienced force. The Australian commander, Lieutenant-General Sir Leslie Morshead, was a demanding taskmaster who had trained his men well; a tough, even ruthless tactician, he could be relied upon to achieve his tasks. Seeking to surprise the enemy, Montgomery therefore ordered the 9th Australian Division to attack northwards towards the coast, while the 1st Armoured Division continued the offensive to the west along the original axis.

The attacks began on the night of 25 October. The 1st Armoured Division failed to make progress, but the attack by the 26th Brigade succeeded brilliantly. Supported by a huge concentration of artillery, it was pressed home with courage and initiative. A high point, known as Trig 29, was taken and 300 Germans were captured.

The Australian attack had a crucial effect on the final outcome of the battle. Thwarted across the remainder of his front, Montgomery now turned to the Australians to maintain the momentum of his advance, while he withdrew the New Zealanders and the

10th Corps from operations to prepare for a later thrust. The other infantry divisions shuffled to the right to fill the gaps left by the New Zealanders and the 20th Australian Brigade, which was to make the next attack. Montgomery prepared to launch his armoured forces north once the Australians had cleared the way.

Across the whole northern part of the front the British forces were facing constant attacks by German tanks, supported by artillery and infantry, but it was the Australian thrust which worried Field Marshal Rommel. If the Australians broke through to the coast they would get behind his main defences and would also cut off the 164th German Division around Thompson's Post. He therefore launched the 90th Light Division against the exposed Australians and ordered the 21st Panzer Division north from the southern front.

Despite the German counterattacks, on the night of 28 October the 20th Australian Brigade struck north from the area of Trig 29. One of the battalions, the 2/13th, had been fighting for five days and nights and its companies had been reduced from 120 to barely 35 men. Again the Australians seized important German positions. Morshead kept up the pressure and passed the tired, understrength 26th Brigade through the 20th Brigade for another attack on the night of 30 October.

Montgomery's chief of staff, Brigadier Freddy de Guingand, wrote later:

> [in] this area the enemy's defences were very strong, and their garrison predominantly German. I think this area saw the most determined and savage fighting of the campaign. No quarter was given, and the Australians fought some of the finest German troops to a standstill, and by their action did a great deal to win the battle of El Alamein.

The Australian attack with tired troops on 30 October was over-ambitious. Important ground was taken, but casualties were heavy. By the following night the 2/48th Battalion was down to 41 men, having begun the battle on 23 October with 30 officers and 656 other ranks. The brigade then consolidated its position as it held off determined heavy German counterattacks.

That night Morshead ordered the 24th Brigade, which had been holding the area next to the coast, to relieve the 26 Brigade. Relief-in-place, at night, in the face of the enemy is one of the hardest military operations, but when dawn came fresh battalions were waiting to meet the German assault. It was a tribute to the excellent staff work within the division and the training of the battalions. That day the full might of the German Afrika Korps hit the brigade. The brigadier was killed but the position held.

By now the Australians had achieved their mission. They had drawn onto themselves the full force of the German reserves of tanks and mechanised infantry. Rommel had expended valuable fuel and tanks against the Australians. The way was clear for the major British armoured offensive which Montgomery ordered to be mounted further south. Within days the British had broken through and the Germans were in retreat.

On 4 November, when victory was assured, Montgomery went straight to the headquarters of the 9th Division to thank Morshead. Later Montgomery wrote: 'We could not have won the battle in 12 days without the magnificent Australian Division'.

The total Eighth Army casualties were 13 650. The 9th Australian Division alone accounted for 2694. The 51st Division was next with 2495 casualties. Providing perhaps one-tenth the attacking force, the Australians suffered 22 per cent of the casualties. The 2/24th Battalion alone had lost 369 officers and men; the 2/48th had lost 346.

On average, during the battle each gun of the 30th Corps fired more than 1900 rounds. The artillery regiments of the 9th Australian Division fired over 50 per cent more than the corps average, reflecting the Australians' big share of the fighting.

The commander of the 30th Corps, General Leese, was quick to recognise the Australians' achievement and later wrote:

The Australians . . . established a very difficult salient beyond Point 29 which they held against continuous Panzer counter-attack. If the front of that Division had been penetrated during their four-days' ordeal, the whole success of the 8th Army plan could have been prejudiced. As it was, they suffered over 5000 [sic] casualties, but they beat off all enemy attacks, withstood intense hostile shelling and maintained a firm base for subsequent operations by the 8th Army. They drew on their front most of the Panzer Corps of which they destroyed a great part by their anti-tank guns. It was a magnificent piece of fighting by a great Division, led by an indomitable character, Leslie Morshead.

The Germans also recognised the quality of the Australians. The Panzer Army Africa intelligence summary of 22 August 1942 noted that out of all the enemy divisions, the 9th Australian Division could be considered the best. As a German intelligence officer observed: 'a not undeserved accolade in view of our experience with the Australians'.

General Horrocks, the commander of the British 13th Corps, which fought south of the 30th Corps, thought that the success of the final break-out was 'largely due to the 9th Australian Division'. After the battle he hurried to congratulate Morshead on the work of his division. Morshead's reply was a classic understatement. 'Thank you, General. The boys were interested.'

It would be absurd to claim that the Australians alone won the battle of El Alamein. A range of factors contributed to victory, including the British predominance in men, equipment and supplies. Rommel could never make up for his shortage of fuel. Nevertheless, with all these advantages, the Eighth Army ultimately had to win in battle. And it was here that the Australian role was critical. They were the fulcrum on which turned the successful breakthrough. By their dash and courage in attack they gave Montgomery the initiative. By their resolution in defence they gave him victory.

Alec Hill

Lieutenant-General Sir Leslie Morshead[*]

WHEN the 9th Australian division moved 'secretly' into Egypt in the last week of June 1942, Lord Haw-Haw, in one of his news bulletins, announced the arrival of Ali Baba Morshead and his 20 000 Australian thieves. If this did not quite match Churchill's chivalrous mention in Parliament of Rommel as a great general, it may nevertheless be counted as a rare distinction for an Australian general to be 'mentioned in dispatches' by the enemy.

Leslie James Morshead was 53. A schoolmaster and lieutenant of cadets, he had served in the old AIF on Gallipoli and in France. Commanding a platoon at the landing, he was wounded leading a company at Lone Pine, trained the 33rd Battalion in Monash's division and led it with acclaim from Messines, until the end in the Hindenburg Line. He came home a lieutenant-colonel, CMG, DSO, French Legion of Honour, with six mentions in dispatches, one of the outstanding younger commanders of the AIF.

Between the wars Morshead combined soldiering with business, becoming Sydney manager for the Orient Line in 1938. He was commanding a brigade in 1939 when chosen to command the 18th Brigade in the 6th Australian Division. They arrived in the Middle East in time for Morshead to see the assault on Tobruk on 21

---

[*] First published under the title, 'Morshead won respect from friends and enemies alike', in *The Weekend Australian Special Edition*, 24–25 October 1992.

January 1941. His inspection of its defences may well have helped him on his next visit ten weeks later as commander of the 9th Australian Division when he did battle with Rommel and the Afrika Korps.

Morshead's initiation as a divisional commander could scarcely have been more difficult, owing to the reorganisation of the 7th and 9th Divisions before Greece. The best trained brigades went to the 7th, so Morshead was left with the least effective units but under orders to move into Cyrenaica and help hold the desert flank. Luckily, his new brigades had received sound individual training but they lacked tactical training at company and battalion levels. As he was also short of major weapons, equipment and transport, his most desperate need was a lengthy quiet period. Instead he encountered an eager Rommel commanding troops flushed with victory.

Morshead's defence of Tobruk, April–October 1941, after a successful withdrawal, established his reputation. He organised an aggressive defence, prescribed tactics for dealing with penetration by tanks and insisted: 'We should make no man's land OUR land'. He worked well with the British armour and artillery which provided matchless support throughout the siege. An unfortunate result of the early months was that he was little known to his soldiers except as a stern disciplinarian: 'Ming the Merciless' soon became 'Ming'. Better days were to come. The defence of Tobruk won time for the preparation of a counteroffensive from Egypt, forced Rommel to divide his army and even to build a bypass road out of gun range; it also denied him the use of the port. In the process the 9th Division learned much about war. Tobruk was a great feat of arms for which the award of Knight of the British Empire conferred on Morshead in 1942 seems very moderate recognition.

Much was to interfere with the division's training after Tobruk and it was not complete when it was called urgently back to the desert in late June 1942. This time Morshead commanded a complete division, better trained although short of weapons and equipment. While these were being obtained, the division was responsible for the defence of Alexandria and Morshead was having a stormy confrontation with General Auchinleck, his commander-in-chief. Auchinleck's order to form the 9th into 'battle groups' and to send one up to the Eighth Army had angered Morshead, who was determined to have his troops fight as a division. Having obtained agreement on that, Morshead agreed to send a brigade as a temporary measure, provided the supply of its equipment and transport was completed. On General Blamey's return to Australia in March 1942, Morshead had become a lieutenant-general and commander of all Australian troops in the Middle East, but his main concern was the 9th Division.

In the hard and costly battles of July and October–November, Morshead and the 9th Division won new laurels, especially in the latter battles. General Leese, commander of 30th Corps, writing after the battle said: 'But I am quite certain that this break-out was only made possible by the homeric fighting over your divisional sector'. Morshead saw much of that for himself as he went forward often several times a day to see brigade and battalion commanders. Nor did he overlook the wounded in his field ambulances. After the battle he told his commanders: 'Don't forget a good word to the cooks'. Never one to waste words, when General Horrocks of 13th Corps congratulated him, Morshead replied: 'Thank you, general. The boys were interested.' Three VCs were among the decorations awarded in the 9th Division at El Alamein and Morshead was made Knight Commander of Bath.

In the South-West Pacific, it was not until October 1943 that Morshead became commander of the 2nd Corps, when the Japanese were trying to regain Finschhafen. He ensured the 9th Division was reinforced in time to meet this threat and went forward to see the troops. 'Wherever General Morshead went the troops made it evident that they were glad to see him. News of his visit rapidly spread . . . and produced a general feeling of confidence', records one of the war diaries.

Morshead was a strong commander, prepared to take on a British commander-in-chief or an American admiral. He moved easily among his soldiers, far more so than Blamey, could talk and laugh with them, as he had when he played football in the 33rd Battalion's team. He was, in Barton Maughan's words: 'Unsparing, unforgiving, outspoken in criticism . . . yet quick to commend and praise'. Thousands of such men turned out for his funeral in Sydney in September 1959. 'Whenever men speak of the 9th Australian Division's feats at Tobruk and El Alamein', Maughan says, 'this great and resolute commander will be remembered. Its victories were his.'

Greg Pemberton

Australia's case for a higher command appointment*

A USTRALIA'S 9th Division at the battle of El Alamein was only one of the British eighth Army's ten divisions but suffered 20 per cent of the casualties and played a critical role in that famous World War II victory for the Allies. Despite its great performances there and earlier, in the legendary siege of Tobruk, its men and their battle-experienced commander, Lieutenant-General Sir Leslie Morshead, had to undergo the indignity of having less experienced and capable British junior officers placed above them because of the British refusal to allow dominion officers to hold senior commands, even when the bulk of the troops were not British. Australia's leading military historian, David Horner, has written in his authoritative book *High Command* that 'Morshead's experience at El Alamein from July to November 1942 shows that the British had still not yet understood the independent status of the Dominions'.

The story of Australia's military history has been that of a struggle for Australia to establish an independent identity for and control over its own armed forces against the efforts of British leaders and some supporters in Australia to integrate Australian and other British Commonwealth forces into British-controlled formations. In addition, even though British leaders wanted to compel the rest of the

---

* First published under the title, 'Hero Morshead humiliated by British military arrogance', in the *Weekend Australian Special Edition*, 24–25 October 1992.

Commonwealth to share its military burden, they have always been reluctant to allow non-British officers to exercise any significant authority.

This pattern, established in the years leading up to and including World War I, seemed set to be repeated during World War II. Senior Australian Army officers, such as Generals Brudenell White and Birdwood, well remembered the battles they had joined with the British high command during the Great War, such as at the first battle of Bullecourt. They were determined that the situation not be repeated.

Yet in 1940 all three chiefs of staff in Australia were British officers. When Australia's first military personnel—airmen—arrived in England in the early stages of the war, British leaders deliberately sought to submerge their national identity into the British forces. With respect to ground forces, Australian senior officers had drawn up a charter for the service of the 2nd AIF overseas designed principally to preserve the identity of Australian forces under Australian commanders, subject only to the general approval of the Australian Government. Their fears were well-founded. When Blamey arrived in Egypt, he found that the British Commander-in-Chief of the Middle East theatre, General Sir Archibald Wavell, was already planning to disperse the first Australian brigades of the 6th and 7th Divisions among British formations. He put a stop to that but failed to assert himself over British plans to use these divisions for the disastrous Greek campaign without full consultation of the Australian commanders or the Australian Government.

If the Greek campaign was a dreadful failure then the situation in Cyrenaica was little better in mid-1941. The three most senior British officers were captured within days, leaving only Morshead as commander of the 9th Division. It was only in this time of crisis that Wavell turned, albeit temporarily, to an Australian, Lieutenant-General Lavarack of 7th Division, to take over command in Cyrenaica. During his six days of command before being replaced by a more junior British officer, Lavarack appointed Morshead fortress commander at Tobruk. There Morshead conducted an imaginative, active, skilful and ultimately successful defence against the Germans, which salvaged Britain's position in the Middle East and possibly even more widely.

Morshead, a former schoolteacher, businessman and citizen-soldier was known as 'Ming the Merciless' after a popular cartoon character of the time because of the demands he made upon his subordinates for efficient and effective performance. German propaganda referred to him and his men as 'Ali Baba and his 20 000 Thieves'. The British relieved Lavarack of his command but retained Morshead, who held out over the passing months while the poorly planned and executed operations of Wavell failed to achieve the relief of the garrison.

Wavell was succeeded by General Sir Claude Auchinleck, and Blamey had to hammer the British commander, backed by London, to replace the exhausted 9th Division. Eventually the Australian Government added its weight to what developed into a rancorous political crisis prefiguring the even graver one the following year when Churchill diverted Australia's Middle East divisions to Burma. In October 1941 Morshead finally turned over his Tobruk command and led the 9th to the quieter theatre in Palestine, while the 6th and 7th would soon return home to meet the Japanese threat.

Blamey too returned to Australia for good in March 1942 in order to organise the Australian Army for the defence against the Japanese. British commanders were pleased to see him go because of his determination to preserve Australian control over Australian forces. Their joy was premature, as Blamey had turned command of the AIF in the Middle East over to Morshead. He had also left Morshead with clear instructions that the Australian force was not to be broken up among the British formations. Morshead understood these instructions completely but once he began to move the 9th from Syria to Egypt, in the wake of the Eighth Army's defeat at Gazala, he soon found that the British commanders had very different views.

Morshead arrived in Alexandria along with the 24th Brigade of the 9th Division in early July 1942, when the British forces were still reeling from a succession of defeats and forced withdrawals at the hands of Rommel's Afrika Korps. Even Tobruk, which Morshead had successfully held, had now fallen. Morshead was immediately confronted by orders from British headquarters to break the 9th Division into battlegroups and send one brigade forward to participate in a British offensive against Rommel on the Alamein line. Morshead knew that all the division's brigades lacked essential equipment and he still had Blamey's directions ringing in his ears.

He agreed to have the 24th Brigade prepare to go to the front line the next morning but also sought to clarify the situation with Auchinleck.

Morshead later recalled Auchinleck's 'brusque' conversation with him at that meeting:

> *Auchinleck*: I want that brigade right away.
> *Morshead*: You can't have that brigade.
> *Auchinleck*: Why?
> *Morshead*: Because they are going to fight as a formation with the rest of the division.
> *Auchinleck*: Not if I give you orders.
> *Morshead*: Give me the orders and you'll see.
> *Auchinleck*: So you're being like Blamey. You're wearing his mantle.

David Horner has observed that Auchinleck 'still seemed unable to grasp the fact that the Australian commander was guided by a series of strict principles, laid down by his government, which he had a duty to uphold'. Sensitive to the operational situation, Morshead did compromise. The 9th would not be broken up but it would be placed under Britain's 30th Corps commanded by Lieutenant-General Norrie. Morshead reluctantly agreed to temporary detachment of a brigade group, noting in his diary: 'This detachment cuts completely across the policy of the Australian government and the AIF'. Two days later Norrie ordered Australia's 24th Brigade to attack some German anti-tank guns without the artillery support Morshead thought necessary. He refused to allow the attack to proceed and then got Auchinleck to postpone the attack until the artillery support could be provided.

Within a few days Morshead had to digest Auchinleck's decision to replace Norrie with Major-General W. H. C. Ramsden, a British officer of wide experience but of junior rank to himself. In comparison to Morshead's tremendous achievements in the siege of Tobruk, Ramsden's performance as commander of the 50th Division had not been, in the words of Horner, 'spectacular'. Morshead held doubts about Ramsden's ability to command. Relations between the two commanders deteriorated and Ramsden complained twice to Auchinleck about Morshead's attitude.

Morshead believed that some British commanders failed to apply basic military principles and in so doing jeopardised the lives of his

Australians. He also thought that they did not recognise that he alone had the authority granted by the Australian Government to detach elements of his force for separate operations. Morshead was livid when on 15 July Auchinleck, without any prior consultation, redeployed his 20th Brigade. He called Auchinleck to complain about this 'theft' and insisted upon its return, although he agreed to wait until the situation had eased.

Pondering on the less than impressive performance of some of the senior British commanders, Morshead told Blamey later that it was 'abundantly clear' that dominion officers were ineligible for command of a corps in the Middle East, even when the corps consisted wholly of dominion troops. Ramsden had already blithely informed Morshead that should he (Ramsden) become a casualty, command of the corps would pass to Major-General Briggs, a recently promoted British divisional commander.

Soon after, Churchill, among other changes, replaced Auchinleck with General Montgomery and made General Alexander commander-in-chief of the theatre. Although this did improve the situation, Blamey complained to Curtin over the lack of consultation by the British: 'In view of the fact that a considerable body of Australian troops are involved, the matter is not one of indifference to us'. He added that none of the new British officers appointed had had 'the same experience of desert warfare or the same success in army warfare' as Morshead. The Australian divisional commander, he continued, could not but feel humiliated at having these inexperienced British officers placed over him.

Blamey pulled no punches in his typically blunt petition to his national leader. He wanted Curtin to press London to give fair consideration to the claims of dominion officers to high command. He complained: 'The disregard which British authorities have invariably shown to Australian officers in this aspect in the Middle East is notorious, and a very great deal of feeling has been aroused in the Australian Army by this latest demonstration of attitude'. Curtin did take up the question with Churchill, who smoothly reassured him that Morshead, for whom he personally had formed a high opinion, had been 'carefully considered' and that his 'undoubted qualifications for a higher appointment' would be taken into account in any subsequent appointments.

Churchill was probably sincere, as he did believe Morshead was suitable as a corps commander, but he had given Montgomery a free hand in such appointments. Montgomery decided that Ramsden should be replaced not by Morshead, but by Lieutenant-General Leese, who was flown out from Britain. Montgomery and Alexander agreed that as Morshead was not a regular soldier, he did not have the requisite training. Morshead explained the situation to Blamey on 4 September, who immediately passed it to Curtin, adding his own assessment:

> This brings out clearly the repugnance of the British command to accept Dominion officers, however successful, in higher commands because they have not been turned out on the British pattern. This attitude of unconscious arrogance has created more ill-feeling against British commanders amongst senior Australian officers than should be allowed to develop. General Morshead is still a divisional commander, but it is safe to say there is no corps commander operating in the Middle East who has had the same amount of successful operational command, both as an independent commander and under a superior, than he.

So when the Commonwealth artillery commenced its massive barrage against Rommel's forces at El Alamein on 23 October, Morshead was in charge of the 9th Division on Montgomery's right flank, next to the coast. In the two weeks of hard fighting that followed, the 9th played a critical role in Montgomery's famous victory. Partly because of its heavy losses, it did not take part in the pursuit of the German forces. It had more pressing commitments to meet closer to home. In November 1942 the British Government reluctantly agreed that the 9th should return to Australia. There it joined with the 7th Division and two brigades of the 6th as II Corps in Blamey's army, on Australian soil, under an Australian commander-in-chief and alongside other senior Australian commanders. Morshead was finally granted the recognition and responsibility he so well deserved—command of that corps.

David Horner

The role of intelligence*

THE victory by the British Eighth Army in the Battle of El Alamein can be attributed to a number of factors. These include the careful planning and cool control of the Eighth Army commander, Lieutenant-General Bernard Montgomery, the British superiority in men and equipment, the supply difficulties faced by his German opponent, Field Marshal Erwin Rommel, and, not least, the outstanding fighting qualities of the 9th Australian Division and the New Zealand Division. Without the skill, endurance and determination of the Australian and New Zealand infantrymen, Montgomery's thorough plans might well have failed.

However, any explanation of the victory at El Alamein must take into account the events of the preceding four months. On 22 June 1942 Rommel's forces had seized Tobruk, and with it over 30 000 prisoners, plus priceless fuel and supplies. Britain's fortunes were at their lowest ebb. Within days Rommel's forces were pushing deeply into Egypt and, by the end of the month, he had reached the El Alamein position, just west of Alexandria. There, throughout July, the British commander, General Sir Claude Auchinleck, directed a series of sharp counterattacks and Rommel was forced to

---

* First published under the title 'How intelligence outwitted the Fox', in *The Australian Special Edition*, 24–25 October 1992.

halt. In any case, he was running short of supplies, and for the moment could go no farther.

But Rommel was determined on one final thrust to bring his forces to the banks of the River Nile. In mid-August Auchinleck was replaced by Montgomery, and between 30 August and 7 September, under a new commander, the Eighth Army defeated Rommel's offensive at Alam Halfa. This successful battle provided the foundation for the eventual victory at El Alamein: it weakened Rommel's forces, raised British morale, and gave Montgomery time to retrain the Eighth Army.

Although these events have been well known for fifty years, they have been the subject of considerable controversy. On the one hand Montgomery claimed that when he took over, the Eighth Army was in disarray. He cancelled all plans for withdrawal and immediately began preparing for his two later triumphs, Alam Halfa and Alamein.

Montgomery's critics claimed that Auchinleck had defeated Rommel in July and had already begun planning for the Alam Halfa battle when he was relieved. As the historian Corelli Barnett put it in the *Desert Generals*, Montgomery appropriated this plan and then, 'wearing a second-hand coat of glory, set out for the top'. Contrary to Montgomery's later assertions, Alamein did not go as planned, and disaster was averted only by the valiant Australians and New Zealanders. Then, when Rommel's forces were broken, Montgomery failed to seize the opportunity and allowed large numbers of the enemy to escape.

Thus was the state of the argument in 1974 when Frederick Winterbotham's book, *The Ultra Secret*, revealed for the first time that British code-breakers had been able to decipher the German top-level operational messages, transmitted on the Enigma cipher machine, for most of the war. As more information was revealed in the late 1970s and early 1980s it raised important questions about the conduct of many British campaigns, not the least being the battle of El Alamein and the period of four months leading up to it.

British intelligence success during this period was achieved in two areas. Firstly, British authorities had to deny information to the Germans, and secondly they had to obtain information of their own. In the first half of 1942 Rommel had developed a remarkable capacity to forecast British intentions, organisation and strengths.

After the United States entered the war in December 1941 a US military attaché, Colonel Bonner Fellers, was sent to Cairo with wide-ranging access to British staff and top secret information. An energetic and meticulous officer, Fellers visited the British forces on operations and reported regularly to Washington by coded telegrams. His reports included the numbers of British aircraft and tanks available for operations and their locations, forthcoming Commando operations, and defensive plans.

Remarkably, all this information was read by Rommel and the German General Staff. The previous year Italian military intelligence had broken into the American Embassy in Rome and had copied the code later used by Fellers. From what he called his 'good source', Rommel had a valuable insight into the British strategy, strengths and plans. He learned of British tank losses before his assault on Tobruk in June and, encouraged by news of an atmosphere of panic in Cairo, he decided on his risky advance that brought him to Alamein at the end of the month.

By this stage the British were reading the German Air Force and Army Enigma traffic and eventually they deduced that Feller's telegrams were being intercepted and read by the Germans. Abruptly, on 29 June, Rommel's 'good source' ran dry. Thereafter the US military attaché used a different means of informing Washington.

Rommel also received information from his own signals intelligence organisation. His principal field signals intelligence unit was the 621st Radio Intercept Company, commanded by a brilliant and ambitious officer, Captain Alfred Seebohm. This unit had developed a high level of expertise; it had become adept at listening to British radio traffic and, either by traffic analysis or breaking British codes, had given Rommel forewarning of British intentions during operations.

When Rommel's forces reached Alamein at the end of June Seebohm moved his unit well forward on the coast near Tel el Eisa, but also near a high point from which he would be able to intercept the maximum amount of British radio traffic. The position was exposed, but was protected by an Italian division.

As part of his effort to seize the initiative from Rommel, Auchinleck now ordered Lieutenant-General Sir Leslie Morshead, commanding the 9th Australian Division, to capture Tel el Eisa.

The 26th Australian Infantry Brigade, heavily supported by artillery, attacked on 10 July and, in a brilliant operation, reached the feature. As part of the attack the 2/24th Battalion moved along the coast, brushed aside the Italians, and overran the 621st Radio Intercept Company. Captain Seebohm was wounded and later died, while one hundred men of the company, plus valuable documents and equipment, were captured.

Rommel was furious at the loss of Seebohm and his experienced, English-speaking operators, for he was effectively denied his foremost intelligence source for the next month; indeed his signals intelligence capability was not full-restored until the following April. Furthermore, the British captured some German codes, as well as evidence of the extent to which the Germans had broken the British codes and were listening to British radio traffic. The British therefore improved their own radio procedures to deny further information to the enemy.

The Australian official historian, Barton Maughan, wrote in 1985 that if he 'were to choose a date for the turning of the war in Africa, and indeed of the entire war between the ground forces of Germany and the western allies' he would choose 10 July 1942. There were three reasons for selecting this date. First, the Eighth Army had taken and held against counterattack the most commanding ground in the crucial coastal sector. Second, the attack forced Rommel to cancel a planned offensive further to the south which was aimed to break through towards Alexandria. And third, the capture of the German signals intelligence unit might 'have influenced the course of future battles and hence, in some degree, the outcome of the opposing armies' struggle for supremacy'.

In the space of eleven days Rommel had lost his two most important intelligence sources, and now his third main source, aerial reconnaissance, was to be reduced. With shortened supply lines the planes of the Royal Air Force could dominate the battlefield, and daily more planes arrived in the theatre. It took two more months before the British achieved a measure of air superiority, but British aircraft would play a major role at Alam Halfa and would deny air reconnaissance to the Germans before El Alamein later in October.

Meanwhile, as measures were being introduced to deny information to Rommel, the Eighth Army began to receive an increased flow of Enigma intercepts—the so-called Ultra intelligence. As early as March 1942 Ultra had begun to produce periodic German tank strength returns, and during May and June Ultra enabled the commander of the Eighth Army to forecast Rommel's intentions. With this background, the British defeats at Gazala in June and the subsequent loss of Tobruk are hard to understand.

By mid-June the flow of Ultra information had increased even further. The British code-breakers at Bletchley Park in England, had broken the codes used by the German air liaison officers accompanying Panzer Army Africa and, in July, had begun to read German Army supply messages. As Ralph Bennett, who worked on Ultra in Cairo at the time, wrote: 'From being an occasional blinding flash of light in darkness, Ultra became a standard ingredient of military intelligence'.

There is disagreement over how well Auchinleck used Ultra. Supporters, such as Corelli Barnett, claim that it was his reliance on Ultra that enabled him to direct the successful attack on 10 July. But Montgomery's official biographer, Nigel Hamilton, states that the Eighth Army intelligence officer, Brigadier Bill Williams, was frustrated by the 'pathetic use to which this unique intelligence had been put'. Williams recalled his excitement after first meeting Montgomery: 'God, he's the sort of chap who's going to be able to *use* Ultra'.

Whatever the truth about Auchinleck's use of Ultra, there can be no doubt that Montgomery recognised its importance. Already he had planned to defend the Alam Halfa position when, on 17 August, he started to receive Ultra information that Rommel was intending to attack in that area on 26 August. The German attack was delayed till 31 August, giving Montgomery more time to prepare. Furthermore, Ultra also revealed that the Germans had not detected the British preparations to meet the attack—a direct result of the closing down of Rommel's 'good source' and the capture of Seebohm's unit.

Once the battle of Alam Halfa was under way Montgomery was kept abreast of the changes in Rommel's plans. For example, at noon on 1 September Rommel decided to halt his advance and go onto the defensive. A decrypted Enigma signal announcing Rommel's decision was received by Headquarters Eighth Army in the early hours of 2 September. Later Enigma decrypts would be even more timely.

Rommel had been caught in an unexpected British minefield and had suffered under air attacks, but the main reason for halting his advance was lack of fuel, and this related directly to the success of Ultra. Forewarned by Ultra, British submarines and aircraft had intercepted Italian shipping operating between Italy, Greece and northern Africa. During June and July only 20 000 tons of Axis shipping were lost, but in August the total rose to over 60 000 tons. An Enigma intercept on 18 August revealed that Rommel had sufficient petrol stocks to last until 26 August. When he decided to attack on 30 August he had fuel for only four and a half days' fighting. The loss of eight Italian tankers or transports between 27 August and 4 September meant that Rommel could not continue his offensive.

As Montgomery prepared for his major attack at El Alamein towards the end of October he continued to receive valuable Ultra intelligence. For example, on 10 September he learned that Rommel had returned to Europe for medical treatment and had been replaced by General Stumme. Intercepts of German tank numbers showed that on the eve of the battle the Axis forces would have 204 tanks, against about 1000 British tanks. Similarly, on 20 October an intercepted reported showed that Panzer Army Africa included 49000 Germans and 54 000 Italians. That same day the Eigth Army numbered 195,000 men.

Montgomery received details of the serviceability and numbers of German and Italian aircraft, and Axis fuel shortages. Then on 17 October the British intelligence staff decrypted the complete Axis tanker program for the period 21 to 29 October, and this would have a decisive effect on the coming battle.

Ultra was not the only source of British intelligence. Aerial reconnaissance and ground reconnaissance by units such as the Long Range Desert Group, contributed important information. Perhaps the most valuable tactical intelligence was provided by the British Y Service—that is, field signals intelligence units that listened to the enemy's tactical radio traffic and deduced his intentions by direction finding and listening to call–signs and changing volumes of traffic, even when the actual codes could not be broken.

Before the beginning of the battle on 23 October Montgomery had received unparalleled information, but once the fighting began Ultra provided little information of direct operational value. With the death of General Stumme on the first day of the battle Rommel rushed back from Europe to assume command. He made only two significant moves during the battle, the redeployment of a Panzer division from the south to the north, and the release of his reserve division. Neither moves were reported quickly by Ultra but were detected early by Montgomery's Y Service.

It is true that Montgomery was kept informed of the deteriorating strength of Rommel's Army during the twelve grinding days of battle but, as in the earlier Alam Halfa battle, Ultra's crucial role was in directing British submarines and aircraft onto Axis tankers. On 23 October a decrypt revealed that the next Axis tanker, the *Proserpina*, with 45 000 tons of fuel, was due on 25 October, but that its fuel could not reach the front until 29 October. Unless fuel was sent by air, the Panzer Army's stocks would be exhausted. In the early hours of 25 October Bletchley Park signalled the *Proserpina's* route to the Middle East and in the evening of 26 October she was set ablaze by British bombers. A second, smaller ship with 1000 tons of fuel and 1000 tons of ammunition was sunk. Rommel described the news as 'shattering'.

On the evening of 2 November Rommel sent two signals to Hitler. The first said that his army was exhausted, that he could not prevent an enemy breakthrough, and that he had insufficient fuel to move more than a short distance. The second signal advised that he had ordered a fighting withdrawal. Soon after dawn the following morning Montgomery read these signals. He could have no doubt that he had won the battle.

With this wonderful intelligence, Montgomery might have seized the opportunity to prevent Rommel's escape. Certainly he had a clear picture of his opponent's problems. Perhaps he felt that his own forces needed to be reorganised. Perhaps he still mistrusted their level of training. In any case, he had achieved a smashing victory. It was a victory with many ingredients. Once battle was joined it relied to a large extent on the courage and skill of the infantrymen, but equally, it was set up by successful intelligence. In this achievement the 2/24th Australian Battalion near Tel el Eisa had played a major role.

12
Conscription

Cameron Stewart

Curtin's changes to the National Service Act*

FIFTY years ago Australia's wartime Prime Minister, John Curtin, took what Arthur Fadden described as the most courageous decision of his political career. On 17 November 1942, Curtin defied Labor Party tradition and proposed that limited conscription be introduced to force Australian militia forces to serve outside Australian territories for the first time. It was a remarkable decision for a man who was sentenced to gaol for his staunch anti-conscription activities during World War I and who had, even during the darkest days of the Japanese advance a few months earlier, consistently maintained that conscription was unnecessary.

The real reasons behind Curtin's puzzling change of heart did not become apparent until the release of defence records many years after his death. They show that Curtin's controversial conscription proposal was not crafted primarily to help defend Australia against the Japanese threat, as was generally believed at the time. It was instead a brave diplomatic stunt which Curtin initiated at the request of the American regional commander General Douglas MacArthur to pacify growing criticism in the United States and Britain of Australia's war effort, which both Curtin and MacArthur felt could jeopardise their constant requests for more military aid to the

---

*   First published under the title 'Curtin and the Call-Up', in the *Weekend Australian*, 7–8 November 1992.

South-West Pacific Area. Curtin's skill in persuading his party to abandon its anti-conscription stance and approve his conscription proposal was a masterpiece of political manipulation, especially given that Curtin was obliged to keep secret the fact that MacArthur had asked for it—a request which would have been seen as an unprecedented interference in domestic politics by a US general.

Prior to Curtin's conscription proposal, the army was divided into two separate forces—the volunteer Australian Imperial Force, which served overseas, and the conscripted Citizens' Military Force, which was permitted only to serve within Australia and her territories, including Papua New Guinea. Curtin proposed that the boundaries of the Defence Act be altered to allow the conscripted militia to serve outside Australian territories within an area defined as the South-West Pacific Area which included the Solomon Islands, Timor and most of Java, Borneo and the Celebes. This amounted to what Arthur Calwell described as 'a stepping stone instalment of conscription' because of its territorial limitations, but it was nevertheless Australia's first commitment to compulsory overseas military service.

When Curtin made his proposal on 17 November he announced that conscription was a military necessity for the defence of Australia, despite the fact that both he and MacArthur privately knew it would almost certainly never be implemented. The *Sydney Morning Herald* reported on 21 November: 'One army under one command was now a military necessity in the South-West Pacific, the Prime Minister John Curtin said today. Australia, he said, was now being defended on an outer screen of islands including Timor . . . these islands were in the South-West Pacific Area (SWPA) and were vital to the holding of the Commonwealth.'

However, by mid-November 1942 Australia's military situation was hardly one that would have led Curtin to propose conscription for fear or security if he had rejected it earlier in the year when the Japanese threat was far greater. By this time the rapidly increasing Allied forces in PNG consisted of the 6th and 7th Australian Divisions Milne Force and the 32nd US Division. In addition, four other US divisions were in the SWPA, four were in Hawaii and 100 000 US troops were in Australia. By mid-November, Allied forces in PNG had regained control of the crest of the Owen Stanley Range from Wau to Milne Bay, had retaken Kokoda and had pinned the only remaining Japanese forces in PNG around Buna on the north coast. In addition to this, Allied air power in the area was far superior to that of the Japanese, who had suffered severe losses in the Coral Sea and Midway Island battles.

The successes in PNG and the changing tide of the Solomons' campaign by mid-November makes it difficult to disagree with President Roosevelt's assessment, made two months earlier when the situation was not so clear cut: 'After considering all the factors involved, I agree with the conclusions of the combined chiefs of staff that your present armed forces, assuming they are fully equipped and effectively trained, are sufficient to defeat the present Japanese force in PNG and to provide for the security of Australia'. MacArthur also had no plans to use the CMF in any offensive operations outside Australian territory. He told Australia's secretary to the War Cabinet, Frederick Shedden, that although he would use the 6th, 7th and 9th AIF divisions in an Allied expeditionary force, he did not consider the CMF was fit for such an offensive. In fact, MacArthur, who initiated the conscription proposal, admitted that it was unlikely to be of any military use when he told his British liaison officer: 'It [conscription] didn't really matter except that it looks bad on paper for the Aussie government [i.e. not having conscription]'.

Curtin's public emphasis on conscription being a military necessity reflects his shrewd appreciation of the tactics required to pass such a sensitive Bill without splitting party and country, rather than a belief that the improving military situation in November 1942 required conscription. It is unlikely that a traditionally explosive issue like conscription would be accepted at both a party and public level totally on the grounds that it was diplomatically useful when much of the important 'behind the scenes' diplomacy was still classified information, even to party members. It was in Curtin's interests to play up the more tangible and superficially more acceptable view that conscription was a strategic necessity and, by playing on security fears, reduce resistance to his proposal at both a party and public level.

But why then did Curtin spend so much time and effort attempting to pass a potentially divisive Bill that both he and MacArthur knew to be militarily irrelevant? The answer was, as MacArthur conceded, that Australia's failure to introduce conscription by November 1942 was looking increasingly 'bad on paper for the Aussie government'. The fact that Australia alone among the Allies had refused to introduce conscription for service outside its territorial boundaries when US conscripts were fighting to defend Australia made Australia susceptible to Allied criticism of her war effort. By November 1942 the Australian press reported more frequently on increasingly anti-Australian feeling in the US and Britain over the failure to introduce conscription.

Both MacArthur and Curtin had reason to be concerned with how their allies perceived Australia's war effort. If it was being argued in the US and Britain that Australia was failing to put forth a full war effort, then Curtin's constant demands for more Allied aid and attention to the SWPA was hardly likely to receive serious or favourable attention. There is ample evidence of growing criticism of Australia in 1942 for failing to introduce conscription. The reaction of an editorial in the *Times* to the decision of the special federal ALP conference to refer Curtin's conscription proposal to the State executive branches reflected the general English dissatisfaction with the Australian war effort:

> The reluctance of the conference to extend compulsory military service to territories outside the Commonwealth but well within the Commonwealth's defence zone may seem odd to those unfamiliar with Australian politics and who recall the Commonwealth's declaration of its determination to share with the Allies the burdens and perils involved in the struggle.

Australia's war effort attracted even greater criticism in the US, where the failure to introduce conscription was seen as isolationist. US Admiral King, chief of the US navy and one of the Joint Chiefs of Staff, said he had added the Bismarcks and the Solomons to MacArthur's command because he 'felt it was necessary to engage the attention of Australia to the defences of the approaches to their country and shake them out of their isolationist attitudes'. Nelson Johnson, the US Minister in Canberra during the war, engaged in frequent correspondence with US State Department political adviser Stanley Hornbeck, most of which was passed on to President Roosevelt. Johnson writes that he was disgusted with Australia's war effort and perceived the average Australian as living 'like a parasite on the body of the Empire, having refused to spend adequate sums on defence preparations and yet now seeming to expect us to do everything for him, fight for him, work for him; [he is] incapable of seeing beyond his surfing beaches, isolationist and unable to face facts'.

US General Marshall, under instructions from Roosevelt, prevented *Colliers* magazine in the US from publishing an article on the Australian war effort. The magazine claimed:

> [that] contrary to the impression in America, the people of Australia are not stalwart physical specimens determined to defend their country from attack, but are physically inferior people who are indifferent to the fate that is on their doorstep. Instead of a preparation for war, one sees in Australia a life of horse racing, beer drinking and long vacations on its beaches.

While this is a somewhat extreme reaction, it is an indication of how Australia's war effort, in particular its failure to introduce conscription, was perceived by its allies.

Both Curtin and MacArthur were fully aware of how this criticism could undermine their attempts to secure more military aid for the SWPA. MacArthur was very much a political general and his driving ambition to make the SWPA the main theatre of war placed him in continual conflict with the combined chiefs of staff in Washington and especially Roosevelt, who had agreed on a 'beat Hitler first' strategy. Both MacArthur and Roosevelt were political and personal opposites and MacArthur was convinced that Roosevelt was seeking ways to restrict his success (and rumoured political ambitions) by emphasising the European theatre at the expense of the Pacific and in particular MacArthur's SWPA.

Curtin was also aware that this political conflict was affecting the flow of aid to Australia. In records of confidential press briefings with Curtin, journalist F. T. Smith noted: '[Curtin said] there are no achievements yet [in North Africa], but they have a commander there who, unlike MacArthur, is not a Republican [General Eisenhower]. The American government does not want MacArthur to be too great a man—there is clear evidence that American politics are coming into the question of aid for us.' Therefore, MacArthur was highly sensitive to Allied criticism of Australia's war effort and told Australia's secretary to the War Cabinet, Frederick Shedden, that in finally proposing conscription Curtin had 'not moved a day too soon as there were reports from America that a campaign was being insidiously built up on this matter'.

Shedden also recorded in January 1943 that 'General MacArthur stated in the strictest confidence that he had received an entirely reliable report that Admiral Leahy, personal assistant to the President, had said that if Australia did not remove the limits on the use of its forces in the SWPA, he would urge the President to withhold lend-lease assistance to the Commonwealth'. In another report on confidential press briefings given by Curtin, F. T. Smith records that 'the request on the one army question [as the conscription issue was known at the time] came to Curtin from MacArthur in Perth [but] Curtin does not want it said however that MacArthur actually asked for it because technically MacArthur should have no concern with a political matter'.

Despite enormous political differences between Curtin and Mac-Arthur, the two men enjoyed a very close working relationship and it appears that—given Curtin's persistent and often futile attempts to secure more military aid for the SWPA—Curtin was highly receptive to MacArthur's arguments on the conscription issue. In giving reasons for this conscription proposal at the special ALP conference on 17 November, the records state: '[Curtin said] the US had saved Australia and the government had had a desperate fight to get aid for Australia. He did not want to live those months again. Now the position was that a barrage of criticism in Australia and the US was directed at Australia that it would have Americans defend Darwin but not Australians fight for the Philippines.' But Curtin also saw that the conscription proposal could be used not only to quell Allied criticism of Australia's war effort, but also as a tool through which more aid could be secured. Curtin made a point of requesting more aid as soon as he made his conscription proposal on 17 November and believed it could contribute to persuading Roosevelt and Churchill to agree to the return of the 9th Division to Australia from the Middle East. But Curtin was not merely a 'rubber stamp' for MacArthur's requests. His own calculation of the chances of successfully passing the conscription proposal without splitting party and country was pivotal.

Throughout 1942 the Opposition and the media had been demanding that conscription be introduced so Curtin was aware that the only serious obstacle to his proposal was his own party. Curtin rejected a referendum on the issue and chose to propose conscription at the special federal ALP conference on 17 November, which he was attending, not as prime minister but as one of the Western Australian delegates.

Curtin's decision to use the conference to propose conscription was a shrewd means of avoiding public criticism from Caucus members such as Arthur Calwell and E. J. Ward. By obtaining from the conference the decision to refer the matter to the State executives, the matter became *sub judice* and therefore Caucus and Cabinet were restricted in their right publicly to criticise or oppose the motion. Curtin realised this would give him time to argue his proposal fully before the State executives met in January. He was right. Through this skilful manipulation of the ALP's organisational structure he received approval from the State executives and the Bill was eventually passed by Parliament on 14 February 1943.

It was indicative of Curtin's single-minded dedication to Australia's success in the Pacific War that he modified his traditional anti-conscription ideals when he perceived that the country stood to benefit from a proposal which ran contrary not only to his own beliefs, but also to those of his party. Ironically, after conscription was introduced, no CMF units were ever engaged in fighting outside Australian territory. But this would have come as no surprise to Curtin or MacArthur because they never believed conscription was a strategic necessity. Rather, it was the complex politics of wartime relations and questions of military aid that led to this landmark decision in Australia's military history.

Index

aircraft carriers, 19
Allen, Major-General Arthur, 229, 230, 231
Anderson, Lieutenant-Colonel Charles, 50–1, 52, 81
Anderson, Herbert, 176–7, 180
Andrew, Reginald, 183–4
ANZUS, 42, 166
Arizona, USS, 4, 11
Asian invasion, threat of, 28–9
atomic bombs, 42
Auchinleck, General Sir Claude, 269, 270, 271, 274, 277
Australia
  air power of, 86
  defence of by British, 29–30, 33, 39
  defence policy of, 32, 132–8
  during war years, 120–3
  economy of, 41, 43–4
  evacuation of, 136
  invasion of by Japanese, 28–9, 30–1
  military history of, 267–8
  relations with Britain and, 162–4
  relations with US and, 165–7

sovereignty of, 84–91
threat of invasion to, 1, 20–3, 28–9, 126, 133, 155–6, 157, 159, 160, 208
US troops in, 41, 135
Australian Imperial Force, 40, 78
Australian troops
  encounters with Japanese troops, 46–8, 49–52, 58–9
  mobilisation of, 30, 36, 38, 41, 48, 56, 79, 81, 86, 156–7
Australian–American Association, 165, 166

Ballard, Galen, 11–12
Ban, Sub-Lieutenant Katsuhisa, 174, 177–85 *passim*
Bennett, Major-General Henry Gordon, 46–7, 54, 57, 63–5, 79, 81, 94–5, 98
Blamey, General Sir Thomas, 129, 136, 137, 157, 210, 211, 228, 229, 231, 269, 271
bombers, 7
bombs, 9; atomic, 42
Bradford, Dale, 12

289